The Yale-Hoover Series on Stalin, Stalinism, and the Cold War

Edited by

PAUL R. GREGORY and NORMAN NAIMARK

The Lost Politburo Transcripts

FROM COLLECTIVE RULE TO
STALIN'S DICTATORSHIP

Hoover Institution
Stanford University
Stanford, California

Yale University Press
New Haven &
London

Published with assistance from the foundation established in memory of Philip Hamilton McMillan of the Class of 1894, Yale College.

Set in Sabon by Keystone Typesetting, Inc., Orwigsburg, Pennsylvania.
Printed in the United States of America by Thomson-Shore, Inc., Dexter, Michigan.

Library of Congress Cataloging-in-Publication Data
The lost Politburo transcripts: From collective rule to Stalin's dictatorship / edited by Paul R. Gregory and Norman Naimark.
    p. cm. — (The Yale-Hoover series on Stalin, Stalinism, and the Cold War)
    "Published in cooperation with the Hoover Institution on War, Revolution and Peace, Stanford University."
    Includes bibliographical references and index.
    ISBN 978-0-300-13424-7 (cloth : alk. paper)
1. TSK KPSS. Politbiuro — History — Sources. 2. Soviet Union — Politics and government — 1917–1936 — Sources. I. Gregory, Paul R. II. Naimark, Norman M.
JN6598.K7L598 2008
324.247'075 — dc22
2008021449

A catalogue record for this book is available from the British Library.

The paper in this book meets the guidelines for permanence and durability of the Committee on Production Guidelines for Book Longevity of the Council on Library Resources.

10 9 8 7 6 5 4 3 2 1

Contents

v

Acknowledgments

There are any number of institutions and individuals who made this publication possible. It would not have been possible without the support of the Hoover Institution, which entered into a cooperative agreement with the Russian State Archive for Social and Political History (Kirill Anderson, Director), the Russian Archival Service (V. P. Kozlov, Director) and Rosspen publishers (Andrei Sorokin, Publisher) to organize and publish the thirty-one newly discovered Politburo transcripts in their entirety.

The decision to initiate this project was a bold one, for at the time there was little information as to whether the transcripts covered substantive Politburo meetings. We therefore wish to thank John Raisian, Director of the Hoover Institution, and Richard Sousa, Senior Associate Director, for their support. We wish as well to thank Lora Soroka of the Hoover Institution for her considerable assistance. The painstaking work of compiling the transcripts was done admirably by a team of archivists, led on the Russian side by Oleg Khlevniuk and Alexander Vatlin, both of whom have contributed essays to this volume. We also thank the dedicated staff of Russian archivists headed by Marina Astakhova who scoured the transcripts and pieced together fragments from other archives to provide a complete record.

Thanks are also due to Yale University Press, in particular to Jonathan Brent, for assistance in establishing the joint Yale-Hoover series, of which this volume serves as one of the first publications. We are grateful for the careful reading of the manuscript and comments by Lynne Viola. We also would like to acknowledge the contribution of Hiroaki Kuromiya, who read the manuscript in full and made valuable comments. Gavin Lewis is also to be thanked for his excellent editing work.

Paul Gregory
Norman Naimark

PART I

Introduction

Findings and Perspectives

NORMAN NAIMARK

The fall of the Soviet Union in 1991 ended a seventy-four-year experiment in the building of a socialist society in what was territory of the former Russian Empire. It would be hard to look at that three quarter-century history without a sense of relief that it is over with. The lives needlessly expended, the resources squandered, and the suffering inflicted on society know few parallels in the annals of human history. The damage done to the members of what was called the East European bloc was immense. The countries of the region have broken with the past and joined the European Union, but the history of communism there has produced bitter and long-lasting legacies. The former Central Asian, Caucasian, and Baltic republics of the Soviet Union are also doing the best they can to break away from their Moscow-dominated past and start afresh. But especially in the case of those regions that shared the Soviet experience from the beginning, serious political reform and economic transformation come very slowly. In both the Russian Federation and Ukraine, the heavy burden of the Soviet past continues to weigh on politics, culture, and society, despite attempts to democratize and institute a market economy. Post-Soviet Russia sometimes appears as controlling and authoritarian as the Soviet state. The "new Russians" often seem garish, crude, and as self-satisfied with their extreme material prosperity as their Soviet predecessors were with their special privileges as members of the *nomenklatura*. There is no turning one's back on history and starting completely anew. The Bolsheviks learned that lesson after 1917; in some ways, history itself shattered their dreams and crushed their aspirations.[1]

The opening of the Soviet archives after 1991 has greatly improved the ability of both Russian and Western historians to understand the development of the Soviet experiment and its successes and failures. This book provides a first look at the "lost" transcripts of the Politburo for the period 1923 to 1938, which have now been added to the growing collection of archives from the highest decision-making bodies of the Soviet Union.[2]

Access to the Soviet state and party archives has not followed a linear path of increased openness and ease of use. The publication of verbatim transcripts of Politburo meetings, after years housed in closed archives, is no exception.[3] Each scholar will have his or her own story to tell about successes and disappointments with the use of new materials on the Soviet period.[4] But there can be no question that the number of important documentary publications has grown by leaps and bounds. More and more interesting and useful historical material is being made available to researchers by the Russian archives, and, more widely, in published form. For historians of the Soviet Communist Party, the collections of RGASPI (Rossisskii gosudarstvennyi arkhiv sotsial'noi-politcheskoi istorii/Russian State Archive of Social and Political History), which covers the pre-1953 period, and RGANI (Rossiiskii gosudarstvennyi arkhiv noveishei istorii/Russian State Archive of Contemporary History), for the post-1953 period, have been absolutely critical in generating new and exciting developments in the historiography. In fits and spurts, new materials from the Presidential Archive are being transferred to RGASPI and RGANI and declassified. The process seems painfully slow and uneven to scholars who are anxious to get to the most crucial archival sources for their research. But given the political and institutional restraints in Russia on declassification, one can be grateful for significant incremental improvements.

The availability of new materials provides important stimuli to new research and writing on Soviet Russia. The fall of the Soviet Union also ensured that the discussion about the Soviet past will not just take place among Western historians. The addition of Russian historians to the scholarly mix marks a significant moment in the historiography, given the highly restricted ability of historians in the former Soviet Union to exchange ideas and materials with their colleagues in the West. Still, we can be reasonably certain that the political foundations of the historiography of the Soviet Union will not disappear anytime soon. As the eminent Soviet historian Ronald Grigor Suny emphasizes in his introduction to the recently published volume III of *The Cambridge History of Russia*, politics have always played an unusually prominent role in the writing of the history of the Soviet Union.[5] Lev Borisovich Trotsky himself served as an important interpreter of the Soviet past, but, of course, from his position as the loser in the power struggle with Stalin and as an opponent of the bureaucratization of Soviet politics that he saw occurring during the "Thermidor" of the 1930s.[6] Sympathizers of Trotsky, the redoubtable Isaac Deutscher and Boris Souverin, further shaped the way scholars and students approached the Soviet past.[7] E. H. Carr's marvelous fourteen-volume *History of Soviet Russia* was no doubt influenced by a generally positive evaluation of the Soviet experiment, if not a specifically Trotsky-like understanding of where it went awry.[8]

The professionalization of Russian historiography after World War II took place under the ubiquitous influence of the Cold War. Politics infused scholarship on Russia, as the West struggled to understand its new postwar opponent. In part because there were relatively few accessible documents and even fewer reliable archival sources, most academic historians stayed away from the Soviet period, leaving it to political scientists like Adam Ulam, Robert Daniels, and Robert Tucker, and historians outside the profession like Robert Conquest. That so much of what these scholars wrote has held up under the scrutiny of newer generations of historians with far greater access to primary documents is a tribute to their detective skills and perspicacity.[9] The intense ideological war waged between the Soviet Union and the United States in the 1950s gave considerable credence to the totalitarian model and fostered new studies of Soviet politics and society based on the Nazi analogy.[10]

Politics again inserted themselves into the historiography of the Soviet Union in the late 1960s and 1970s, when the war in Vietnam and the emergence of a large and more diverse cohort of young scholars in the universities created a perceived need to reassess "Cold War" interpretations of the Soviet Union and world communism and look at the historiography of the USSR from a fresh viewpoint. This trend corresponded, as well, with new, if limited possibilities of communicating with Soviet scholars and conducting research in the Soviet Union. Sheila Fitzpatrick and Moshe Lewin were among the most influential proponents of the social history paradigm, which tried to get away from the totalitarian model and the focus on politics in general, and instead emphasize the nature of social change and the past experiences of normal men and women, workers, peasants, and intelligentsia, in the Soviet Union.[11] But the social history "turn" gave way to yet more diverse challenges to the traditional historiography precipitated by the emergence of Gorbachev and the imminent collapse of the Soviet Union. The study of nationalities and of Russia as empire grew by leaps and bounds.[12] At the same time, the actual collapse of the Soviet Union under the weight of its own history invigorated a wave of scholarship from what might be called the neototalitarian school. Generally belonging to the Right of the political spectrum, the neototalitarians emphasized that the original sin of communism (whether committed by the French Revolution, Marx and Engels, or Lenin) had caught up with its Kremlin heirs and brought them down.[13]

Sweeping historical judgments about the Soviet experience and its socialist experiment represented a serious and major tangent of postcommunist scholarship. At the same time, given new and stimulating access to Russian archival sources, micro-level studies of Soviet institutions and of social groups became much more widespread.[14] Historians of the Soviet Union also became much more interested in the subjective individual experiences of Soviet citizens, as they attempted to create some kind of equilibrium in their own lives, faced with the ideological, social, and political demands surrounding them.[15] The publication of important documents became a way for Russian archival administrations and Western scholars and institutions, hungry for new materials for research, to cooperate and serve the needs of this new wave of scholarship on the one hand, and the financial needs of the archives on the other. The Yale University Press Annals of Communism series has been an important institutional focus of this important work.[16] But many presses, scholars, and institutions around the world, in Russia and in the West, have also contributed.[17]

It is within this historiographical context that the present volume should be seen. Generally, the emphasis over the past dozen years has been on document publication, more than on the analysis and contextualization of these materials. This book reverses that balance, and asks eleven leading scholars of the Soviet past, significantly from both Russia and the West, to analyze newly available documents from the perspective of their interests and specialties. The documents are previously inaccessible Politburo transcripts ("stenograms"), minutes taken verbatim from twenty-eight Politburo meetings during the 1920s and 1930s. The transcripts were recently declassified after being transferred from the Presidential Archives to RGASPI. The distinguished economic historian of Russia, Paul Gregory of the University of Houston, working under the auspices of the Hoover Institution, put together the concept for this book of essays on the transcripts, which we have jointly edited. The transcripts themselves are being published simultaneously in their entirety in Russian in three volumes by the Rosspen publishing house, the Russian Archival Service, and the Hoover Institution.

The Politburo transcripts enlighten the history of the interwar Soviet period in several important ways. First, they demonstrate the depth of policy discussions and the multiplicity of factors that were taken into account by the Soviet leadership when deciding administrative, economic, and foreign policy matters. Second, they make apparent the quintessentially political content of virtually all decision making at the highest level of the Soviet party and state. If the discussions about economic matters, especially the recurring grain crises, appear to be more substantive than those regarding administrative and foreign affairs issues, every policy discussion is shot through with political determinants and outcomes. Sometimes, the political struggle of the 1920s and early 1930s is the very subject of the transcripts; sometimes, it underlies them. But in every case, the battle for political supremacy between Stalin, Grigory Zinoviev, and Lev Kamenev, on one side and Leon Trotsky on the other, between Stalin, Nikolai Bukharin, Aleksei Rykov, and Mikhail Tomsky on one side and Zinoviev and Kamenev and Trotsky (the "United Opposition") on the other; and between Stalin, Molotov, Voroshilov, and Mikoyan on one side, and Bukharin, Rykov, and Tomsky (the so-called "Right Opposition") on the other, in these different combinations as time goes on and alliances shift, infuses the Politburo discussions. No one was yet aware — perhaps not even Stalin himself — that this would become a life-and-death struggle between the *vozhd'* and his alleged enemies. This fact makes the arguments, accusations, and counteraccusations all the more poignant.

The transcripts also are riveting examples of the internal personal interactions between the leaders of the Politburo in the 1920s and 1930s. The way they argue among themselves, address each other, and correct their opponents' alleged errors provides raw material for psychological portraits, individual and collective, of the main Politburo rivals. Their verbal jousting and sometimes good-natured kidding reveal a great deal about the atmospherics of leadership at the very pinnacle of Soviet power. The special language they use — episodically brutal, crude, cynical, immodest — speaks reams about the background and environment in which Bolshevik politicians were formed and operated. In some ways, we are witnesses to the rough-and-ready internal struggling within a close and affectionate Mafia family; in others, we can wonder at the highly personalized character of the criticisms of political rivals. In the transcripts, we can glean something of the ideological fabric and common background that kept the Bolsheviks together. We also learn a lot about the fundamentally different approaches to the serious problems of state and society that tore them apart.

Paul Gregory's chapter in this volume focuses on the provenance of the transcripts and examines the way they fit into the other Communist Party documents available to us from the interwar period. Clearly, the Politburo was the pinnacle of power in the Soviet system, and the transcripts were treated by those who had access to them as gospel from on high. The Politburo used the transcripts very purposefully as a way to circulate information from the inner circle of party leaders to the Central Committee and state and party leaders in the regions. They were also intended to discipline regional leaders and make them more responsive to the Kremlin's policies, eliminating much of the autonomy that had been enjoyed by these leaders. The Politburo oligarchs sometimes debated at length whether a particular meeting should have a transcript recorded or not. Important sessions that were planned to deal with political and economic issues were deemed appropriate for verbatim transcripts that in turn would be passed on to party and state hierarchs. In some cases, however, the transcripts were withheld from distribution because Politburo leaders determined that the discussions were too sensitive or indiscrete for dissemination.

Hiroaki Kuromiya's contribution examines Stalin's vaunted drive for ascendancy in the party in light of the new Politburo documents. His central observation, which is generally shared by all of the authors in this book, is that Stalin was a master tactician when faced with opposition and resistance among his comrades. He knew just when to back off and show restraint and he understood when he was free to attack and browbeat his opponents. Stalin took great pains, Kuromiya tells us, to portray himself as interested only in principled issues, not in his own political power and influence. In Stalin's rhetoric, the party was the only thing that mattered; the class struggle was the soul of his Manichean view of the universe. He managed in this way to portray himself as the party's humble servant. Kuromiya also emphasizes, as do a number of authors in the book, Stalin's hypersensitivity to perceptions of Soviet Communist Party politics outside the country. There could be no demonstrations to the outside world of party weakness or divisions in the ranks; otherwise the capitalist powers, in Stalin's view, would be tempted to intervene. Even if there were factional struggles, every effort had to made to conceal them, while bringing them to an end.

Robert Service, an estimable biographer of Stalin, focuses like Kuromiya on Soviet politics in the late 1920s.[18] In particular, Service analyzes the transcript from the joint meeting of the Politburo and the Central Control Commission Presidium of September 8, 1927. This famous meeting was the denouement of the political struggle between Stalin and Bukharin on the one hand, and the "United Opposition" (Trotsky, Zinoviev, and Kamenev) on the other. Service underlines the fact that the arguments on both sides were remarkably open and frank. Trotsky and his allies could say pretty much everything that was on their minds. Although Stalin and V. M. Molotov were direct and sharp in their criticisms of Trotsky's historical role in the party, by their very restraint in allowing him to speak, they gave Trotsky rope to hang himself through his own extreme, intemperate, and self-important rhetoric. Service's fascinating portraits of Trotsky's self-destructive behavior and of Bukharin's weakness in face of the critical importance of this Politburo meeting provide the reader with a deeper understanding of why Stalin and his clique emerged supreme in this confrontation.

Alexander Vatlin's essay on the transcript of the June 3, 1926 Politburo meeting demonstrates that the British General Strike (May 1926), the exclusive subject of the session, served as a lightning rod for the Bolsheviks' differences over foreign policy in the 1920s. Trotsky, Zinoviev, and Kamenev were advocates of a more radical policy to support insurgent British workers against the supposed reformism of the trade unions. In Vatlin's account, their common views of the issue helped to cement the foundations of the "United Opposition" between the Leningraders Zinoviev and Kamenev, on the one hand, and Trotsky and his supporters on the other. Rykov and Tomsky (Stalin was absent from the meeting) favored a more measured approach to the British trade unions. Arguments over "foreign policy," in this case and others, were a substitute for serious internal political struggle. Vatlin's reading of the transcript on "The Lessons of the British General Strike" fits well with the interpretations of the other authors in the volume. Fundamentally, the transcript's history supports the argument that the dissenting views of the "United Opposition" did not reflect the majority of the party, which tended to side with Stalin's more restrained and cautious approach to foreign and domestic policy issues. Once again, Trotsky's extreme views do not appear to have made much headway in the confrontation with Stalin's supporters. Zinoviev's energetic support of the radical position on the strike precipitated his dismissal from the Politburo in July 1926, and reinforced Stalin's determination to seek his removal as head of the Comintern.

Few historians have made more significant contributions to sorting out the meaning of new Russian archival sources for Soviet history than Oleg Khlevniuk.[19] In this volume, Khlevniuk focuses on the transcript of the joint session of the Politburo and the Presidium of the Central Control Commission of November 4, 1930, on the Syrtsov-Lominadze affair. There can be no question, Khlevniuk states, that the dismal failures of forced collectivization, which had been launched the previous year, raised serious questions in the middle levels of the party and state apparatus about Stalin's effectiveness. Sergei Syrtsov and Vissarion Lominadze, both members of the Central Committee, and their sympathizers in the party reflected this dissatisfaction and growing discomfort with Stalin's dictatorial power in the party. At the same time, as Khlevniuk emphasizes, Syrtsov and Lominadze were not part of the "Right Opposition's" critique of forced industrialization and collectivization. Instead, they represented a more reasonable iteration of the "Leftist" direction. But this did them no good with Stalin, who, with the relatively decent harvest of 1930, initiated the "Second Great Break," pushing forward with radical collectivization and dekulakization. The message of the Syrtsov-Lominadze affair was that not even moderate dissent would be tolerated. The two were removed from their prominent positions and demoted. Syrtsov was shot in 1937; facing imminent arrest, Lominadze committed suicide in 1935.

Stalin's renewed collectivization drive produced more misery and a growing sense of endemic crisis in the countryside. The upheaval in the villages rankled Old Bolsheviks and led to criticism of the party leadership, even to talk of removing Stalin. Charters Wynn analyses the transcript of the joint session of the Politburo and Presidium of the Central Control Commission of November 27, 1932. This session was dedicated to exposing the "Smirnov-Eismont-Tolmachev affair," an alleged conspiracy of party members unhappy with Stalin and the failures of collectivization. The charge stemmed from a late-night social gathering, where two inebriated Old Bolsheviks, Nikolai Eismont and Vladimir Tolmachev, talked about Stalin's responsibility for the tragic state of affairs in the countryside. Wynn points out that the sharpness of the attack on this "antiparty counterrevolutionary group" revealed Stalin's spiraling fears of opposition groups within the party that might seek to remove him in a "terrorist" plot. In some ways, the Smirnov-Eismont-Tolmachev group was treated as the reincarnation of the "Right Opposition" of the late 1920s. Alexander Smirnov, a former Minister of Agriculture and well-known opponent of collectivization, was directly linked to Eismont and Tolmachev through his presence at the drunken social gathering. In Stalin's eyes, Smirnov's friendship with the "Rightist" Mikhail Tomsky and their common absence from the Politburo session that condemned the anti-Stalinist "Riutin platform" (September 28 to October 2, 1932) aggravated Smirnov's sins and especially those of the much more influential Tomsky. In fact, in Wynn's reading, Tomsky was the main figure in the dock at this Politburo session; for Stalin to succeed, the party's chief workers' tribune had to be brought down, and the transcript of the session was used specifically for that purpose.

The growing unhappiness of Stalin and his pro-NEP allies with the work of the Central Statistical Administration (TsSU) in the mid-1920s is the subject of R. W. Davies's contribution dealing with the transcript of the Politburo session of December 10, 1925. Davies, a pioneer in the study of the Soviet 1920s and 1930s, links the political struggle between Stalin and the Left, especially Zinoviev and Kamenev, and the problem of grain production. P. I. Popov, the venerable chief statistician of the Central Statistical Administration, made the fateful decision to publish material about potential grain sales in 1925 and 1926 according to distinct groups of peasant households by size of holdings. Kamenev immediately jumped on the results as demonstrating, in his view, the increasing social differentiation among the peasantry and the reliance of the bulk of grain production on a small percentage of prosperous peasants, some of whom could be categorized as "kulaks." The proponents of NEP, committed to notions of the importance of the "middle and small peasants," did not want to hear this. As a result, at the December 10 Politburo meeting, Popov became a target for removal, with Stalin suggesting that statistics needed to be more "scientific" and "objective," meaning subservient to the political whims of the Politburo. There was no way that Stalin could tolerate an independent statistical apparatus. Yet the future *vozhd'* — as in the other transcripts — appears calm, cagey, and focused, even when Popov openly criticizes his view of statistical sciences. Though Popov was removed in the end, Davies notes that this was not the kind of "witch hunt" that would become so common by the end of the decade. Popov's successor at TsSU continued to maintain a modicum of independence for the statistical administration. Moreover, the critical issue that a disproportionately large percentage of grain was provided by well-to-do peasants did not go away until full-scale collectivization wiped out the group as a whole.

The grain supply was of central importance to the Bolsheviks because of their need to feed the cities. Even more crucial in the mid-1920s was the role of grain in Soviet exports, which in turn financed the growth of industry. In connection with the dependence of grain exports and investment in industry on state price mechanisms, meager Soviet gold reserves, and the weak Soviet trade balances, David M. Woodruff examines three sets of Politburo transcripts from October 26 and November 2, 1925, and February 22, 1926, that focus on macroeconomic policies. In these meetings, the People's Commissar of Finance, Grigory Sokol'nikov, sought to use a combination of import restrictions and tight monetary policy to insure a favorable trade balance and increase the supply of gold. Sokol'nikov was opposed by the industrial bureaucrats, led by Vesenkha (Supreme Soviet of the National Economy) chief Feliks Dzerzhinsky, who were desperate for greater imports of machinery and increased credits from the state to fuel factory expansion. For the time being, the Politburo, encouraged by Stalin, chose the more conservative strategy of preserving the gold supply and cutting back imports. Stalin insisted on the maintenance of a positive trade balance both to maintain the value of the Soviet currency and to avoid excess dependence on foreign markets. Woodruff observes, however, that macroeconomic policymaking devolved too easily into discussions of penalizing the microeconomic behavior of specific groups and classes, a phenomenon that persisted in the development of Stalinist economics in the 1930s. Stalin and his supporters sometimes denounced the speculative behavior of procurement agents as the problem; sometimes, they focused on the excess price demands of the cooperatives. Not surprisingly, Sokol'nikov's support of Kamenev and Zinoviev earned him Stalin's enmity. He was removed from his post, even if his more conservative monetary policies were, for the time being, those favored by Stalin.

Price setting, especially in the context of the urban-rural market, was crucial to Politburo economic policies. The maintenance of the *smychka* — the alliance between the peasants and proletariat — was considered the central feature of the New Economic Policy of the 1920s. Mark Harrison looks at the discussion of the setting of prices in the transcript of the January 2, 1927, Politburo meeting. Here, the party hierarchs confronted the ongoing problem of the "scissors crisis": relatively high industrial prices that inhibited the production of agricultural goods and the grain supply. The Politburo already had embarked on a program of reducing retail prices to deal with the urban-rural market equilibrium. The food procurement crisis of 1928, which set off Stalin's "Great Break," had still not hit the economy with force. Harrison points out that by 1927 the policy of price controls on industrial goods no longer worked as effectively as it had earlier because of a serious goods famine in industry. The cost of industrial goods production, including workers' salaries, was going up faster than production itself. Contrary to expectations, the policy was actually driving peasants and the regime farther apart because it was destroying the urban-rural market equilibrium, and with it, the vaunted *smychka*. Like Woodruff, Harrison underlines the fact that Stalin sought microeconomic solutions to macroeconomic problems by attacking the ability of the cooperatives and trading agencies to resist price controls. More important, Harrison concludes, the calculating, forceful, and even brutal way Stalin sought to impose the solution of lower prices was a foreboding of the draconian measures of breakneck industrialization and collectivization to follow. Both Harrison and Woodruff point to the fact that the leadership's unwillingness to accept market forces — the insistence on maintaining an overvalued exchange rate in foreign trade and on setting procurement and industrial prices domestically — meant that Stalin had to resort to "administrative," meaning repressive, measures to accomplish his economic goals.

No scholar can read the transcripts of the Politburo meetings without the sense that the words of both accusers and defenders in the political struggle and in the debates about economic policy carried meanings beyond their normal usages. Ideological presuppositions and political practice shaped the impact of certain terms and phrases. But also, according to Leona Toker's contribution, a linguistic battle went on at these Politburo sessions over the very content of words. She analyzes the transcripts of the October 8 and 21, 1926, and September 9, 1927, meetings, which centered on the party's attempts to discipline the

"United Opposition." She is interested in the use of several particular constructions and words: "that, which"; "elementary"; "normal" (in the context of party relationships); "party" ("the party" and "our party"); "falsification"; and "slander." Toker also points to the ways in which Stalin, in particular, was able to transform linguistically certain otherwise commonplace and innocuous notions into dangerous affairs (for example, "love of discussion" into criminal anti-party gossiping). She also points out the nefarious implications of the seemingly childish trading of insults that went on among party leaders, Trotsky and Stalin in particular. The verbal abuse heaped on the opposition, she suggests, was only a kind of dress rehearsal for the physical abuse that would follow. The cooptation of language against the Old Bolsheviks prefigured their sentencing to death for their participation in fantastic plots.

Rustem Nureev analyzes the transcript of the October 11 and 12, 1938, Politburo session, which discussed the publication of the *Short Course: The History of the All-Union Communist Party (Bolsheviks)*. The timing of the Politburo session was significant; the Great Purges would conclude only a month later. Almost all of the Old Bolsheviks had been arrested or eliminated. Now the *Short Course* was published to erase their role in the history of the party and the building of the Soviet state, leaving only Stalin as the true and natural successor to Lenin. The earlier transcript of September 9, 1927, discussed by Toker, Kuromiya, and Service, contained a bitter exchange between Stalin and Trotsky about "Lenin's Testament," which had called Stalin "too rude" to lead the party. At an earlier Central Committee meeting of May 24, 1924, Zinoviev and Kamenev had already exculpated Stalin from this accusation, though Trotsky was not hesitant to bring it up again in 1927. In any case, the testament was never published in Stalin's lifetime, even if the notion of Stalin's "rudeness" remained alive in party circles until all those who knew or talked about it were dead. Nureev emphasizes that the *Short Course*, which became the mandatory historical and ideological primer for party members, wiped the slate clean and created a new Stalinist party history. The book was meant primarily for the use of party propagandists, usually from the new Soviet intelligentsia, who would then spread the gospel to the workers and peasants. In the place of bloody purges, which had taken an enormous toll on the party and the country as a whole, Stalin and his hierarchs aimed to employ the propaganda of Marxism-Leninism in the *Short Course* to build and maintain a loyal and dedicated party.

The contributors to this volume demonstrate the unusual historical value of the "lost" Politburo transcripts, especially when used in concert with other available sources, including memoirs and published documents. The transcripts capture Bolshevik deliberations at the actual point of decision making, though, of course, the outcomes were often known well beforehand. The earlier transcripts from the 1920s make it apparent that the Politburo was a genuinely deliberative body. But it was also in transition, from a Bolshevik leadership forum that could produce compromise solutions and tolerated criticism to one that excoriated dissenters and exacted strict obedience from its members.

The internecine political struggles within the Bolshevik elite are highlighted by the arguments over policy, history, and economics. The transcripts demonstrate that by the end of the 1920s, Stalin was able to achieve his objectives of fully politicizing economic questions and turning statistics into an "objective," meaning completely controlled scientific enterprise. Stalin and his stage manager, Molotov, determined the agenda and the flow of discussion within the Politburo, while allowing their opponents to speak their piece. Stalin was not yet a dictator.[20] He was a teacher (Mark Harrison), an ideologue (Robert Service), and a brilliant tactician (Hiroaki Kuromiya). But he also systematically consolidated his power in the party and state and convinced broad segments of the rank and file that he was the true defender of socialism and leader in the class struggle. The Politburo sessions that attacked Syrtsov and Lominadze and Smirnov, Eismont, and Tolmachev gave warning signals about the limits of criticism and argument. In this sense, they presaged the trials and persecutions of the "Great Terror" of 1937–38. The transcripts also reinforce the contention that Stalin seized power in the "Second Revolution" discursively, as well as politically.[21] He corrupted the use of ideological terms and constructions for his own purposes. Through innuendo, accusation, and inference, he removed the Old Bolsheviks from political power and established himself as the voice of the party and the interpreter of its history.

Notes

1. See Kotkin's intriguing *Armageddon Averted: The Soviet Collapse 1970–2000.*

2. Khlevniuk, Gregory, and Vatlin, *Stenogrammy zasedanii Politbiuro TsK VKP(b), 1923–38.*

3. The publication of the transcripts of the Politburo for the period 1923 to 1938 is the result of a joint project among the Hoover Institution, Stanford University, the Russian Archival Service, and Rosspen. For more on this, see Paul Gregory's chapter in this volume.

4. See especially the special issue of *Cahiers du Monde Russe*, nos. 1–2, 1999, entitled "Assessing the New Archival Sources," which includes valuable contributions by Andrea Graziosi, Oleg Khlevniuk, and Terry Martin, among others. See also Getty, "Russian Archives: Is the Door Half Open or Half Closed?"; Naimark, "Cold War Studies and New Archival Materials on Stalin"; and Haslam, "Russian Archival Revelations and Our Understanding of the Cold War."

5. See Suny's "Introduction," *Cambridge History of Russia: The Twentieth Century,* vol. 3, pp. 1–64.

6. See, especially, Trotsky, *The Revolution Betrayed: What Is the Soviet Union and Where Is It Going?*

7. Service, *Stalin: A Biography,* p. 4.

8. Haslam, *Vices of Integrity: E. H. Carr, 1892–1982,* pp. 33–34.

9. See the following: Ulam, *Expansion and Coexistence: Soviet Foreign Policy, 1917–1967;* Tucker, *Stalin as Revolutionary 1879–1929: A Study in History and Personality;* Daniels, *Conscience of the Revolution: Communist Opposition in Soviet Russia;* and Conquest, *The Great Terror: Stalin's Purge of the 1930s.*

10. See Gleason, *Totalitarianism: The Inner History of the Cold War.*

11. See Lewin's foundational *Russian Peasants and Soviet Power: A Study of Collectivization* and Fitzpatrick's *Education and Social Mobility in the Soviet Union, 1921–1934.*

12. Suny, *Revenge of the Past: Nationalism, Revolution, and the Collapse of the Soviet Union;* Slezkine, *Arctic Mirrors: Russia and the Small Peoples of the North;* and Martin, *The Affirmative Action Empire: Nations and Nationalism in the Soviet Union, 1923–1939.*

13. See especially Furet, *The Passing of an Illusion: The Idea of Communism in the Twentieth Century;* Todorov, *Hope and Memory: Lessons from the Twentieth Century;* Courtoise et al., *Black Book of Communism: Crimes, Terror, Repression;* and Malia, *Soviet Tragedy: A History of Socialism in Russia, 1917–1991.*

14. See Viola, *Peasant Rebels under Stalin: Collectivization and the Culture of Peasant Resistance;* Fitzpatrick, *Stalin's Peasants: Resistance and Survival in the Russian Village after Collectivization;* Hoffmann, *Peasant Metropolis: Social Identities in Moscow, 1929–1941;* and Kuromiya, *Stalin's Industrial Revolution: Politics and Workers, 1928–1932.*

15. For different perspectives on a similar question, see Kotkin, *Magnetic Mountain: Stalinism as a Civilization;* and Hellbeck, *Revolution on My Mind; Writing a Diary under Stalin.*

16. Among other archival materials on the period relevant to this volume, the Yale series has published Lih, Naumov, and Khlevniuk, eds. *Stalin's Letters to Molotov, 1925–1936;* Davies, Khlevniuk, and Rees, *The Stalin-Kaganovich Correspondence 1931–1936;* Banac, *The Diary of Georgi Dimitrov;* Dallin and Firsov, *The Dimitrov-Stalin Correspondence;* Viola, Danilov, Ivnitsky, and Kozlov, *The War against the Peasantry, 1927–1930;* and documents on the Great Purges, such as Getty and Naumov, *The Road to Terror: Stalin and the Self-Destruction of the Bolsheviks, 1932–1939.*

17. These institutions include, for example: the Hoover Institution; the Feltrenelli Foundation; the Cold War History Projects at the Wilson Center, at Harvard University, and at the London School of Economics; and the University of Toronto Russian Archives Project.

18. Service, *Stalin: A Biography;* see also Kuromiya, *Stalin: Profiles in Power.*

19. See, most recently, Khlevniuk, *The History of the Gulag: From Collectivization to the Great Terror.*

20. See Khlevniuk, *Politbiuro: Mekhanizmy politicheskoi vlasti v 1930-e gody.* See also Gorlizki and Khlevniuk, "Stalin and his Circle," pp. 243–58.

21. See Hellbeck, *Revolution on my Mind; Writing a Diary under Stalin,* and Halfin, *Terror in My Soul: Communist Autobiographies on Trial.*

The Politburo's Role as Revealed by the Lost Transcripts

PAUL GREGORY

The "holy grail" of scholars studying the Soviet system has been to view its highest level of political and economic decision making. Although thousands of pages of party congresses, party platforms, official speeches, decrees, and Central Committee plenums have been published, they mostly capture ritualistic presentations of decisions made earlier at the highest level — by the Politburo, or by Stalin alone.

The essays in this collection provide a first glance at thirty-one "lost" verbatim transcripts (called "stenograms" in Russian) of Politburo meetings from 1923 to 1938. These verbatim transcripts cover primarily the 1920s and early 1930s. The 1938 stenogram on Stalin's *Short Course* of October 1938 was six years after the next-to-last stenogram of November 1932 on "The Group of Smirnov, Eismont, and Others." These stenograms have been published in their entirety in Russian.[1]

These stenograms provide verbatim records of discussion, debate, and formulation of decrees and resolutions that took place on the floor of the Politburo. Their coverage ranges from routine economic matters to the highest party politics, such as the expulsions of Leon Trotsky and his allies in the "United Opposition" and the suppression of the last opposition to Stalin's one-man rule.

From the first days of Bolshevik power, the Politburo of the Central Committee was the highest political authority, with Lenin clearly the first among equals. Stalin would attain this position in the late 1920s; in the meantime, he had to maneuver within the confines of a collective leadership. The Politburo's preeminence is taken as a matter of fact throughout the stenograms. As declared by the chair (Lev Kamenev) of the October 26 and November 2, 1925 session "About Questions of Grain Collections and the Import-Export-Currency Plan":[2]

> KAMENEV: It is necessary to give a firm directive to curb inflation no matter what. It is the Politburo that must say this.

In the February 25, 1926 meeting "About Necessary Economic Measures in the Near Future," the chair (Aleksei Rykov) cut off another member's (Mikhail Kalinin's) defense of agriculture by reminding him that agriculture had not met the Politburo's target on grain collections:[3]

> RYKOV: And what about the requirement to fulfill a Politburo decree?

In the January 3, 1927 meeting "About Lowering Retail Prices," Stalin berated trade commissar Anastas Mikoyan for not fulfilling a decree (which originated with the Politburo but was issued by the executive branch) to lower industrial prices:[4]

> STALIN: I have in my hands the decree and I must say that this decree is a high-level directive to the trade commissariat and to other agencies to lower the prices of industrial goods. I underline this because in actual fact Mikoyan has carried out a policy that has reversed this decree.

The practice of allowing Stalin as party General Secretary to organize Politburo meetings went back at least to 1922, as is evidenced by Lenin's handwritten letter to him: "Comrade Stalin. I believe it necessary to show this letter [a denunciation of a recent congress of physicians] to Dzerzhinsky [Feliks Dzerzhinsky, the head of the secret police, or OGPU] with extreme secrecy (no copies) and to all members of the Politburo and to prepare a directive to order Dzerzhinsky to prepare measures and report to the Politburo (two week deadline?).[5] Throughout the entire period covered, the setting of the agenda was firmly in the hands of Stalin's secretariat. In the 1920s, the "Secret Department" of the Central Committee set the meeting date, invited guests, and saw to the preparation of materials.[6]

In other societies, the lack of candid records of decision making at the highest level can be substituted for by other sources, such as diaries, autobiographies, and memoirs of political leaders and state officials. In the Soviet case, there are relatively few memoirs; the most prominent, such as those of Nikita Khrushchev and Anastas Mikoyan,[7] contain little inside information about the activities of the Politburo. The correspondence of party leaders, released after the opening of the official archives, provides invaluable information, especially the candid letters between Stalin and his trusted deputies, Molotov and Kaganovich.[8]

These stenographic records were transferred to the Russian State Archives of Social and Political History (RGASPI) from the Archive of the President of the Russian Federation (APRF) in the early years of the new century. We will not know conclusively whether we have the complete stenographic records until the Presidential Archives, the main repository for Politburo documents, is open for systematic research. Fragments of stenograms of the climactic joint meetings of the Politburo and Central Control Committee Presidium of January 30 and February 9, 1929 on the "Right-wing Deviation," have been found, but it is suspected that these stenograms were destroyed. Fragments of stenograms can also be found in the Trotsky archive,[9] particularly on the issue of the inner-party struggle.[10]

The period covered by these lost stenograms is propitious. After Stalin's death, the Politburo (renamed the Presidium) kept short summaries of debates from 1954 to 1964.[11] The inclusion of these thirty-one new stenograms provides a record, albeit fragmentary, that completes much of the 1923 to 1964 period.

Information gleaned from these stenograms can be supplemented by the agendas (*povestki dnia*) of Politburo meetings, which have been published and provide voluminous but often routine information on decision-making processes.[12] They reveal the myriad of questions discussed, by which agencies or persons the questions were raised, and the main participants in discussion of each issue.

As an example, the Politburo discussed twenty separate questions in its March 18, 1926 session, including, among others, reports from the foreign affairs ministry on Japan; agricultural subsidies; Lenin's mausoleum; and various personnel appointments.[13] Each question was presented by from one to four participants, including Politburo members such as Leon Trotsky, Lev Kamenev, Aleksei Rykov, Valerian Kuibyshev, and Mikhail Kalinin, and by fifteen participants from outside the Politburo. This Politburo meeting also handled five items voted on either by telephone or by written vote (*opros*) on March 15 and earlier in the day. Of these twenty questions, only item 11 was stenographed and was published as "Stenogram of the Meeting of the Politburo of the Central Committee of the All-Union Communist Party (Bolsheviks) of March 1926 'About the Question of the Chairmanship of the Leningrad Soviet,' March 18, 1926, stenographic record."[14]

The published Politburo agendas can be telling for their silences as well. The bitter struggle between the Politburo majority and the "United Opposition" of Leon Trotsky, Grigory Zinoviev, and Lev Kamenev in the October 8 and 11, 1926 sessions (covering over two hundred pages of transcripts) is described in the October 8 and 11 agendas only as "Detailed Discussion of the Decision of the Politburo from October 7, point 1."[15] There is no mention of the combined Politburo–Central Control Commission meetings of January 30 and February 9, 1929 on the "Right Deviationists" other than item 11 of the January 31, 1929 Politburo agenda: "to call a combined meeting of the Politburo and Presidium of the Central Control Commission."[16] The most significant Politburo decisions, such as the initiation of dekulakization on January 30, 1930[17] and the initiation of the Great Terror on July 3, 1937[18] were hidden behind bland designations "About Measures Associated with Kulaks" and "Question of the NKVD" and buried in top-secret "Special Files."

We also have isolated lists of Politburo meetings of the 1930s, which show who was present (full and candidate Politburo members, members and candidate members of the Central Committee, and members of the presidium of the Central Control Commission), the number of questions considered, and decisions from earlier meetings taken by written vote.[19] As an example, the combined session of the Politburo and the Central Control Commission of November 27, 1932 was attended by thirty Politburo and Central Control Commission members and by seven invited members of the Central Committee (most summoned to be censured because of their criticism of Stalin's one-man rule). In this case, there was only one topic, "About the Case of Eismont and Tolmachev," and the Politburo's decision was to "exclude Eismont and Tolmachev from the party and turn their case over to the OGPU."[20] This meeting was stenographed in full as "Combined Meeting of the Politburo and the Presidium of the Central Control Commission "On the Question of the Group of A. P. Smirnov, Eismont, and Others" of November 27, 1932 and covers more than 160 pages of transcripts.

We can sometimes link Politburo meetings with later Central Committee actions. Questions that had been previously discussed at Politburo meetings were formally approved as Central Committee plenum resolutions, as was the case with discussions about additional export resources (October 26 and November 2, 1925), reductions in consumer prices (January 3, 1927), and supplies for workers and trade development (July 22–23, 1931). Plenum participants either read Politburo stenograms or attended expanded Politburo meetings (as in the case of the July 22–23 plenum), and adapted their positions accordingly.[21]

This collection of Politburo stenographic records originates in the June 14, 1923 Politburo decision to make stenographic records of the main reports and concluding remarks on the principal agenda items of each meeting.[22] The debates (*preniia*) were to be stenographed only if the Politburo itself so decided. The first Politburo stenogram (from August 2, 1923: "Question about the Export of Grain") appeared in the archives of the Politburo one and a half months later. The published Politburo agendas are not accurate guides to whether stenograms were taken of questions in the meeting. The December 24, 1924 and January 3, 1925 questions were stenographed but this fact is not shown on the agenda, while item 8 of the February 25, 1926 agenda ("About Necessary Economic Measures for the Near Future") is correctly listed as "stenographed" in the agenda.[23]

The June 1923 decision to prepare stenographic records of the main agenda reports of Politburo meetings was not observed from day one. Only two stenograms were made of fifty-five Politburo meetings for the rest of 1923. In 1924, four of seventy-five meetings, in 1925 three of fifty-three meetings, and in 1926 only eight of seventy-one meetings had points that were stenographed.[24] The thirty-one verbatim records of single questions at Politburo meetings represent a tiny fraction of Politburo discussion. For the period 1923 to 1926, stenograms were made in only 6.6 percent of Politburo meetings. These stenograms cover about two-tenths of 1 percent of the questions discussed before the Politburo during this period. Yet, the fact that they require three lengthy volumes to be printed in their entirety suggests that their importance far exceeds these modest percentages.

The relatively few stenographic records can be understood from a technical point of view. It was simply not possible to record the thousands of separate questions discussed at Politburo meetings. From 1930 to 1935, the Politburo discussed 20,911 separate questions.[25] If each question required thirty pages of transcripts, the number of pages would have been over 600,000. The preparation of a single stenographic record was incredibly time-consuming. Remarks by each participant recorded "from voices" had to be distributed to that speaker for review, editing, and sometimes significant additions or even changes of positions. This practice allowed debate to continue after Politburo meetings as participants "corrected" and added to the texts of their remarks, sometimes attaching lengthy statements. The preparers of the stenographic report of the October 3, 1926 meeting "About the Inner-Party Situation" complained in a letter that Trotsky had almost doubled the length of his remarks, a fact that Stalin and his faction duly reported.[26] The edited versions then had to be pieced together into the final reports. The stenographic records were then typeset and distributed as brochures, called "red books" because of the red-pink color of the binding.

The limited number of stenographic records is also explained by the Bolshevik penchant for secrecy. What went on within the Politburo was a matter of controlled secrecy. The Politburo's (Stalin's) decisions to launch terror campaigns in 1930 and 1937 were first relayed to designated regional officials as top-secret Politburo directives.[27] A broader audience of executors then had to be informed through operational decrees, which converted the substance of Politburo decisions into concrete plans of action. Published decrees, the most important of which were either issued by the Politburo alone or jointly with the state administration, provide little insight, because over five thousand decrees of the 1930s were classified as top secret, far exceeding the number of published decrees.[28] Those officials receiving directives from the Politburo were "categorically forbidden to reveal that these are instructions of the Central Committee."[29] The "special file" decisions on European foreign policy have been published and enrich our knowledge of Politburo decisions in the area of foreign policy.[30] Redacted versions of the special files have been released but have yet to be studied.[31]

The Politburo itself decided on the circle to be informed of its decisions and how much they were to be told. Stenograms usually included decrees of the Central Committee "About Acquainting Persons with the Distributed Secret Stenograms of the Meeting of the Politburo." The distribution of the October 8 and 11, 1926 stenogram "About the Inner-Party Situation" was limited to secretaries of regional party committees and heads of control commissions, Communist youth organizations, Communist university cells, and chairs of the USSR Central Executive Committee and of the Central Committee of Trade Unions.[32] Recipients had to return their copies within a set period of time or face severe penalties to prevent "outlaw" circulation outside the narrow group, but recipients of even top-secret Politburo documents were known to be careless, such as a Central Asian Central Committee member who was punished for leaving such documents in his room at the Hotel National.[33]

The Politburo had in its ranks extremists, such as candidate member and OGPU head Feliks Dzerzhinsky, who wished for a thick veil of secrecy around the body. At the June 14, 1926 meeting, the issue of stenographic records provoked the following squabble between Dzerzhinsky and Trotsky:[34]

> DZERZHINSKY: I believe that to keep a record of what we talk about is a crime.
> TROTSKY: Of the fact that we talk? If so, we must direct the OGPU to force us to stop talking; this will simplify everything.

Stalin and other Politburo members emphasized the importance of discretion when Politburo meetings were stenographed. In the February 25, 1926 meeting "About Necessary Economic Measures in the Near Future," Stalin rebuked two Politburo members (Mikhail Kalinin and Mikhail Tomsky) for speaking out against a Politburo consensus:[35]

STALIN: Now I want to answer Comrade Kalinin (and also Tomsky on peasant matters). Kalinin's speech, which he delivered here, should not have been made before the Politburo. It is not possible to do this. What is written will be read in the localities, and I want to say that this is dangerous and incorrect.

Mikhail Kalinin in the October 11, 1925 meeting about the internal party situation warned Politburo members to think twice about statements that were being stenographed:[36]

KALININ: If we conducted discussions only in the Politburo, without stenograms, without announcements, we could allow ourselves more leeway. But this discussion is tied into an extraparty milieu and in a significant degree has weakened Soviet power.

There were also efforts to remove crude remarks from the stenographic records that were eventually published. In the February 25, 1926 meeting "About Necessary Economic Measures in the Near Future," the presiding chairman rang the bell, noting that Mikhail Kalinin had already spoken seven minutes and asking whether he should be given more time: [37]

KALININ: Keep in mind that I am the only defender of agriculture here.
TROTSKY: Then don't give him more time.
VOROSHILOV: It is not necessary to place that remark in the stenogram.
KALININ: No, it is absolutely necessary (Bell rings again)

Given that speakers could edit their spoken remarks, they could remove undiplomatic, or in the case of Stalin, unstatesmanlike utterances. Notably, Stalin edited out about half of his remarks in the meeting called to attack "deviationists" on November 27, 1932, many of them wisecracks or caustic remarks, such as: "He (Smirnov) is not capable, like others, of deftly hiding things. It just bursts out of him."[38]

The ultimate method of nondisclosure was to not publish and distribute the stenographic records. The stenographic reports of the June 14, 1926 session on the report of the Moscow City Party Committee summarizing its political and economic work, the August 2, 1926 session on results of establishing state and collective farms, and the December 31, 1928, meeting on the work of Donugol [the complex of mining enterprises] were not published.[39] Stenographic reports of the November 25, 1930 session on collectivization in the northern Caucasus, of the June 22 and 23, 1931 sessions on improvement in supplies for workers and development of Soviet trade, and of the October 11 and 12, 1938 sessions on party propaganda in connection with publication of the *Short Course* were also not published.[40] Individual documents from attachments to stenograms were sent to a narrower circle than those to whom the "red books" were normally be sent. Mikhail Tomsky's report summarizing his work in Paris during the General Strike in Great Britain was sent only to Central Committee members and to members of the Presidium of the Central Control Commission.[41]

Some stenograms were withheld for political reasons, like those revealing objectionable facts about and frames of mind of, or impolitic behavior on the part of Politburo leaders. Other stenograms were withheld because the tasks put forward at that Politburo meeting had not been fulfilled, such as the failure to complete the steps of collectivization and dispossession of the kulaks.

What makes these stenographic records more significant than their small number is the fact that the questions stenographed were selected for a reason. Someone in the Politburo majority or minority had to request that a stenographic record be made. In effect, when Politburo sessions were stenographed, speakers knew they were addressing a wider audience of party officials than just those present.

In the early 1920s, stenographic records were made on economic issues to inform members of the Central Committee and regional party and state officials about the Politburo's economic policies. The message of the August 2, 1923 "Question about the Export of Grain" was that the internal costs of producing and transporting grain had to be reduced and that cooperatives were preferred to private trade.[42] The message of the August 16, 1923 session "About a Single Agricultural Tax" was to free small farms from the tax and to warn that taxes from other producers must be collected without fail. The December 24, 1924 meeting "About Former Estates" announced the danger posed by returning landowners and the need to purge them from local Soviets.

As divisions within the Politburo became more apparent, economic discussions spilled over into politics. The December 10, 1925 meeting "About the Work of the Central Statistical Administration on Grain Balances" was called to fire the director of the statistical service for issuing statistics that contradicted the agrarian policy of the majority of Politburo members.[43] The August 2, 1926 meeting "About the Results of State Farm and Collective Farm Development" announced the Politburo's preference for cooperatives, collectives, and state farms (over private farms) but concluded not to move against private farmers by force.[44] The January 3, 1927 session "About Lowering Retail Prices" was called to publicly rebuke Trade Minister Anastas Mikoyan for not reducing industrial prices as the Politburo had decreed.[45]

The economic discussions, especially of the mid-1920s, were freewheeling. Each Politburo member as well as invited experts could express their opinion. Sessions of economic issues were called to resolve competing claims for resources among various state agencies. The February 25, 1926 session "About

Necessary Economic Measures in the Near Future" records bitter departmental battles over cuts in imports and cuts in investment budgets and makes the case (as supported by Stalin) for an investment-in-industry-first program.[46] The contentious October 26 and November 2, 1925 meeting "About Questions of Grain Collections and the Import-Export-Currency Plan" dealt with reductions in imports, budget cuts, and reductions in investment finance to reduce inflationary pressures.[47] The verbal battles fought in such meetings were waged by competing departmental interests. In the October 26–November 2, 1925 session, Finance Ministry representative G. Y. Sokol'nikov led the battle for cuts (and for less inflation) against industry czar Feliks Dzerzhinsky's impassioned pleas to spare industry from cuts:[48]

> SOKOL'NIKOV: I am fighting for the reduction of grain collections and for the lowering of prices (adds: well, convict me for a crime against the state). . . . I am protecting state interests from departmental egoism.
> DZERZHINSKY: Comrade Sokol'nikov, in that case, it would not be necessary to engage in stupidities. It would not be necessary to export a hundred million worth of gold, or to engage in magic tricks.

The representative of military departmentalism, Kliment Voroshilov, then entered the fray to defend the military from budget cuts:

> VOROSHILOV: The situation with the Red Army is extreme and exceptionally difficult. The Politburo needs to know this . . . and if this becomes known to our enemies — then we cannot rule out all kinds of adventurism.

Dzerzhinsky was not above using threats to avoid cuts in his beloved industry, such as at the February 25, 1926 meeting "About Necessary Economic Measures in the Near Future:"[49]

> DZERZHINSKY: Now I want to point out what these figures about supplemental needs for imported raw materials mean in terms of cutbacks in production. We would have to stop cotton textiles factories more than 14 days, factories another 40 days, and let 58,000 workers go.

The end result of economic discussions was normally a Politburo decree, worked out on the basis of compromise. In some cases, especially after inconclusive debate, a Politburo commission would be appointed to draft the decree. The October 26 and November 2, 1925 meetings "About Questions of Grain Collections and the Import-Export-Currency Plan" ended with the appointment of a commission and Stalin's proposal "to give the commission a fixed date and if they agree unanimously consider it a decision of the Politburo."[50] In order to achieve a consensus, Politburo members holding minority positions were included in these commissions, as in that formed at the end of the November 2, 1925 meeting:[51]

STALIN: In view of the fact that Comrade Dzerzhinsky is not in complete agree-
ment with Comrade Sokol'nikov, I propose to include him in the commission.
RYKOV: I propose as members of the commission Comrades Kamenev, Stalin,
Rykov, Sokol'nikov, Bukharin, Dzerzhinsky, and Rudzutak.
KAMENEV: Because we are dealing with grain collections, then it is necessary
to include also Comrade Sheiman [an official of the grain collections agency].

In the contentious February 25, 1926 meeting on "Necessary Economic
Measures in the Near Future," the Politburo meeting ended with a drafting
session on the wording of the decree to be issued:[52]

RYKOV: I propose, in general, to confirm the proposals of the commission in
the area of economic policy; in connection with numerical proposals to consider as a minimum a 100 million budget reserve.
TROTSKY: This is unclear. We have a figure of 133 in the commission protocols, which is independent of another 15 million, which yields 148 million.
STALIN: In general, it comes out to 133 million, of which 100 hundred million
is a reserve and we'll spend the rest.
TROTSKY: In that case, it is necessary to say it as such.

The Politburo then went on to delegate detailed cuts to the Council of
Peoples' Commissars. Further editing followed from Mikhail Tomsky, the
head of Soviet trade unions:

TOMSKY: I object to giving the increase in labor productivity as a firm directive to the labor unions and enterprise managers, noting the exact percentage
increase. I object not because such an increase is not possible but because
there is a commission that is working on this matter. I insist that we await the
final work of the commission.

Although economic issues remained a constant factor in the life of the Politburo, its most consuming issues were political. The period from Lenin's death
to Stalin's consolidation of power would be eventful, deciding not only the
succession but also the fundamentals of political, social, and economic policy.
Although Lenin left behind a political testament highly critical of Stalin, it
pointed out the faults of other Bolshevik leaders, and there was no anointed
heir. Only Leon Trotsky enjoyed a wide following. Hence, the first concern of
other Politburo members was Trotsky. Grigory Zinoviev, the head of the Comintern, Lev Kamenev, chairman of the Moscow Soviet, and party General
Secretary Stalin formed a ruling troika to block Trotsky. Stalin was included
because of his control of the party apparatus, but the other two thought that
Lenin's testament removed him from contention. The glue that held the dispa-
rate members of the Politburo together was "party discipline" — the principle
that Politburo members were free to express their opinions but once a Politburo decision was taken, all members had to publicly support that decision.

At the date of the first stenogram (August 2, 1923), the Politburo had seven full members and six candidate members.[53] By the end of 1930, of the thirteen full and candidate members of 1923, only four remained in the Politburo (Stalin, Molotov, Kalinin, and Jan Rudzutak). The others had been expelled and had been replaced by Stalin loyalists (full members: Kliment Voroshilov, Lazar Kaganovich, S. M. Kirov, S. V. Kosior, Valerian Kuibyshev, and Sergo Ordzhonikidze; and candidate members: Anastas Mikoyan, G. I. Petrovsky, and V. Ya. Chubar').[54] It was these Politburo members who formed Stalin's Politburo majority which oversaw collectivization, dekulakization, and forced industrialization in the early 1930s. Of the twenty-two Politburo members serving between 1923 and 1930, four died of natural causes, two committed suicide, and ten were executed.

The atmosphere of the Politburo sessions of the mid-1920s under the Kamenev-Zinoviev-Stalin troika is described by Stalin's secretary Boris Bazhanov (who fled to the West and miraculously escaped assassination):

> Two tables faced each other in the long, narrow room, with red table cloths on them. At one end was the Politburo chairman's chair, originally occupied by Lenin, but now occupied by Kamenev, who presided over the sessions. The other members sat side by side facing each other, with space between the two tables. Stalin was on Kamenev's left, and Zinoviev on his right. Between Zinoviev and Kamenev, a small table was set right against the larger table and that is where I sat. On the little table was a phone linking me with my staff who waited in the next room. Persons due to appear also waited in that room. When one of my staff called me, a small light went on. I would tell her who to send in for the next point on the agenda. As each point was settled I would note its disposition on the file and pass it to Stalin, sitting facing me. Usually he glanced at it and gave it back to me, signifying "no objection." If the case was very important and complicated, he would pass it back to me via Kamenev who examined it and wrote "OK" in the margin. The other members sat lower down the table than Stalin and Zinoviev. Nikolai Bukharin was usually next to Zinoviev, then Molotov (still a candidate member), then Mikhail Tomsky. Next sat Trotsky, with Mikhail Kalinin, sometimes behind him, sometimes behind Tomsky. At the end of the room, a closed door led to the next room, full of people waiting to appear before the session. Almost all the peoples' commissars were there, in full force. . . . Kamenev was an excellent chair, guiding the discussion well, cutting short superfluous conversation, and quickly arriving at decisions. The fact that the troika members sat next to each other at the end of the table was very helpful in their conspiracy. They could exchange notes whose contents were shielded from the rest and whisper comments or agreements to each other.[55]

The main speakers usually submitted their reports prior to the meeting, and only oral summaries were presented at the meeting. Oral presentations were freely interrupted by questions from the audience (Stalin was one of the most frequent questioners); discussion (*preniia*) followed. Discussion was ended by proposal of the chair, such as Kamenev's "I move that we end discussion" which ended the debate on the December 24, 1924 meeting "About former Estates."[56] At the December 10, 1925 meeting on the Central Statistical Administration's grain balances, twelve participants, including Stalin, Trotsky, and other Politburo members, plus the head of the statistical administration and Gosplan officials, took part in the debate.[57]

The Politburo meetings of the period of the Kamenev-Zinoviev-Stalin troika were chaired by Kamenev. After Kamenev and Zinoviev joined forces with Trotsky, Aleksei Rykov, who also served as prime minister, typically chaired. As the "Right Opposition" of Rykov, Bukharin, and Tomsky parted company from the Stalin majority, Politburo meetings were chaired either by the then prime minister, Molotov, or by his deputy, Ya. Rudzutak. The chairman's job was to move the meeting along in an orderly fashion and to hold speakers and debate participants to agreed-upon time limits. If a speaker exceeded his allotted time, the chairman would ring a bell and determine whether more time should be allowed.

In the Politburo meetings of the mid-1920s, debate took place in a generally congenial atmosphere. There were attempts at humor and "laughter" (*smekh*) was noted in the stenogram. Kalinin elicited laughter in the December 24, 1924 Politburo meeting "About Former Estates," with a telling quip that showed the Bolsheviks' low regard for the peasantry:[58]

> KALININ: Yes, peasants will complain even about a saint if it is possible to take something from him (laughter) I am convinced that if Saint Paul had seven desyatinas, what do you think, would the peasants let him keep them? (Laughter)

Even after bitter debate, there was an effort to end on a positive note. The December 10, 1925 meeting "On the Question about the work of the Central Statistical Administration on Grain Balances" ended with the firing of its director, P. I. Popov. In his concluding remarks, the chairman (Aleksei Rykov) reiterated the statistical agency's mistakes but noted:[59]

> RYKOV: I am sure that these comrades worked with the best of intentions. I am sure that these comrades consider themselves true Leninists.

In the mid 1920s, Stalin lacked the power to suppress dissent and had to tolerate the transcribing of Politburo sessions in which his political opponents made their cases. In 1926 and 1927, Stalin's nemesis was the "United Opposition" of Trotsky, Kamenev, and Zinoviev. In 1928 and 1929, it was the "Right Opposition" of Rykov, Bukharin, and Tomsky, who had been his allies in the struggle against the "United Opposition."

Someone had to request that a Politburo meeting be stenographed. Prior to Stalin's ascent to one-man rule, such requests were often met with suspicion. At the October 11, 1926, meeting, Lev Kamenev defended his request for a stenogram as follows:[60]

> KAMENEV: Somebody mentioned here that I spoke for the stenogram, to be able to "wave a paper." I did not request a record, and if you let me speak without a stenogram, I am willing to speak. I dare say that I am not on record now. There indeed have been moments in the Central Committee when a stenogram was used as a weapon.

It was Kamenev's political ally, Zinoviev, who requested transcribing "On the Lessons of the British General Strike" (June 3, 1926) and "About the 'Draft Platform' of Trotsky, Zinoviev, Muralov, and Others" (September 8, 1927). Representatives of the majority, in their turn, accused the opposition of using stenograms for factional goals. At the meeting of March 12, 1926, Stalin stated that Zinoviev had refused to submit a written notification about leaving his position as the head of the Leningrad Soviet because "he wanted to make a case for today's stenogram." Answering Kamenev, who reproached the majority for using verbatim records to discredit the opposition, Stalin noted at the same meeting:[61]

> STALIN: Stenograms have been taken during Politburo meetings for two years. Stenograms have been taken at somebody's request. Today you demanded stenograms not for cooperation, but for struggle. That is how the question of cooperative work is put at the Politburo. The Politburo is not to be blamed if you look for and create material for struggle.

When the Stalin majority moved to unseat the "United Opposition" leader, Zinoviev, from his chairmanship of the Leningrad Soviet, Zinoviev's ally E. G. Evdokimov (notably not a Politburo member) demanded that the March 18, 1926 session "On the Question of the Chairmanship of the Leningrad Soviet" be stenographed:[62]

> EVDOKIMOV: I said, when I requested that Comrade Rykov stenograph this question, that I consider it of extreme importance, not only as a general party question but as a general political issue, not only internal but also external. I am not able to say all that I would like to say because I reserve the right to prepare a written declaration addressed to all members of the Central Committee and to the Central Control Commission. Is there anything else that I can add to what I have said?
> VOICE: Think it over.
> EVDOKIMOV. There is nothing to think over. I get upset, comrades, when I speak. I am a temperamental person and I do not always have the necessary clarity of thought and self-control when it is required.
> STALIN. That is dangerous for the health.

Later in the meeting, chairman Rykov summarized the motivation for a stenographic record:

> RYKOV: We are stenographing the debate on the chairmanship of the Leningrad Soviet according to the proposal of Comrade Evdokimov. Evidently, Comrade Evdokimov is operating on the proposition that our debates should be known to a wider circle of party members than the Politburo itself.

The Politburo also granted the requests to stenograph the clash of the October 8 and 11, 1926 session between the Stalin majority and the "United Opposition." This transcript, which covers almost two hundred pages of text and resolutions, includes a decree of the Central Committee for distribution to regional party secretaries, secretaries of the Central Committee of the Communist Youth, and a number of bureau heads. The main point of contention was the "United Opposition's" demand to present its platform to the forthcoming Party Congress, which Stalin opposed at the October 8, 1926 session:[63]

> STALIN: Proposing peace and simultaneously sending Zinoviev to Leningrad for battle, the opposition, apparently, hoped that it could come to the Central Committee for negotiations with Leningrad in its pocket in hopes that Zinoviev would "win over" Leningrad organizations. But their calculation did not work out and this explains the moderate tone of their proposals. But what would have happened if Zinoviev had returned from Leningrad with a series of opposition proposals from the Putilov factory, or the Trekhugol'nik works?

There could even be lighter moments that evoked laughter, sometimes genuine but often derisive. After Kalinin questioned whether Trotsky held the majority for fools in his refusal to back away from his factional work, there was the following exchange:

> KALININ: Comrade Trotsky knows how to make a molehill from a mountain.
> STALIN: And from a molehill a mountain. (Noise in the hall. Laughter).

Likewise when Kamenev tried to formulate a compromise solution:

> KAMENEV: You told us that you want an admission of factionalism and an agreement to cease and desist, and we formulated our response as best we could (laughter). I do not understand why you are laughing. We said that we honestly will subordinate ourselves.

Or again:

> TOMSKY: I don't like to relate private conversations and correspondence but I yesterday asked Kamenev why Grigory [Zinoviev] was not present? Was he ill? And the answer was "His father is ill." (laughter)
> UGLANOV: (Moscow party secretary): How can he be ill? He works at a dairy farm.

TOMSKY: I was amazed at the newly discovered good son, Comrade Zinoviev, who appears to be a gentle and loving son, who is capable of putting aside issues of great political importance to fulfill his duties as a faithful son. But it turns out that either Kamenev misinformed me or Grigory [Zinoviev] misinformed him.

Within a year of this meeting, all pretense of collegiality and compromise had disappeared. The no-holds-barred tone of discourse is reflected in the following exchanges from the Combined Politburo–Central Control Commission meeting of September 8, 1927 on the "United Opposition":[64]

STALIN: Comrade Trotsky demands equality between the Central Committee, which carries out the decisions of the party, and the opposition, which undermines these decisions. A strange business! In the name of what organization do you have the audacity to speak so insolently with the party?
ZINOVIEV: Each member of the party has the right to speak before the Party Congress, and not only organizations.
STALIN: I think that it is not permitted to speak so insolently as a turncoat to the party.
ZINOVIEV: Don't try to split us; don't threaten, please.
STALIN: You are splitting yourselves off. This is your misfortune. [After a diversion, Stalin returns to his general attack.] Judge now the value of your idle chatter about the governance of the party. . . . Only those who have joined the camp of our enemies could go so far. But we wish to pull you out of this dead end.
TROTSKY: You should pull your own self out of the swamp first. (Noise, shouting, the bell of the chairman.)
ZINOVIEV: You should get out of the dead end yourself. We are on Lenin's road, and you have left it.

After Stalin's charge of "complete intellectual and political bankruptcy," the discussion ended with the chair turning to another speaker, despite Trotsky's petty protest:

CHAIRMAN [RUDZUTAK]: Comrade Yaroslavsky has the floor.
TROTSKY: Comrade Stalin spoke 25 minutes.
CHAIRMAN: Exactly 20 minutes.
TROTSKY: Comrade Stalin spoke 24 minutes.
CHAIRMAN: Your watch must be more reliable than the sun. Comrade Yaroslavsky has the floor.

As Stalin's dictatorship tightened in the 1930s, fewer and fewer Politburo sessions were stenographed, and the Politburo became a closed book for the party membership except when Stalin himself wished to inform them of certain matters, such as treachery by high party officials. Most Politburo decisions were made by telephone or by small groups of party leaders appointed by Stalin.[65]

Stalin now displayed zero tolerance towards party officials who questioned the correctness of his policies and his personal authority, even towards those, such as S. I. Syrtsov, candidate member of the Politburo and chair of the Council of Peoples' Commissars of the Russian Republic, who shared his general political views. When denunciations were received (perhaps organized by Stalin himself) that Syrtsov was criticizing the party line and calling for Stalin's removal, a combined Politburo–Central Control Commission meeting "On the Factional Work of Comrades Syrtsov, Lominadze, and Others" was held on November 4, 1930 with Stalin's ally Sergo Ordzhonikidze serving as the chief prosecutor.[66]

> ORDZHONIKIDZE: (recounting Syrtsov's interrogation): Syrtsov began with the point that not all is well in the party, that there is a closed circle of leadership, that such members of the Politburo as Voroshilov, Kalinin, Kuibyshev, and Rudzutak are isolated and are only mechanical members and so on, and that there are a large number of deficiencies to which no one is paying attention and so on and so on. [Ordzhonikidze goes on to relate the contents of denunciations of Syrtsov] What is the main point and most disturbing in this matter? Of course, there can be vacillation and disagreement in such a large party, especially in such a period when it is necessary to carry out the colossal work of socialist reconstruction. . . . But every member of the party must come to his party if he has doubts. The party should help such a comrade resolve his own doubts, to save him, and set him on the right course. If he does this, no one will call him to his party responsibility. But when he does these things in secret, this becomes an antiparty matter. Can we have such people in our leadership who try to tear it down?
>
> STALIN: It is impossible

Syrtsov mounted the following defense:

> SYRTSOV: I did not doubt for one minute the need for the liquidation of the kulaks as a class. . . . I believe that the leader can move forward in any order, but I believe that, in addition to slogans, it is necessary and correct to have a detailed discussion of the implementation of these measures in a Central Committee plenum or a detailed meeting of the Politburo. It seems to me we could have avoided many of the costs by doing so.

As to the accusation that he had not informed the party of his doubts, Syrtsov argued:

> SYRTSOV: I did not keep my fears about the political situation, the economy, to myself and Sergo [Ordzhonikidze] and others know that I attempted to bring

all such questions that disturbed me before the Central Committee. . . . At the end of the XVI Party Congress I agreed with Comrade Stalin to discuss all these questions in detail. But it did not work out.

The result of the meeting was the "Decree of the Combined Meeting of the Politburo and the Presidium of the Central Control Commission about the Factional Work of Syrtsov, Lominadze, and Others," approved on November 5, 1930, which decreed, among other things, to expel Syrtsov from the Central Committee.

As Stalin solidified his power, he redefined disloyalty to include the failure to support the party line with sufficient zeal and vigor, as evidenced by the attack on the former prime minister, Aleksei Rykov, earlier expelled from the Politburo, at the November 27, 1932 meeting:[67] The frustrated Rykov took the floor to protest that he had actually been prevented from publicly supporting the party:

> RYKOV: I asked for the floor to answer the charge addressed against me about my lack of public speeches outside the boundaries of my ministry.
> ORDZHONIKIDZE: Speak openly so that the country can hear.
> RYKOV: I wanted to speak publicly two times. Once I wanted to hold a lecture at the Union House . . . in defense of the general party line, but in the end this did not happen because some kind of party organization did not want this.
> KAGANOVICH: Where?
> RYKOV: In Moscow. The second time I organized a large meeting in the Park of Culture and Rest, where it was announced and publicized that I would appear. But when I arrived I was told that the regional party committee sent comrade Uvarov, the head of communications of Moscow city, in my place. . . . I conclude from these facts that for some reason it has been decided that my public appearances have become inappropriate, consequently, it is best for me to stay out of sight.

After Stalin's full accession to power, there was no real debate, only harassment of those who had purportedly expressed doubts about Stalin, such as Central Committee member A. P. Smirnov, accused of calling for Stalin's replacement at a private party. Smirnov was placed in the awkward position of having to prove a negative (that he had never doubted Stalin).[68]

> SMIRNOV: Yes, yes. It is difficult to prove my innocence.
> MIKOYAN: But you must help us to prove it.
> SMIRNOV: But to disprove gossip and defamation is even more difficult.

Stalin's advice to Smirnov provided little comfort:

> STALIN: You can have a negative position, but it is necessary to report this to the Central Committee. When you take a position against the party and gather people illegally for a break, this is improper.

The window of open and free discussion was shut tight after Stalin established his dictatorship in the 1930s. By 1932, any informal meeting in which Stalin's policies were discussed in a negative light had become a political crime.

One of the most important contributions of these early Politburo steno-grams is to provide information on the development of Stalin's own thinking on economic policy, the use of force, and agricultural policy. As noted by Boris Bazhanov, Stalin's personal secretary, Stalin had the extraordinary gift of si-lence, a trait that was unique in a country that said too much.[69] In these early stenograms, Stalin participated regularly in debates; he often provided useful summaries of the discussion, and some of the characteristics of the future Stalin-dictator can be read from his comments.

Stalin was a consistent supporter of the notion of firm plans that had to be fulfilled as a matter of law. In the August 2, 1923 meeting "Question about the Export of Grain," Stalin argued in favor of a firm plan for the amount of grain exports. "Otherwise our plans will fall apart. If we don't make these calcula-tions we will be like a blind man at the wheel." In the August 16, 1923 meeting "About a Single Agricultural Tax," Stalin favored a tough policy with respect to collecting the taxes: [70]

> STALIN: Now about legality. Of course, legality is necessary. But legality con-sists not only of avoiding insulting the peasants during the collection of taxes, but also in the full collection of taxes. If taxes are not 100 percent collected this is a violation of the law.

Stalin's conviction that no excuses should be allowed to those who failed to fulfill Politburo tasks is reflected in the October 26 and November 2, 1925 meeting "About Questions of Grain Collections and the Import-Export-Currency Plan":[71]

> STALIN: Increasing grain prices, cutting back collections and so on — all this, it is said, is a matter of geology and not economic regulation. This is, of course, not true. . . . We must free ourselves from these deficiencies. We require a real and not bloated plan of collections that corresponds to our possibilities and we must adopt all measures that force the peasant to sell his grain on the market. . . . It is time to form a unified front of grain collectors.

In the same meeting, Stalin expressed confidence that economic problems could be surmounted by planning.

> STALIN: We must arrange things so that we regulate trade and that trade does not regulate us.

Stalin downplayed the burden of taxes and collections on agriculture. In the August 16, 1923 meeting "About the Single Agricultural Tax," he pointed out that the tax burden on agriculture was well below the estimated 20 percent figure.[72] In the February 1926 meeting "About Necessary Economic Measures in the Near Future," Stalin clearly expressed his preference for an industry-first policy that evidently followed the arguments of the Trotsky wing of the party:[73]

> STALIN: Agriculture can still develop without special expenditures and without new technology. It has considerable potential for this, already considerable technology that is developing further. . . . Such possibilities are not present in industry, because industry cannot develop further without a serious increase in capital investment in new technology and in better equipment. . . . We are beginning a period where the growth of industry is the main means of developing the economy and in the end improving the lot of the peasantry.

Notably, Stalin was echoing the views of Trotsky expressed at the same meeting:

> TROTSKY: It seems to me that in asking the question about the interrelationship between industry and agriculture, there have been several mistakes [made by Kalinin]. Industry pushes agriculture ahead and it is industry, by its very nature, that is to a greater degree than agriculture to be the leading and main initiator of development.

As of the August 2, 1926 meeting "About the Results of State Farm and Collective Farm Development," Stalin was still not ready to endorse force in the countryside. Instead he spoke of using state farms as demonstrations of the superiority of "more advanced forms of agriculture." Collective farms should be given tax advantages and subsidies and "peasants should be directly told that we prefer this form."[74]

Scholars have just begun to probe into these "lost transcripts" of the Politburo. The essays in this collection are a first look at them. It is clear that our understanding of the Soviet and Stalinist systems has been transformed by the opening of the Soviet state and party archives. The opening of the first verbatim records of Politburo deliberations provides fresh information primarily on that vital period of collective rule by a group earlier united by the vision of socialist revolution but now disagreeing on how to "build socialism." This material should inform scholars on the inevitability of the emergence of one-man rule under these circumstances, which, if unchecked, could lead to the horrors of extermination and purge. Or would it have indeed been possible to operate with a collective rule with some minimal checks and balances?

Notes

I am grateful to the Hoover Institution for their support of this work. I would also like to express my gratitude to Lora Soroka, Carol Leadenham, and Linda Bernard of the Hoover archives. I wish as well to thank the National Science Foundation for their support of this and related research.

1. Khlevniuk, Gregory, and Vatlin, *Stenogrammy zasedanii Politbiuro TsK VKP(b), 1923–1938*.

2. RGASPI Fond 17, op. 163, del. 533.

3. RGASPI Fond 17, op. 163, del. 680.

4. RGASPI Fond 17, op. 163, del. 703.

5. Khaustov, Naumov, and Plotnikova, *Lubianka: Stalin i VChK-GPU-OGPU-NKVD, ianvar' 1922–dekabr' 1936*, pp. 39–42.

6. RGASPI Fond 17, op. 85, del. 3, 7, 123.

7. Khrushchev, *Memoirs of Nikita Khrushchev*, vol. 1: *Commissar (1918–1945)*; Mikoian, *Tak bylo: Razmyshleniia o minuvshem*.

8. Kosheleva, Lel'chuk, Naumov, Naumov, Rogovaia, and Khlevniuk, *Pis'ma I. V. Stalina V. M. Molotovu, 1925–1936 gg.: Sbornik dokumentov;* Lih, Naumov, and Khlevniuk, *Stalin's Letters to Molotov, 1925–1936;* Khlevniuk, Kvashonkin, Kosheleva, and Rogovaia, *Stalinskoe Politbiuro v 30-e gody;* Khlevniuk, Davies, Rees, and Rogovaia, *Stalin i Kaganovich: Perepiska 1931–1936 gg.;* Davies, Khlevniuk, and Rees, *The Stalin-Kaganovich Correspondence 1931–1936;* and Kvashonkin et al., *Sovetskoe rukovodstvo: Perepiska, 1928–1941*.

9. Fel'shtinskii, *Kommunisticheskaia oppozitsia v SSSR: Iz arkhiva L'va Trotskogo*, vols. 1–4.

10. Vilkova, *RKP (b) i vnutripartiinaia bor'ba v dvatsatye gody, 1924: Dokumenty i materialy*.

11. Fursenko, *Prezidium TSK KPSS 1954–1964: Chernovye protokolnye zapisi zasedanii, stenogrammy, postanovleniia v 3 tomakh*.

12. Adibekov, Anderson, and Rogovaia, *Politbiuro TsK RKP(b)-VKP(b): Povestki dnia zasedanii*, vol. 1: *1919–1929;* ibid., vol. 2: *1930–1939;* ibid., vol. 3: *1940–1952*.

13. Ibid., vol. 1: *1919–1929*, pp. 445–6.

14. RGASPI Fond 17, op. 163, del. 682.

15. Adibekov, Anderson, and Rogovaia, *Politbiuro TsK RKP(b)-VKP(b): Povestki dnia zasedanii*, vol. 1: *1919–1929*, pp. 491–92.

16. Ibid., p. 666.

17. Ibid., vol. 2: *1930–1939*, p. 16.

18. Ibid., p. 876.

19. Khlevniuk, Kvashonkin, Kosheleva, and Rogovaia, *Stalinskoe Politbiuro v 30-e gody*, pp. 183–255.

20. Ibid., p. 222.

21. Khlevniuk, Gregory, and Vatlin, *Stenogrammy zasedanii Politbiuro TsK VKP(b), 1923–38*, Introduction.

22. Question 13: "Proposal of the Secretariat of the TsK and Zinoviev about the Work

of the Politburo," in Adibekov, Anderson, and Rogovaia, *Politbiuro TsK RKP(b)-VKP(b): Povestki dnia zasedanii*, vol. 1: 1919–1929, p. 223.

23. Ibid., p. 440.

24. These figures were compiled from Adibekov, Anderson, and Rogovaia, *Politbiuro TsK RKP(b)-VKP(b): Povestki dnia zasedanii*.

25. Khlevniuk, *Politbiuro: Mekhanizmy politicheskoi vlasti v 1930-e gody*, pp. 288–91.

26. Khlevniuk, Gregory, and Vatlin, *Stenogrammy zasedanii Politbiuro TsK VKP(b)*, 1923–38, Introduction.

27. Vert and Mironenko, *Massovye Repressii v SSSR*, pp. 93–104, 267–80.

28. Davies, "Making Economic Policy," p. 63.

29. Khlevniuk, Kvashonkin, Kosheleva, and Rogovaia, *Stalinskoe Politbiuro v 1930-e gody*, pp. 83–84.

30. G. M. Adibekov et al., *Politbiuro TsK PRP(b)-VKP(b) i Evropa: Resheniia "osoboi papki," 1923–1939*.

31. These special files (OP) are available in RGASPI as Fond 3, op. 74, various delo.

32. RGASPI, Fond 17, op. 3, del. 700.

33. Khlevniuk, Kvashonkin, Kosheleva, and Rogovaia, *Stalinskoe Politbiuro v 30-e gg.*, p. 78.

34. RGASPI, Fond 17, op. 3, del. 688.

35. RGASPI, Fond 17, op. 3, del. 680.

36. RGASPI, Fond 17, op. 3, del. 680.

37. RGASPI, Fond 17, op. 3, del. 680.

38. RGASPI, Fond 17, op. 3, del. 1011.

39. RGASPI, Fond 17, op. 3, del. 687, 696, 835.

40. RGASPI, Fond 17, op. 3, del. 1011, 1218.

41. RGASPI, Fond 17, op. 3, del. 687.

42. RGASPI, Fond 17, op. 3, del. 425.

43. RGASPI, Fond 17, op. 3, del. 535.

44. RGASPI, Fond 17, op. 3, del. 696.

45. RGASPI, Fond 17, op. 3, del. 703.

46. RGASPI, Fond 17, op. 3, del. 680.

47. RGASPI, Fond 17, op. 3, del. 533.

48. RGASPI, Fond 17, op. 3, del. 533.

49. RGASPI, Fond 17, op. 3, del. 680.

50. RGASPI, Fond 17, op. 3, del. 533.

51. RGASPI, Fond 17, op. 3, del. 533.

52. RGASPI, Fond 17, op. 3, del. 680.

53. The full members were Grigory Zinoviev, Lev Kamenev, Vladimir Lenin [who died January 21, 1924], Aleksei Rykov, Josef Stalin, Mikhail Tomsky, and Leon Trotsky. The candidate members were Feliks Dzherzhinsky, Mikhail Kalinin, V. M. Molotov, Jan Rudzutak, G. Ya. Sokol'nikov, and M. V. Frunze (who died under mysterious circumstances in October of 1925). This information is from Adibekov, Anderson, and Rogovaia, *Politbiuro TsK RKP(b)-VKP(b): Povestki dnia zasedanii*, vol. 1: 1919–1929, pp. 751–52.

54. Khlevniuk, Kvashonkin, Kosheleva, and Rogovaia, *Stalinskoe Politbiuro v 30-e gg.*, p. 93.

55. Bazhanov, *Bazhanov and the Damnation of Stalin,* pp. 44–45.
56. RGASPI, Fond 17, op. 3, del. 526.
57. RGASPI, Fond 17, op. 3, del. 535.
58. RGASPI, Fond 17, op. 3, del. 526.
59. RGASPI, Fond 17, op. 3, del. 535.
60. RGASPI, Fond 17, op. 3, del. 700.
61. RGASPI, Fond 17, op. 3, del. 682.
62. RGASPI, Fond 17, op. 3, del. 682.
63. RGASPI, Fond 17, op. 3, del. 700.
64. RGASPI, Fond 17, op. 3, del. 705.
65. Khlevniuk, *Politbiuro: Mekhanizmy politicheskoi vlasti v 1930-e gody,* pp. 249–56.
66. RGASPI, Fond 17, op. 3, del. 1011.
67. RGASPI, Fond 17, op. 3, del. 1011.
68. RGASPI, Fond 17, op. 3, del. 1011.
69. Bogdanov, *Strogo-sekretno: 30 let v OGPU-NKVD-MVD,* p. 83.
70. RGASPI, Fond 17, op. 3, del. 424.
71. RGASPI, Fond 17, op. 3, del. 533.
72. RGASPI, Fond 17, op. 3, del. 425.
73. RGASPI, Fond 17, op. 3, del. 680.
74. RGASPI, Fond 17, op. 3, del. 696.

PART II

The Power Struggle

3

Stalin in the Light of the Politburo Transcripts

HIROAKI KUROMIYA

The Politburo of the Communist Party, the de facto highest decision-making body of the Soviet Union, was long believed to have taken no verbatim transcripts of its meetings or, if it did, not to have preserved them. This assumption has been proven wrong. Thirty-one verbatim transcripts, dating from the 1920s and 1930s, have been declassified and transferred into open Russian archives. It is unlikely that there are more extant transcripts somewhere deep in the secret depositories of Moscow.[1] Whatever the case, these new Politburo stenographic reports, albeit limited in number, are of utmost importance to the study of Stalin and his rule.

Iosif V. Stalin was an enigma for many years. He left few personal documents (such as diaries and memoirs) and the many relevant official documents remained classified in the former Soviet archives. This situation improved dramatically, first, with the glasnost and perestroika campaign, and then, with the collapse of the Soviet Union. These events unleashed a flood of previously unknown documents penned by Stalin. In addition, some who had worked with him or knew him personally left memoirs and testimonies. A few who survived the Soviet regime have given oral testimonies and interviews.[2]

Fifteen years of intensive research have generated much work on Stalin and his era and, consequently the person of Stalin has become less enigmatic. Nevertheless, in comparison with, for instance, Hitler and the Nazi regime, the study of Stalin and his regime continues to suffer from the unknown number of possibly critical archival documents still classified in the so-called Presidential Archive in the Kremlin, the FSB (secret police) archive, the Foreign Ministry archive, and elsewhere. Yet new documents, like these Politburo transcripts, continue to surface through declassification and, perhaps, by accident as well.

A preliminary examination of the Politburo transcripts suggests that, although these new documents may not revise our knowledge of Stalin radically, they update and refine it substantially. Three areas of interest emerge from these transcripts: first, Stalin's view of himself as a political figure; second, Stalin's view of politics and its function in the Soviet system; and third, Stalin's views of the policies he sought to implement and eventually succeeded in executing, that is wholesale collectivization, dekulakization, and rapid industrialization, or, in a word, Stalin's "revolution from above." This essay discusses these three points.

I

Unlike many modern political leaders, Stalin left few personal accounts. Like some others, however, Stalin promoted the cult of himself, later called his personality cult. Yet, in the prewar years covered by the transcripts, this cult had not yet reached the grotesque dimensions it would assume after World War II. Whether Stalin entertained the same kind of vanity as Hitler or Mussolini is a question that has a direct bearing on his style of politics. The new Politburo documents, fortunately, shed some new light on this question.

The most famous characterization of Stalin as a political figure is that of the first leader of the Soviet government and Stalin's immediate predecessor, Vladimir I.Lenin. In his December 25, 1922 document from the collection of dictated memoranda later known as his "testaments," Lenin compared Stalin and Lev Trotsky, the two main contenders for power. Lenin noted that Stalin had acquired "boundless power" as the General Secretary of the Communist Party, but he was "not sure whether he [Stalin] will always be capable of using that power with sufficient caution." As for Trotsky, Lenin felt that he was "personally perhaps the most capable man in the present C.C. [Central Committee of the party]," but he had "displayed excessive self-assurance and shown excessive preoccupation with the purely administrative side of the work." Lenin does not say who would be more suitable for the leadership of the party.

Although Lenin had helped Stalin to become the General Secretary of the party a few months earlier, no one at the time thought that the position would become the locus of power and leadership that it did. Hence Lenin's concern as expressed in his "testaments." Yet two days after the dictation of his testament, he conveyed his wish that Stalin be removed from his position as the party's General Secretary, because he was "too rude" and "intolerable" for a General Secretary. Two months later, just before a stroke left him totally incapacitated, Lenin demanded an apology from Stalin after Stalin allegedly insulted his wife Nadezhda Krupskaya ("You had the rudeness to call my wife on the telephone and berate her"). Stalin sent his apologies to Lenin and thus managed to retain his position, which he used to ultimately defeat successive challenges to his power by Trotsky, Nikolai Bukharin, and others.[3]

The Russian historian Valentin Sakharov has recently claimed that the "testament," at least some of the documents most damning to Stalin (including one demanding Stalin's removal), were forged by Lenin's entourage to discredit Stalin.[4] Sakharov's claim has generated much controversy and little consensus.

No one, including Stalin himself, denied that he was "rude." Obviously he did not adhere to the proper manners of "respectable society," insisting instead that his vulgar language and rudeness reflected the straightforwardness and bluntness of the working masses. Historians disagree as to whether Stalin was sincere or disingenuous in such claims. Yet they tend to agree that Stalin played the political game well, managing to remain in power. On appropriate public occasions, Stalin could humbly accept Lenin's criticism, promise that he would work to correct his rudeness and mend his manners, and even tendered his resignation at least three times. His offers of resignation were not accepted by the party.[5]

The new Politburo documents illuminate his masterful and tactful treatment of a serious dispute with Trotsky over Lenin's "testament" that arose during the time of challenge to his power in the 1920s. At the meeting of the Politburo of September 8, 1927, Trotsky accused Stalin of secreting Lenin's "testament." Stalin refuted this accusation in the following exchange, claiming Trotsky to be a "liar" and adding that it was rather Trotsky and his allies that Lenin had wanted to "repress"[6]

> TROTSKY: And you hide Lenin's testament? Lenin in his testament revealed everything about Stalin. There is nothing to add or subtract.
> STALIN: You lie if you assert that anyone is concealing the testament of Lenin. You know well that it is known to all the party. You know also, as does all the party, that Lenin's testament demolishes exactly you, the current leader of the opposition. . . . Is it true or not that Lenin in such a decisive moment as the October uprising demanded the expulsion of Comrades Zinoviev and Kamenev [Trotsky's allies] from the party? Is this a fact or not? What does this all tell us? It tells us that Lenin recognized the necessity of repression no better or worse than the Central Committee of our party.

Stalin's use of language such as "liar" and "repress" is characteristic. Trotsky's accusation of Stalin is odd in light of the fact that, even though Lenin's testament was not widely circulated, it was known to the party in 1924 and Stalin had acknowledged himself, at least on the surface, that Lenin was right in his criticism. Stalin was blunt and rude, but his speeches suggest that he took pains to represent himself as taking positions that were principled and not "selfish." Stalin repeatedly accused Trotsky and his supporters of trying to turn the party from decision making and action into a "discussion club."[7] Stalin cited a case during the Civil War in which Trotsky, having failed to gain the support of the Politburo on military matters, petulantly refused to show up for work and had to be persuaded to return. Little is known of this incident, but Trotsky did not refute Stalin's account.[8]

Whether Stalin's characterization of Trotsky's conduct was accurate or not, Trotsky is known to have been a difficult colleague who looked down on others. This made him an easy target for Stalin. Already in 1924, Stalin had effectively discredited him, stating that: Trotsky has "set himself up in opposition to the CC and imagines himself to be a superman standing above the CC, above its laws, above its decisions"; when told that CC members could not refuse to carry out CC decisions, Trotsky "jumped up and left the meeting [of the CC]," so the CC had to send a "delegation" to Trotsky "with the request that he return to the meeting," but he "refused to comply with the request."[9] In 1927, Stalin mocked Trotsky, stating that he "resembles an actor rather than a hero, and an actor should not be confused with a hero under any circumstances."[10] It is telling that at the September 8, 1927 Politburo meeting, a supporter of Stalin ridiculed Trotsky in a similar vein: "Comrade Trotsky, I know that you have an intelligent brain, but it has ended up in a fool."[11] Stalin seems to have been familiar with Lenin's private thoughts about his archenemy: "Trotsky is a temperamental man with military experience . . . as for politics, he hasn't got a clue."[12]

The Politburo transcripts confirm Stalin's penchant for "rudeness" and that he was adept at insulting and browbeating his political opponents. At the September 8, 1927 Politburo meeting, Stalin confronted Trotsky, "You are pathetic, without any sense of truth, a coward, a bankrupt, insolent and impudent, who allows himself to speak of things completely at variance with reality." So Trotsky resorted to Lenin's key characterization of Stalin: "You are rude." Then he added: "Who is he [Stalin]? A leader or a horse-trader?" (This addition was expurgated, probably by Trotsky himself, from the "corrected" version of the stenographic report of the meeting.) Stalin repeated his insults to which Trotsky responded that Stalin had only revealed his own "powerlessness." Stalin was relentless: "I respond[ed] to you in kind, which you deserved, so that you'd know your place in the party, so that you'd know workers are going to thrash you for such things."[13] Although from these records alone, one may not be able to grasp the battle of words in its full scope, it appears that those who were present understood who had won.

Stalin played politics by presenting himself as a loyal, even impersonal representative of the party, or as the first servant of the party and the working class, as opposed to Trotsky who appeared to many to behave like a "superman" in the party. At the November 4, 1930 Politburo meeting, which discussed the "Syrtsov-Lominadze affair,"[14] Stalin contended that two party functionaries, S. I. Syrtsov and V. V. Lominadze, who had had the temerity to criticize him, think it necessary to "vilify and curse me," but that was their affair, let them, "I'm used to it."[15] Similarly, at the November 27, 1932 Politburo meeting on the "Eismont-Smirnov-Tolmachev affair,"[16] Stalin again presented himself as a party loyalist, unjustly criticized by errant members of the party, who "represent the matter as if Stalin were guilty of everything"; but in fact, it's not Stalin but the political line of the party that matters; "they are fighting not against Stalin but against the party and its line."[17] In a speech at the same meeting regarding an alleged plan for his removal from his post, Stalin asserted: "What matters is not Stalin, but the party. You can remove Stalin, but things will continue just as they are now."[18] Earlier, in the late 1920s when Stalin and Bukharin fought for power, an incident occurred between them. As Stalin was delivering a speech, Bukharin left, apparently in protest, without listening to the end. After Bukharin's departure, Stalin interrupted his speech to demonstrate his moderation and personal restraint: "I'd swear at him, but he's gone, so there's an end of it."[19]

Stalin's identification of himself with the party meant that any attack against him was an attack on the entire party. At the November 4, 1930 meeting, Stalin insisted that those who thought he was the root cause of all alleged economic catastrophes and miseries and that all would go well if he were removed were mistaken. Such "agitation" created the ground for "a host of terrorists."[20]

These documents suggest that Stalin was consistent in insisting that Stalin the person was not important. It is said that Stalin used to tell his son Vasily that he was not a "Stalin": "You're not Stalin and I'm not Stalin. Stalin is Soviet power. Stalin is what he is in the newspapers and the portraits, not you, no, not even me!"[21] Thus Stalin often referred to himself in the third person singular as "Stalin." Stalin also insisted later in life that the cult of Stalin was not something he personally desired but that the Soviet people needed, a sort of new "tsar."[22]

It is difficult to know what private, selfish calculations lay behind these seemingly "selfless" contentions. Yet it is the case that Stalin consistently refused to allow his personal relations and personal factors into politics. Indeed, he ordered the deaths of people close to him without hesitation. It is not difficult to imagine what Stalin thought of people who did not clearly distinguish between politics and personal lives. Bukharin sometimes wanted to have "heart-to-heart talks" with Stalin to resolve differences and misunderstandings.[23] When Bukharin faced possible execution in 1937, he repeatedly requested Stalin's *personal* attention to his case.[24] Stalin ignored such requests. For Stalin, personal relations, feelings, and loyalties had nothing to do with politics. This leads us to the second point of the present essay.

II

The new Politburo documents significantly clarify Stalin's attitude towards politics and its functioning in the Soviet system. He believed that individual intentions, good will, and such had no place in Soviet politics, but that "objective" consequences (as opposed to "subjective" intents) mattered. His criticism of party functionaries implicated in the 1930 Syrtsov-Lominadze affair and the 1932 Eismont-Tolmachev-Smirnov affair is plainly revealing. Whatever weakened the unity and the strength of the party in its struggle against "enemies," both internal and external, was "objectively" harmful to the party and therefore not to be tolerated. Of course, this is familiar logic in all nondemocratic organizations. Stalin took this logic to the extreme.

Faced with the dire economic crisis of the summer of 1930, Syrtsov, a candidate member of the Politburo, and Lominadze, party secretary of the Transcaucasus, had begun to doubt Stalin's wholesale collectivization and rapid industrialization.[25] Syrtsov's "treachery" was brought before the Politburo. In his testimony, he declared that the decline of workers' real wages and living standards posed a real political threat that could not be ignored ("an enormous counterrevolutionary danger emanates from queues").[26] In an undemocratic body politic open criticism is difficult, and therefore secret or semisecret maneuvers become the norm. Stalin called such actions "double-dealing" (*dvurushnichestvo*) — public compliance and private doubts. Stalin suspected that those with private doubts would draw closer together and that, even if they did not, the "objective" result was to harm the party.

Stalin's speeches in this period can be characterized by three recurrent expressions, "double-dealing," "deceptions," and "blocs" (of doubters, vacillators, and critics). He was ready to see dark intentions in everyone and political "blocs" everywhere.[27] Stalin hurled these same expressions against the "enemies of the people" during the Great Terror in 1937–38. The prosecutors in the three famous Moscow show trials used exactly the same language against Stalin's erstwhile rivals and colleagues.

In his attack against Syrtsov and Lominadze, Stalin made his position clear: some "schoolchildren" have gotten together, imagined themselves as politicians, and "played the Politburo." Although such a game would normally not be worth heeding, under the conditions of struggle with "class enemies," all the more intensified by factional divisions within the party, it was a serious political matter.[28] "Playing the Politburo" included floating the idea of removing Stalin from his post. Although little evidence exists that such ideas were openly expressed, Stalin equated them with terrorism. In October 1930 when Bukharin proposed a heart-to-heart talk with Stalin, he was refused. Instead Stalin accused Bukharin of "cultivating the psychology of terrorism." This remark was removed from the "corrected" version of the records of the meeting, however.[29]

There is no doubt that in such a time of crisis some people, even former supporters of Stalin, privately dreamed of removing Stalin from his post. Yet few spoke their thoughts in public, although drink may have loosened tongues in private.

In November of 1932, denunciations of Russian Republic officials Nikolai Eismont and Vladimir Tolmachev, and Central Committee member A. P. Smirnov, reached Stalin's ears. Purportedly, these three had discussed in private meetings the "catastrophic" Ukrainian famine and the necessity of removing Stalin. Whether any of those implicated in the Eismont-Tolmachev-Smirnov affair actually advocated this is not known. Eismont, for example, categorically denied such allegations.[30] His associates sought to defend him on the grounds of his proclivity to drink, claiming that his intoxicated comments did not reflect his true thoughts. Stalin was not sympathetic to the drunkenness excuse. He responded that there were two ways of fighting the party: one was by sober people talking to sober people; another was by getting drunk at parties and "incidentally" talking about a policy platform. Stalin declared: "Outward signs [of struggle] may be absent when people get together for a drink on holidays, but in fact they are recruiting people [for their struggle against the party]." (These remarks were notably removed from the "corrected" version of the records of the November 1932 meeting.)[31] Stalin maintained that within the Eismont, Tolmachev, and Smirnov circle, vodka alternated with "petit-bourgeois criticism of the party's practical policies." Vodka was a vital part of their "platform" and "successfully competed with other [more serious, political] parts of the platform." All the same, Stalin added, this did not and could not change the fact that they were trying to resurrect the platform of the former "Right Opposition" regarding industrialization and collectivization.[32]

While Stalin clearly understood that the affair involved a private drinking party, he insisted that the *objective* result was a political group fighting against the party. In the original transcript, Stalin conceded they may have been half-drunk and talking informally but all the same they constituted a group.[33] Stalin repeatedly attacked the group and its alleged "inspiration" (Bukharin and his former associates) for masking their true colors. This line of reasoning was not lost on those who were criticized by him. At the November 4, 1930 Politburo meeting, Lominadze admitted that even though they claimed they did not constitute a political grouping, "objectively it turns out that we are a kind [of political grouping]."[34]

Stalin was consistent in looking for a political, to his mind "objective," meaning in any seemingly accidental incident and in dismissing "subjective" interpretations. In 1921, a prominent Bolshevik, Fedor A. Sergeev (Artem), was killed in what was in all likelihood an airplane accident. Yet Stalin was wont to say to Sergeev's son (whom he had adopted after the father's death), that the accident may have been "political": "Don't forget about the class struggle."

Stalin's logic was that "If an accident has political consequences, then it is necessary to look closely into it."[35] Curiously, exactly the same logic informed a Politburo decision of April 1937, the time of the Great Terror, regarding a fire that had broken out at the residence of one of its members, L. M. Kaganovich: the Politburo "considers this fire not an accidental event but one organized by enemies."[36] No doubt, the judgment was dictated by Stalin.

Stalin's insistence on the supremacy of the political outcome ("objectivity") over intent ("subjectivity") manifests itself in the Politburo transcripts. Whether Bukharin and others intentionally inspired alleged anti-Stalin groups (such as the Eismont-Tolmachev-Smirnov group) was not important. *Objectively,* Bukharin and his associates were the "inspiration." By sympathizing with Bukharin's moderate course, "anti-Stalin" groups adopted and resurrected the "platform" of the former "Rightists." At one point during the November 4, 1932 meeting, Stalin interrupted remarks by Anastas Mikoyan, stating: "Now they [Trotsky, Bukharin, Zinoviev, and other former opponents of Stalin] are all White Guards." It was almost certainly an inadvertent slip. The remark was removed from the "corrected" transcript of the meeting.[37]

In a similar vein, Stalin insisted that the crisis of collective farms in 1932–33 (the years of the Great Famine) was not a crisis of policy but the result of enemy action. According to Stalin, numerous enemies had made their way to the collective farms, where they were trying to destabilize them from within. Their infiltration, Stalin declared, a "remarkable matter, an entire epic." Enemies hid themselves cleverly in collective farms. Party members had failed to detect these masked enemies and therefore, Stalin emphasized, "revolutionary vigilance" was needed.[38]

Stalin saw links between domestic and foreign enemies. "Enemies" were not merely isolated internal foes but were also agents of the international bourgeoisie and major capitalist countries bent on destroying the Soviet Union. Stalin was not unique in using external threats to disarm internal political opposition. Yet the international isolation of the Soviet Union was indeed *the* defining "objective" factor of Soviet domestic politics. Time and again, Stalin used the specter of war, not merely as a rhetorical device but in Politburo meetings to attack his political enemies and to defend his programs.

Stalin used the war scare of 1927 to attack Trotsky, Zinoviev, and Kamenev. Stalin contended in the September Politburo session that internal conflict created the impression of weakness to external enemies. His opponents had disclosed internal disagreements to the entire world, thereby depriving the Soviet Union of the ability to postpone war "if only for a few years." Their demands and opposition were in essence ("objectively") against the interests of the party and the Soviet state. They did not understand the international situation in which the country was placed. Trotsky and his allies had "lost their heads" in their fight against the party. He went so far as to say that they had "lost their sanity."[39] Stalin relentlessly presented his opponents as "defeatists" and by implication "traitors," for whom the survival of the Soviet Union was less important than their own power. By contrast, Stalin presented himself as a staunch defender of the Soviet Union. The defense of the Soviet Union against external threats was the most important task of the Soviet government. He did not mention that its downfall would have meant his own downfall as well.

The year 1932 was also a dangerous year for the Soviet Union. The foundation of Manchukuo, a Japanese puppet state in northeast China, which bordered directly on the Soviet Union, worsened the international situation and coincided with the economic crisis that culminated in 1932–33 in the Great Famine. Fearing Japanese aggression from the east, the Soviet Union repeatedly proposed nonaggression treaties to Japan, only to be rejected. To consolidate its western borders, the Soviet Union succeeded in 1931 and 1932 in signing nonaggression pacts with France, Poland, Estonia, Latvia, and Finland (and in 1933 even with fascist Italy). Stalin deemed imperative a nonaggression pact with Poland in particular and denounced what he called the "common narrow-minded mania of 'anti-Polonism'" as an impediment.[40]

Stalin used the November 27, 1932 Eismont-Tolmachev-Smirnov Politburo meeting to mount a strong defense of his collectivization and industrialization policies. The nonaggression pacts signed with western neighbors were due to successes of industrialization and collectivization. Capitalism dominates the weak and does not sign pacts with them — such was Stalin's logic.[41] Stalin's interpretation was strained given the grave economic crisis, but his "neighboring capitalist countries," suffering from the Great Depression, followed closely the USSR's rapid industrialization, which they understood would vastly strengthen its defense capability. The military attaché at the Japanese embassy in Moscow, Yukio Kasahara, sent a series of memoranda to Tokyo in 1931–32 warning about the sharp rise in Soviet defense capabilities. At least two such memoranda were intercepted, translated into Russian, and circulated among the Politburo members in December 1931 and February 1932.[42] In one of these, dated December 19, 1931 (after Japan's conquest of Manchuria), the Japanese ambassador in Moscow, Koki Hirota, advised the Japanese General Staff: "On the question of whether Japan should declare war on the Soviet Union — I deem it necessary that Japan be ready to declare war at any moment and to adopt a tough policy towards the Soviet Union." Someone, almost certainly Stalin, underlined this sentence in pencil. Hirota continued: "The cardinal objective of this war must lie not so much in protecting Japan from Communism as in seizing the Soviet Far East and eastern Siberia." Someone, again likely Stalin, circled the phrases "the Soviet Far East and eastern Siberia." Circulating the memorandum, Stalin also sent a copy to the Military High Command: "To Comrade Gamarnik. Important."[43] Stalin reinforced the Soviet military presence in the Far East while trying to placate Japan and securing nonaggression pacts with western border countries.[44] In the end, Japan did not declare war on the Soviet Union. It was the Soviet Union that declared war on Japan in 1945.

Stalin linked the survival of the first socialist state with rapid industrialization. Unless the Soviet Union could close its fifty- to one-hundred-year lag behind advanced capitalist countries in ten years, the Soviet Union would be defeated just as Russia had been beaten by foreign conquerors ("the Mongol khans, the Swedish feudal lords, the Polish — Lithuanian pans, the Anglo-French capitalists and the Japanese barons").[45] Interestingly, in his February 1932 memorandum to Tokyo the Japanese military attaché Kasahara, most probably with this famous speech of Stalin in mind, noted that "the military might of the Soviet Union" would become an extraordinary force "in ten years." These two quoted phrases were underlined in pencil, again, almost certainly by Stalin.[46]

In a remarkable statement at the November 27, 1932 Politburo meeting, Stalin repeatedly emphasized the urgency of rapid industrialization for the survival of the Soviet Union; otherwise the Soviet Union would become like China. Everyone spits on China, because China is weak. China is "bankrupt."[47] Without the socialist transformation of the country, everyone will spit on the Soviet Union as well and foreign countries will intervene in Soviet affairs just as they do in those of China. The choice is "China or a socialist Soviet Union." The industrialization drive (the rejection of the "China path") would make the country strong and defensible against its enemies.[48]

Stalin's repeated reference to China in 1932 reflected his deep concern about the situation in the Far East—Japan's conquest of a large part of China directly abutting the Soviet Union and Japan's secret agenda to capture the Soviet Far East and eastern Siberia. This was particularly disquieting to Stalin who saw the loss of Russia's territory in the 1904–5 Russo-Japanese War as an insult. He was very fond of listening to the prerevolutionary dance tune "On the Hills of Manchuria," and was determined to take revenge.[49] Stalin indeed took revenge in 1945.[50]

Stalin's frank remarks about a weak and feeble China were diplomatically tactless and were not included in the "corrected" transcripts of the November 27, 1932 Politburo meeting (even though it would have been unlikely at the time that the transcripts would ever be made public). This was a precaution. "Bankrupt" though China may have been, it was a force to be used against Japan and Manchukuo. Indeed, when a nonaggression pact with Japan proved unrealizable, Stalin turned in December 1932 to the "bankrupt" China (the Nanjing Government) and resumed diplomatic relations that had been broken since Chang Kai-shek's brutal campaign against the Chinese Communists in 1927.

A strong Soviet Union was Stalin's strategic goal throughout. In 1948, Stalin lectured the French Communist leader Maurice Thorez: "The main thing is that one not be weak. It is important to remember that the enemy takes no pity on the defenseless, the weak."[51]

III

Stalin's industrialization was intended to build a new, centrally planned economy, with heavy industry occupying the central place. China might have chintz, silk, and perhaps rubber boots, but, a Soviet Union, without tanks, guns, and airplanes, would fall victim to growing internal capitalist elements and an external capitalist encirclement.[52] Central planning was part and parcel of the Soviet industrialization drive. After Stalin beat Hitler in World War II, he is quoted as saying: "The main task of planning is to ensure the independence of the socialist economy from capitalist encirclement. This is absolutely the most important task. It is a type of battle with world capitalism. The basis of planning is to reach the point where metal and machines are in our hands and we are not dependent on the capitalist economy."[53] The Soviet industrialization drive, according to Stalin, was as much a political as an economic enterprise.

It was the wholesale collectivization of agriculture and the attendant de-kulakization campaign, according to Stalin, that enabled the decisive turn to rapid industrialization. Once and for all, the sources of potential capitalist restoration (kulaks and nonsocialist, individual farming) had been destroyed. Stalin stated in November 1932 that while the Soviet Union had inherited some industry from the tsarist regime, it received no collective or state farms; they were all Soviet innovations.[54] Stalin boasted that the collectivization was "a completely novel, historically unprecedented event."[55]

Marx and Lenin did not and could not foresee all the details of building a socialist society. Stalin had to decide such things. In his remarks at the October 1938 Politburo meeting called to launch the publication of his *Short Course,* Stalin repeatedly emphasized that small, individual farming was doomed: before the collectivization of agriculture, plots were becoming more divided and smaller, the rural economy was becoming "naturalized," and "marketization" was declining. Without collectivization the cities would have starved, the Red Army would have perished, and the agricultural sector itself would have "degenerated." It was a matter of life and death to break this stalemate, to collectivize agriculture, and thereby to create large, modern agricultural enterprises.[56]

The collective farm system came to symbolize poverty and to be associated with "a second serfdom" in the minds of farmers. Therefore, Stalin's announcement at the October 1938 Politburo meeting that there was "no poverty in the country" was remarkable.[57] Stalin appears to have believed that with the exploiting classes largely eliminated, people must be living better than before 1917. Any lingering problems were a consequence of subversion by the remnants of the enemies.

In the long run, the vastly expanded Soviet heavy industry helped the Soviet Army beat Hitler's formidable armed forces. Whereas during World War I, the old countryside had failed to feed adequately the cities and the army (which had led directly to the downfall of the tsarist regime), the collective farm system, for all its poverty and brutal exploitation, managed to sustain the Soviet cities and the military forces better during World War II.[58] Vyacheslav Molotov, Stalin's right-hand man, contended subsequently that "our success in collectivization was more significant than victory in World War II. If we had not carried it through, we would not have won the war."[59]

Stalin was deeply convinced that his policies of collectivization and industrialization followed the immutable laws of history. Professional revolutionaries like himself had to make the most of these laws with decisiveness and determination. This was axiomatic for him, and he could not understand why Bukharin and his supporters refused to accept his policies. On a number of occasions, Stalin exclaimed out of frustration and disbelief that his critics had "gone mad,"[60] just as in 1927 he had called Trotsky and his supporters "mad" for allegedly not understanding capitalist encirclement.

Those who failed to understand the Marxist laws of history were doomed, according to Stalin. The cardinal sin of his opponents such as Trotsky and

Bukharin was their refusal to succumb to the laws of society and instead entertain pity for "class enemies." Stalin said in 1937 that they could never stomach collectivization (which involved cutting into the living body of the kulak), and they went underground. Powerless themselves, they linked up with external enemies, and promised Ukraine to the Germans, Belorussia to the Poles, the Far East to the Japanese. They hoped for war and were especially insistent that the German fascists launch a war against the USSR as soon as possible.[61]

In his revealing speech at the Politburo meeting in October 1938, Stalin declared that the mortal sin of the Bukharin and Trotsky supporters was their opposition to his "revolution from above": "Well, were they all spies? Of course not. Whatever happened to them? They were cadres who could not stomach the sharp turn toward collective farms and could not make sense of this turn, because they were not trained politically, did not know the laws of social development, the laws of economic development, the laws of political development. . . . How to explain that some of them became spies and intelligence agents? . . . It turns out that they were not well grounded politically and not well grounded theoretically. They turned out to be people who did not know the laws of political development, and therefore they could not stomach the sharp turn."[62] Those who opposed the historical laws of creating a socialist society were by definition counterrevolutionaries. Stalin's "revolution from above" was a historical necessity; any criticism of Stalin and his policy became counterrevolutionary.

Stalin's October 1938 remark before the Politburo implied that he did not believe that Bukharin, Trotsky, and their supporters were actual foreign spies. Stalin probably knew that *subjectively*, by intention, they were in fact all opposed to capitalism. Their true crime was that they had lost faith in the rightness of the party.[63] In his speech at the November 25, 1932 Politburo meeting, Stalin also maintained that the "root" of his critics' problem was that they did not believe in the rightness of the party's (and by implication Stalin's) political course.[64] By their opposition to Stalin and hence to the laws of history and the construction of socialism in the Soviet Union, *objectively* they were no different from foreign spies. Therefore they were to be exterminated as traitors. (In any case, Stalin believed that they had gone mad.) Indeed they were killed en masse in 1937–38, except for Trotsky who was murdered in Mexico in 1940 by Stalin's order. There was a cold logic to Stalinist politics.

IV

The new Politburo documents are valuable sources for the study of many subjects, including Stalin. This essay does not discuss all, or even most, of the speeches and remarks of Stalin that the documents contain, concerning such subjects as Soviet trade and price policies in the 1920s, the factional struggles within the party, and the 1928 Shakhty show trial. Numerous impromptu rejoinders and interventions made by Stalin during speeches by other members also need to be analyzed in detail. They are bound to yield interesting results. There are other sources that have become available recently and still remain to be examined in detail, as outlined in Naimark's introduction.[65] Another recent book, *Stalin's Table Talk*, like the volume of Hitler's table talk, contains numerous less formal speeches of Stalin and remains to be analyzed.[66]

These and other similar documents contain unedited, impromptu remarks by Stalin and others made in the highest organs of decision making, the vast majority of which were not intended to be made public. Stalin is known to have paid close attention to detail and carefully edited his own and others' speeches.[67] The study of unedited versions of documents may uncover the undisguised thoughts and intents of Stalin as well as others. Indeed, they reveal how Stalin and others spoke and comported themselves, what logic and concepts (as opposed to rhetoric for public consumption) they used, how they presented themselves as leaders and politicians, and how they treated their political opponents.

A preliminary examination of the Politburo transcripts reveals three aspects of Stalin particularly well. They show Stalin to have been a skillful and tactical politician capable of presenting himself as a humble, loyal, selfless and even impersonal representative of the state and the party while, simultaneously, capable of delivering sharp and effective attacks against his critics as selfish and spineless. Stalin's overarching concern was the survival of the Soviet Union (and consequently himself) which had established a new, socialist state through collectivization, dekulakization, and industrialization. This was a result of the determined struggle Stalin had waged, but it also, according to Stalin, followed the laws of history. Whoever failed to understand these laws or refused to submit to them was an *objective* enemy of historical necessity whatever their *subjective* intent might be. The cold logic of Stalinist politics reveals itself very clearly in these new Politburo documents.

Notes

1. See Paul Gregory's introductory chapter in this volume.
2. See Norman Naimark's introductory chapter in this volume.
3. Lenin's "testament" is quoted from Tucker, *The Lenin Anthology*, pp. 727, 728, and 748. The classic account of Lenin's testaments and the power struggle in the party is in Lewin, *Lenin's Last Struggle*.
4. Sakharov, *"Politicheskoe zaveshchanie" Lenina: Real'nost' istorii i mify politiki.*

5. Kuromiya, *Stalin: Profiles in Power,* chap. 3.

6. RGASPI, Fond 17, op. 3, del. 705.

7. RGASPI, Fond 17, op. 3, del. 705.

8. RGASPI, Fond 17, op. 3, del. 705.

9. Stalin, *Works,* vol. 6, pp. 14, 39.

10. Stalin, *Works,* vol. 9, p. 289.

11. RGASPI, Fond 17, op. 3, del. 705.

12. Pipes, *The Unknown Lenin: From the Secret Archive,* p. 124.

13. RGASPI, Fond 17, op. 3, del. 705.

14. See Oleg Khlevniuk's essay in this volume.

15. RGASPI, Fond 17, op. 3, del. 1003.

16. See Charters Wynn's essay in this volume.

17. RGASPI, Fond 17, op. 3, del. 1011.

18. RGASPI, Fond 17, op. 3, del. 74.

19. RGASPI, Fond 17, op. 3, del. 1003.

20. RGASPI, Fond 17, op. 3, del. 1003.

21. Quoted in Montefiore, *Stalin: The Court of the Red Tsar,* p. 4.

22. Kuromiya, *Stalin: Profiles in Power,* pp. 137, 162, 191.

23. RGASPI, Fond 17, op. 3, del. 1003.

24. See Getty and Naumov, *The Road to Terror: Stalin and the Self-Destruction of the Bolsheviks, 1932–1939,* pp. 556–60.

25. See Oleg Khlevniuk's essay in this volume.

26. RGASPI, Fond 17, op. 3, del. 1003.

27. One characteristic remark is in RGASPI, Fond 17, op. 3, del. 700.

28. RGASPI, Fond 17, op. 3, del. 1003.

29. RGASPI, Fond 17, op. 3, del. 1003.

30. RGASPI, Fond 17, op. 3, del. 1011.

31. RGASPI, Fond 17, op. 3, del. 1011.

32. RGASPI, Fond 17, op. 3, del. 1011.

33. RGASPI, Fond 17, op. 3, del. 1011.

34. RGASPI, Fond 17, op. 3, del. 1003.

35. Sergeev and Glushik, *Besedy o Staline,* pp. 74–75.

36. RGASPI, Fond 17, op. 162, del. 21, l. 30.

37. RGASPI, Fond 17, op. 3, del. 1011.

38. RGASPI, Fond 17, op. 3, del. 1011.

39. RGASPI, Fond 17, op. 3, del. 705.

40. Davies, Khlevniuk, and Rees, *Stalin-Kaganovich Correspondence 1931–1936,* p. 68.

41. RGASPI, Fond 17, op. 3, del. 1011.

42. Khaustov, Naumov, and Plotnikova, *Lubianka: Stalin i VChK-GPU-OGPU-NKVD, ianvar' 1922–dekabr' 1936,* pp. 291–95, 298–308.

43. Ibid., pp. 292, 295. Ian Gamarnik was Deputy Military Commissar at the time.

44. See Terayama, "Sutarin to Manshu: Sen hyaku sanju nen dai zenhan no Sutarin no tai Manshu seisaku" (Stalin and Manchuria: Stalin's policy towards Manchuria in the first half of the 1930s), *Tohoku Ajia Kenkyu,* no. 9, pp. 89–110.

45. Stalin, *Works,* vol. 13, p. 41.

46. Khaustov, Naumov, and Plotnikova, *Lubianka: Stalin i VChK-GPU-OGPU-NKVD, ianvar' 1922–dekabr' 1936*, p. 299.

47. Of course, Stalin did not mention the fact that the Soviet Union was party to "bankrupting" China: inheriting the Russian Empire's control of the Chinese Eastern Railway, the Soviet Union continued to administer it (although nominally in conjunction with China). In 1929 the country even entered into armed conflict with China over the railway. In 1935, however, the Soviet Union sold it to Manchukuo to avoid further complications with China.

48. RGASPI, Fond 17, op. 3, del. 1011.

49. Sergeev and Glushik, *Besedy o Staline*, pp. 22–23, 78.

50. In 1945 Stalin declared: "The defeat of the Russian forces in 1904 in the Russo-Japanese War left painful memories in the people's consciousness. It left a black stain on our country. Our people waited, believing that the day would come when Japan would be beaten and the stain eliminated. We, the people of an older generation, waited forty years for this day. And now this day has come." Stalin, *Sochineniia*, vol. 2, p. 214.

51. Naimark, "Stalin and Europe in the Postwar Period, 1945–53: Issues and Problems," p. 48.

52. Ibid., pp. 30, 94.

53. Quoted in Pollock, *Conversations with Stalin on Questions of Political Economy*, p. 19.

54. RGASPI, Fond 17, op. 3, del. 1011.

55. Banac, *The Diary of Georgi Dimitrov*, p. 89. Stalin made the same point regarding dekulakization at the July 1931 Politburo meeting. See RGASPI, Fond 17, op. 3, del. 1005.

56. RGASPI, Fond 17, op. 3, del. 1218.

57. RGASPI, Fond 17, op. 3, del. 1218.

58. Alec Nove in Linz, *The Impact of World War II on the Soviet Union*, pp. 83, 89.

59. Molotov, *Molotov Remembers: Inside Kremlin Politics, Conversations with Felix Chuev*, p. 248.

60. Iakovlev, *Kak lomali NEP: Stenogrammy plenumov TsK VKP(b) 1928–1929gg.*, vol. 4, pp. 654, 674. Also see RGASPI, Fond 17, op. 3, del. 1011.

61. Banac, *The Diary of Georgi Dimitrov*, p. 70.

62. RGASPI, Fond 17, op. 3, del 1218. Note that this particular speech was published in *Voprosy istorii*, 2003, no. 4, p. 21. Several historians have utilized this material. See, for example, Vatlin, "Iosif Stalin auf dem Weg zur absoluten Macht: Neue Dokumente aus Moskauer Archiven," p. 105 and Kuromiya, *Stalin: Profiles in Power*, pp. 135–36.

63. Kuromiya, *Stalin: Profiles in Power*, p. 136.

64. RGASPI, Fond 17, op. 3, del. 1012.

65. Iakovlev, *Kak lomali NEP: Stenogrammy plenumov TsK VKP(b) 1928–1929gg.*, vols. 1–5. See also Norman Naimark's introductory chapter in this volume.

66. Nevezhin, *Zastol'nye rechi Stalina*.

67. See Naimark, "Cold War Studies and New Archival Materials on Stalin."

4

"Class Brothers Unite!": The British General Strike and the Formation of the "United Opposition"

ALEXANDER VATLIN

At first glance, there is no direct connection between the British General Strike of May 1926 and the power struggle within the ruling circles of the Bolshevik Party. These two events were widely separated by geography, but the transcripts of the Politburo reveal a direct link. The dueling camps within the ruling Politburo — Leon Trotsky, Lev Kamenev, and Grigory Zinoviev versus Stalin, Nikolai Bukharin, and Aleksei Rykov — had radically different interpretations of the General Strike and offered different policy responses. Their open clash on this issue within the Politburo on June 3, 1926 was one of the first manifestations of the coming bitter split between Stalin and his supporters and the "United Opposition" of Trotsky, Kamenev, and Zinoviev. The heated discussion became a catalyst for the formation of the "United Opposition" against Stalin and his erstwhile allies in the summer of 1926. Initially, Zinoviev and Kamenev joined a troika with Stalin to block Trotsky, but they began to find common ground on issues such as the proper handling of the General Strike.

Bolshevik Policy and the General Strike

Trotsky, Zinoviev, and Kamenev were united in the fact that they considered the weak Russian support of the General Strike a major policy blunder, and they clamored for an early meeting of the Politburo to put their views on record. They pushed for and got a meeting on June 3, 1926. They went into the meeting confident of the superiority of their vision of the current international arena. Stalin's absence from the June 3 meeting (he was on vacation in the Caucasus) gave them added confidence and offered an opportunity to split Stalin's Politburo majority. Additionally, the fact that Politburo stenograms, were regularly distributed among party officials, gave the "oppositionists" a chance to make their case to a wide audience of party functionaries.

The stenogram of the June 3, 1926 Politburo session on the General Strike chronicles passionate, unbridled debate. In its essence, it resembled parliamentary debates between the government, as represented by Stalin's proxy, V. M. Molotov, supported by Rykov and Bukharin, and the opposition, as represented by Trotsky, Zinoviev, and Kamenev. Prior Politburo meetings had discussed policy matters as if in a circle of close allies, but not this one. The heated debate adds historical value to this transcript. It shows the fragility of "collective leadership" and, from a broader perspective, the crisis of collective leadership that ended with its destruction by Stalin's victory in the power struggle.

Grigory Zinoviev, as the head of the Soviet Comintern delegation, served as the Politburo session's referent on the question of the English strike at the June 3 Politburo session.[1] On May 12, after the army had broken through picket lines, the General Council of the British labor confederation, the Trades Union Congress (TUC), which had ordered the strike in the first place had called off the strike. Zinoviev now described this as yet another proof that the leaders of the reformist British trade unions had betrayed the most vital workers' interests. Zinoviev's attack raised questions about the Politburo's strategy of aligning with the TUC as opposed to assisting more revolutionary worker elements. Zinoviev occupied an advantageous position for attacking the "majority." According to his interpretation, the "majority," fearing "to break with reformist trade unionists, continued to collaborate with them, while abandoning the interests of the true worker's movement."

An experienced orator, Zinoviev did not mince his words: "The treason of the Trade Union Council [the name often used in Politburo discussions to describe the TUC and its General Council] passed unnoticed by those who did not want to see it, and by those who are ready for further collaboration with them. Well, let them start a square dance with the dead."

To provide an alternative to the pitfall of political prejudices, Zinoviev appealed for a restoration of the purity of revolutionary ideals: "We have reached the point where our motto on events in England should be 'unity from below.'" That is, Zinoviev was arguing that the Politburo should cast its lot directly in with the workers, not with a treacherous reformist trade union movement. Although in the mid-1920s, such a policy doomed the Communists to a political ghetto in the international community, it nevertheless served as an effective weapon in internal party collisions. Such sentiments appealed to Lenin's authority and to the romantics of the "revolutionary assault."

From Zinoviev's opening report through the ensuing debate, the "oppositionists" assaulted the Politburo majority, accusing them of abandoning the workers' movement in Europe and then trying to sweep major policy errors, such as the failure to give adequate support to British strikers, under the rug. Trotsky led the assault:

> TROTSKY: Almost four weeks have passed since the end of the strike, and we haven't even raised the issue here. By ignoring it, we have placed ourselves in a position where everyone can think what he wants. Any attempts to discuss this question in advance, in order to avoid unnecessary collisions in the Politburo, have been stubbornly resisted. A collective solution is not welcomed. As a result, what we have is a worthless pile of paperwork, decisions overlapping with and contradicting each other. . . . To solve the problem, we have to approach it more seriously, otherwise what use is it of having a stenogram recording?

Trotsky's assault brought forth an emotional response from the head of the Soviet government and frequent chair of Politburo sessions A. I. Rykov:

> RYKOV: A few words on Trotsky's claim that the question has not been discussed. I think no other question has received as much attention from us as recent events in Britain. First of all, a special commission including Stalin, Zinoviev, Rykov, Dogadov, Molotov, Bukharin, Lozovsky, and Chicherin has been created that has regular daily sessions. The last five Politburo sessions, to a greater or lesser extent, touched upon the problem of the strike in Britain. So all questions related to it have been thoroughly worked through. The protocols of these sessions start with the "English question."
> KAMENEV: But, on the other hand, it keeps on getting put off.
> RYKOV: There is no talk of "putting it off." We need practical solutions.
> TROTSKY: That is, a "practical" solution, but what is missing is an adequate appraisal of the political significance of the event.[2]

Trotsky's stance on the British strike was, to a large degree, motivated by his egocentric interests, personal dislikes, and resentment of past slights, as his following remarks show.

> TROTSKY: I just wanted to get fully involved in the discussion of the issue along with other Politburo members and as usual, I was willing to conform to the joint resolution. Why does it always happen that, as soon as I announce that I wish to fully participate in discussion of a serious issue along with

my comrades, Molotov announces that I am a usurper? Isn't it outrageous? Where does it come from? I think it comes from the contradiction Molotov constantly faces: that between his excessive administrative power and his poor mental outlook. This contradiction disrupts the collective decision-making process. Administratively powerful, you [Molotov] are not capable of intellectual reasoning; you don't have the ability to foresee the course of events, take into account multiple factors, raise the right question at the right moment, and draw conclusions. That's why you are always on guard; every attempt to place a new issue on the agenda is interpreted as an encroachment upon your personal power. This is the key to understanding all your actions, and of your stubborn reluctance to collaborate with people who have proven, in spite of all odds, their eagerness and preparedness for collective work. Instead of trying to understand others' ideas, Molotov is searching for the interests of the "bloc" behind them in order to find out whether it is possible, without bothering ourselves with unnecessary inquiries, to revert to repressive measures [against the minority].[3]

Zinoviev's and Trotsky's remarks accurately capture the growing reluctance of the Politburo majority to work with them collegially but they also contain barely concealed malevolence. According to their interpretation, the Stalinist majority, having abandoned the idea of constructive collaboration with "the opposition," were doomed to diplomatic failure. Acting out their "right-wing" tendencies, the Politburo majority was, in the opposition view, preparing the way for peace with social democracy. However, the Politburo's flirtation with the left-wing social democrats was based on a failure to understand that they would betray the revolutionary proletariat at a decisive moment. The TUC's unwillingness to push for revolutionary goals was seen as a concrete example of this betrayal.

Such accusations were received by the Politburo "majority" with indignation. In response, they accused the dissenters of political myopia and an inability to sensibly evaluate the political situation. Zinoviev's point that the British strike had undermined the stability of capitalism in Europe became an especially frequent point of discussion.

In the heat of the debate, the question of the British strike as such was pushed aside; every speech was dictated by the interests of the factions and was aimed at discrediting the opponents' policy.

The consolidation of Trotsky, Zinoviev, and Kamenev into a "United Opposition" was effusively commented upon by the key representative of the Stalinist faction, Molotov.

MOLOTOV: Comrades Trotsky and Zinoviev are using this issue to enter into an alliance. I am sure this is highly erroneous, but what's most important, it runs counter to our principles. Comrades Trotsky and Zinoviev will be little use if they sacrifice the solution of the problem to their tactical alliance.[4]

At the end of the June 3 session, Zinoviev asked the Politburo's permission to defend his political stance at the upcoming Comintern session. He was refused. Zinoviev, regularly forced to carry out orders that ran counter to his political views, played an increasingly formal role in the Comintern. However, he did not want to risk total alienation from the Politburo on the grounds that his dismissal would deprive him of the (admittedly modest) resources of the Communist International in future struggles. In fact, an oppositional presentation by Zinoviev to the Comintern could serve the majority's interest. According to Stalin, such a presentation by Zinoviev would provide an opportunity to call for Zinoviev's dismissal from his post as Comintern chair.[5]

The stenogram of the June 3, 1926 Politburo session reveals the consolidation both of the "United Opposition" and of the Politburo "majority." Even without Stalin present, the latter withstood an assault "from the left" and demonstrated its viability as a worthy opponent of Zinoviev and Trotsky in disputes on international problems. For the majority members, this meant not support of Stalin's power ambitions, but the assertion of their own views of socialist construction in Russia. Their acceptance of the challenge of the "United Opposition" marked the beginning of a new period in the history of the party. It shows that Stalin, at that time, based his Politburo majority on the views of its members on domestic and foreign policy.

The Brewing Storm

The escalation of the internal party struggles, reflected in the stenogram of the Politburo session of June 3, 1926, had its own prehistory. After Lenin's retirement from active political life, the leadership in the Bolshevik party had been concentrated in the hands of a "troika" of Zinoviev, Kamenev, and Stalin. This informal coalition was created to thwart the political ambitions of Trotsky, who (not without grounds) conceived of himself as the natural heir to the dying party leader.[6] The troika, despite its short life, fulfilled its major function: Trotsky was deprived of much of his power.

Stalin's machinations as a troika member did not go unnoticed. Already in the troika's first months, Zinoviev and Kamenev understood Stalin's personal ambitions for party leadership. In his note to Kamenev from July 30, 1923, Zinoviev reported the measures Stalin had undertaken without prior agreement of other troika members. Zinoviev concluded: "If the party is destined to live through a period of Stalin's personal dictatorship — let it be. But at least I personally have no intention to cover up all these 'swinish affairs.' Every faction discusses our troika. I am supposed to have influence in the troika, while in reality there is no troika but just a Stalinist dictatorship. Ilich [Lenin] was a thousand times right" (in his warning to dismiss Stalin before it was too late).[7]

In the autumn of 1925, on the eve of the Sixteenth Party Congress, Zinoviev and Kamenev started a "New Opposition" largely based upon Zinoviev's Leningrad party organization. Its program rested on the concept of the impossibility of the final victory of socialism in one country. Additionally their "New Opposition" objected to the "mutation" of the supreme party leadership and to "kulak deviation" in its ranks, and called for restoration of the Leninist principles of democratic centralism. The supporters of the "majority" proclaimed their preparedness to undertake the most decisive actions against dissenters, or against "the threat of a 'second Kronstadt.' "[8] Manipulating party opinion, Stalin and his allies managed to isolate the Leningrad opposition during the Sixteenth Party Congress, and to rebuff its major proposals there.[9]

The defeat of the "New Opposition" at the Sixteenth Party Congress initiated a purge of its supporters from the party and state organizations at all levels of the administrative hierarchy. Zinoviev was not reelected to the Leningrad Provincial Party Committee. He retained his position as the head of the Comintern as part of a short-lived compromise that required that Comintern decisions be made by the party delegation.[10]

On March 18, 1926, the Politburo met to discuss the question of Zinoviev's dismissal from his post as head of the Leningrad Council of Workers and Peasants' Deputies.[11] At this session, Stalin's mastery of political intrigue was evident. Zinoviev was removed in typical Stalin fashion; according to Stalin the Politburo was simply bowing to the will of the Leningrad party itself. Stalin defended the decision to keep Zinoviev in (nominal) charge of the Comintern: "I don't know of any party in the Comintern that would raise the question of dismissing Zinoviev." Zinoviev's cynical retort was: "Comrade Stalin noted that no foreign party insists upon Zinoviev's dismissal from the Comintern. But after certain 'preparatory measures' are undertaken, some parties will be sure to ask for it, Comrade Stalin." Indeed, within less than a year Stalin decided it was time to remove Zinoviev from the Comintern, as if acceding (as Zinoviev had predicted) to requests of foreign communists.[12]

As the oppositionists lost ground, they appealed to the democratic norms of party life, only to be brushed aside by the majority. At the March 18 session, Zinoviev again appealed for party democracy: "We all have sinned against internal party democracy, our only excuse being the fact that the economic, political, and international situation for a long time forced us to preserve an almost militarized discipline within the party; sometimes it made us go to extremes."

Zinoviev's "confession" only fueled the animosity of his opponents, such as the unforgiving Molotov, who reminded the Politburo that it was Zinoviev who earlier had attempted to expel Trotsky from the Politburo:

> MOLOTOV: Comrade Zinoviev remembers about democracy only when he is in the minority. I think that Comrade Zinoviev is not the one to teach us the rules of the party. With respect to rules, he has always taken the most radical, the most stringent position. From January on, it was Comrade Zinoviev whom the Central Committee had to constantly restrain.

Trotsky's position in the March 18 Politburo debate over the removal of Zinoviev as head of the Leningrad party deserves a detailed analysis. Insisting that it was necessary to correct the internal party regime, Trotsky distanced himself from the struggle over personal power ambitions.

> TROTSKY: Comrade Stalin was right when he said that the victory over the Leningrad opposition [Zinoviev and his supporters] was achieved not only through the pressure of the central apparatus, but also due to the desire of the Leningrad Communists to get rid of excessive pressure from the local party apparatus [headed by Zinoviev]. That's right! But what if they just jumped out of the frying pan into the fire? Does the Moscow regime leave any hope for us to think that the [new] one in Leningrad will be more tolerant?

Through such a strategic move Trotsky condemned not only the opposition as such, but the measures undertaken against it. He stressed that harsh interventions from Moscow unavoidably resulted in "relegation of the status and degradation of the ideological leadership. . . . And what does this degradation mean? It means an inevitable strengthening of the (central) party apparatus. Why? Because the lack of true debate has to be compensated for by coercion."[13]

The significance of the March 18 Politburo stenogram is much broader than the questions on the agenda, or the intricacies of internal party struggles. The Politburo regulated key spheres of life; hence, speeches and comments made during the sessions are of historical significance. Rykov's March 18 remark that "management of the by now highly developed Communist parties in the Comintern deserves more attention than before" is particularly telling. This evasive formulation concealed the unpleasant fact that the Comintern had been transformed into an honorary exile for passé or disgraced party officials. Contrary to the Comintern's internal regulations, where the Soviet party was listed as one constituent of the "worldwide party of the revolutionary proletariat," the leaders of other Communist parties passively waited for instructions from their Russian comrades.[14]

The bitter dispute about the head of the Leningrad committee revealed that a reconciliation was unlikely and that, sooner or later, internal party conflict was destined to escalate. What was unclear was the eventual constellation of personalities. In the spring of 1926, new power balances were explored. Trotsky established contacts with Stalin and Bukharin, who expressed a willingness to "reconcile" with the Trotskyites to prevent their alliance with the remnants of the "Leningrad opposition."[15] Aware that he would not be able to single-handedly change the power balance, Trotsky was also looking towards the Zinovievites, contempt for whom he never bothered to conceal. Already in April, the Politburo majority learned that Trotsky and his ally Grigory Piatakov "undertook an attempt to involve Kamenev and Zinoviev in their plans."[16] With such flux, other consolidation within the party leadership became only a question of time.

The General Strike: Moves in Advance of the Politburo Meeting

The General Strike, which began on May 4, 1926, provided a decisive impetus for the formation of the "United Opposition." Even after the TUC called off the strike, the British coal miners defied the union leadership and stayed out.[17] For the Bolshevik leadership, following these events with acute interest, the strike symbolized a revolutionary upsurge and the disruption of the political stability of Great Britain — the leader of the Western world. It appeared that Trotsky's predictions, outlined in his work "Whither Britain?" (published several months prior to the strike) were correct and that antiquated British imperialism had become the primary base for the next outbreak of the world revolution.

The question of the British strike was raised at every Politburo session after its start. The fact that the strike was directed by trade union leaders whom the Communist press had incessantly designated as "lackeys of the bourgeoisie" added a certain oddness to the situation. On May 4, the Politburo proposed to adopt a more moderate position towards the TUC: "The party and the Soviet press should maintain a calm, detached tone with appropriate critique of such 'Rightists.'"[18] Simultaneously, the Politburo decided to provide two million gold rubles in financial assistance to the strikers on behalf of the Soviet trade unions.[19] The chair of the Soviet trade unions, M. P. Tomsky, left for Paris "to provide operational help to the General Council upon necessity."

The first session of the special commission, created by the Politburo for "operative reaction" to the events in Britain took place on May 7.[20] Its working decisions were not recorded, but were placed instead in the highly-secret "special files." The Politburo commission's appraisals of the British strike had distinctly "Leftist" overtones. Later Molotov, responding to the attack of the opposition, disclosed who stood behind the commission's findings:

> MOLOTOV: Stalin addressed the "core" of the issue, in particular, the task of turning the strike into a political event, and the necessity to advance under the motto "away with Conservative government, long live workers' power!" Stalin outlined the basic ideas of this policy, with which all of us, including you, Comrade Zinoviev, agreed.[21]

On the same day, May 7, the question of the British strike was included in the Comintern Presidium agenda. Stalin, who almost never flattered the Comintern with his presence, appeared at this meeting. Obviously, Stalin was contemplating the best way to attack the defeated, though not fully crushed Zinoviev. Comintern head Zinoviev presented a "loyal" interpretation of events (that had been coordinated with the Politburo), stressing that continuation of the strike could create an opportunity for the seizure of state power by the working class. The Comintern Presidium concluded that "the renewed stabilization of capitalism is out of the question now."[22] To a certain degree, all members of the Bolshevik government shared unrealistic expectations of the outcome of the General Strike.

Each side in the internal party struggle attempted to turn the events of the General Strike to its own advantage. Comintern chair Zinoviev found himself the center of public attention. Full of energy, he composed daily orders to the European Communist parties, demanding support for British workers. This fact did not pass unnoticed by the "majority faction" in the Politburo. Its representatives, apart from Bukharin, had never before displayed interest in the international Communist movement. Despite the fact that they were on unfamiliar ground, they could not avoid accepting the challenge.

In the course of the May 7 sessions, Stalin and Molotov criticized Zinoviev's draft note to British Communists. On May 8, after Zinoviev's hurried corrections, there was a second revision.[23] Stalin took advantage of these revisions to exaggerate Zinoviev's mistakes: "In this draft, as the members of the Politburo can see, there is no place for the slogan 'away with Conservative government, long live workers' power!'"[24] A favorite trick of Stalin was to discredit political opponents by transforming petty omissions into major errors. Two years later, it was Bukharin's turn to fall prey to such a tactic, when he was forced to rewrite the program of the Sixth Comintern Congress.[25]

The atmosphere within the Politburo darkened after a note arrived from Great Britain that the TUC's General Council had rejected Moscow's offer of financial help. The council argued that acceptance of Soviet aid would be used against the strikers. Obviously at a loss, Stalin sent a telegram to Tomsky in Paris: "Please help, what can we do?"[26] When news of the end of the strike arrived from London, Tomsky, filled with a spirit of social compromise, addressed an optimistic telegram to the Politburo. Tomsky recommended that the British Communist Party proclaim that the abortive strike "denotes the failure of the Conservatives' ideas and the partial moral victory of the proletariat," and that "by transforming the struggle into conditions that might turn out more favorable than the current ones, it contributes towards the solution of major political questions."[27]

Tomsky's interpretation created the opportunity for Zinoviev and his allies to accuse their opponents of "Right-wing Deviation" and of playing along with the "traitors from the Trade Union Council." Zinoviev composed an indignant letter to the Politburo, describing Tomsky's position as "deeply erroneous and in principle incorrect." Zinoviev wrote, as usual without tempering his language: "The unconditional capitulation of the Trade Union Council, without even guaranteeing that the workers at least get their jobs back, is an unprecedented act of betrayal in the history of the international workers' movement. If the British Communist Party submits to this ignominious decision and expresses its loyalty to the Trade Union Council, it would become an accomplice in this crime."[28]

At the extraordinary Politburo session of May 14, Zinoviev's angry note was rejected, but Tomsky's policy was also discredited. Stalin telegraphed Tomsky in Paris: "We are inclined to believe that what happened was not compromise but treason. Submission to the Trade Union Council's decision is not appropriate when the workers wish to continue the strike. Instead we should criticize and expose the mistakes of the Trade Union Council and its leadership. The masses should be educated to their mistakes. Let's propose to the Politburo commission to cancel its resolution and replace it with one in agreement with the current telegram."[29]

For Zinoviev, the majority's backtracking and indecision marked an unquestionable personal success. He was planning his next steps to advance his position in the Politburo. However, in the course of the May 7 Comintern session, he preferred not to expose his cards. He proposed instead not to hurry conclusions, for "in a couple of days the situation will be clear."[30] The Comintern refrained from decision making on those very issues for which it was founded. The Comintern Presidium limited itself to refutations of (justified) British press claims that it had imposed "Russian revolutionary methods" on British Communists.[31]

In general, the defeat of the British strike played to the advantage of the dissenters within the party leadership. It gave them the opportunity to accuse the Stalinist faction of "betrayal of revolutionary Marxism" and "defeatism." The oppositionists could also accuse the majority of endangering the principle of the "unified workers' front," accepted by both the Bolshevik leadership and the Comintern in December of 1921.[32]

The Unified Workers' Front

The 1921 policy of the "unified workers' front" was a reaction of the Communist parties to the malaise in the worldwide revolutionary movement. It called for cooperation of Communist parties with socialist parties "in the struggle for the interests of the proletariat." Actually in a veiled form, the "unified workers' front" conceded the hopelessness of the world revolution, the goal for which the Comintern was created. Although the turn towards a "unified workers' front," hallowed by the name of Lenin, was not openly questioned, its feasibility was a subject of heated disputes within the party leadership.

Each approach of the European Communist parties to the social democrats was resisted by ultraleftist elements, unwilling to sacrifice the "purity of their principles." Political compromise was not a strong suit of the communist movement, as Lenin's complaint of "the childish malaise of leftism" in the spring 1920 highlighted. Zinoviev decisively opposed the imposition of a unified workers' front "from above,"[33] and he saw the failure of the British strike as yet another proof of the treacherous nature of the trade unions' bosses.

The Anglo-Russian Trade Union Committee was formed at a joint London conference of the Soviet and British trade unions on April 6–8, 1925 to restore the unity of the international trade union movement. For Soviet ruling circles, the treaty meant acknowledging that the Moscow-based Red International of Trade Unions (Profintern) had failed to win over the world's working class. Soviet trade union leader Tomsky, in his speech to the Sixteenth Party Congress, conceded that the Bolsheviks should be prepared to follow the working classes even if it meant "into hell or even to the Pope in Rome."

It was the demand for an immediate break with the "traitors" (withdrawal of the Soviet trade unions from the Anglo-Russian Trade Union Committee) that paved the way for the alliance between Zinoviev and Trotsky, who, upon his return from protracted therapy in Berlin, was ready to immerse himself in politics. Trotsky's memo on the British workers' movement from May 18 characterized the Anglo-Russian Committee as a "purely tactical compromise, which did not withstand the trial of real struggle."[34] Although he did not call for an immediate break with the Anglo-Russian Committee, Trotsky's message was clear, and it was immediately supported by Zinoviev.

The "epistolary" phase of the struggle ("statements against statements")[35] began on May 22, when the Soviet Comintern delegation found it "necessary to report on the lessons of the British strike on behalf of the Comintern Presidium."[36] Zinoviev took advantage of Stalin's departure to the Caucasus to impose his own interpretation. Already on May 26, he distributed his draft among Politburo members, which stressed that the strike had brought the working class close to the seizure of power. His conclusion refuted "the majority's position" that capitalism had entered a lasting period of stability: "The controversy over the issue of capitalism's 'stabilization' has been resolved. Accordingly, the policy based on the assumption that capitalism has overcome the postwar difficulties and has embarked upon a lasting period of its stabilization has turned out to be erroneous."[37]

Zinoviev's draft reflected his desire for revenge. For the first time, he stated clearly that since the leaders of the TUC have "cut off the head of the general strike on behalf of the English bourgeoisie," all contacts with them should be terminated. Shortly thereafter, Trotsky entered the fray with a May 26 *Pravda* article on the lessons of the British strike and the mistakes of the British Communists. To cap things off, the "dissenters" made a joint presentation of their position at Sverdlovsk University.

Representatives of the "majority" immediately sounded the alarm. On June 1, Bukharin and Molotov wrote to Stalin: "We think it is of primary importance for you to urgently get acquainted with the program and tell us what you think. Zinoviev has changed his mind on the question of stabilization and Comintern tactics. Now he is slinging mud at Comintern policy . . . and is launching an initiative for an immediate break with the Trade Union Council."[38] Stalin, who by that time had almost reached the Caucasus, agreed in full with the negative evaluation of Zinoviev's draft. His critical remarks on its margins are telling: "an idiot" (repeatedly), "too hasty," "too rough," "To Trotsky!" Stalin's anger was especially fueled by Zinoviev's insistence on the break with the Anglo-Russian Trade Union Committee, and his statement on "the end of stabilization." Stalin drew his own lesson from the General Strike: "I think the bourgeoisie is launching an attack, and the workers cannot even uphold their previous demands."[39] For an experienced politician the tactics of Zinoviev and Trotsky were clear: "Obviously, by using the 'British question' they want to win their position back."[40]

Thinking they had gained the upper hand, Zinoviev wrote on June 1 that "Discussion of the British question in the Politburo cannot be delayed any longer; following the Politburo, the Presidium of the Comintern has already twice put off discussion. As a result, the Comintern leadership finds itself in an absolutely embarrassing position: they are the only ones who have yet to take a stand on the lessons of the British strike. Although the Sixteenth Party Congress proclaimed a 'more active involvement of the representatives of the foreign parties in Comintern activity,' the opposite has been true. Whenever we create our own commission in the Politburo to work out a solution to an important issue, its discussion in the Comintern turns into empty formality. I seriously warn you that the same should not happen with the British question."[41]

On the next day, Trotsky composed a note with similar contents: "Failing to promptly adopt an adequate position on an extremely important issue, we are pursuing a deeply mistaken policy . . . the party needs an answer." Having argued in support of an immediate exit from the Anglo-Russian Committee, Trotsky laid his cards on the table: "The tactics of understatement and diplomatic maneuvers have found their natural continuation in the desire to preserve the semblance of things that are already nonexistent."[42]

Recognizing the growing tension within ruling circles, Stalin, still in the Caucasus, advised his allies to ignore the claims of the dissenters: "Just put off this question for the next week and let them go to hell." However, the standing of the opposition was still too high to simply ignore the opinion of two Politburo members. Bukharin's associates were busy preparing an alternative political program which, among other things, aimed at "unmasking adventurous petit-bourgeois tendencies (*otzovizm*) in the question of break with the General Council."[43]

The Politburo Session of June 3, 1926
"On Lessons from the English Strike"

The events leading up to the Politburo session of June 3, 1926 devoted to the lessons of the British strike foreshadowed that the meeting would be explosive. Indeed, the June 3 session was marked by extremely heated discussion that lasted an entire day. The drafts of Bukharin, Tomsky, and Molotov were distributed only on the day of the session. Criticizing the "traitors from the General Council," they argued nevertheless for the preservation of the Anglo-Russian Trade Union Committee, that is, for continued cooperation with the British trade union leadership.

Zinoviev, who delivered the major report, insisted that the strike was destined to transform itself into a political campaign that would have created an opportunity for the working class to seize power. No one present was willing to dispute these "basics of communism," but tactical calculations pushed aside strategic issues: Politburo members were willing to pass for "Leftists," but no one desired to be accused of "Right-wing Deviation." Internal party conflict undermined any attempt to transcend basic dogma and disrupted the capacity of the Bolshevik leadership to find a consensus. Tomsky's ill-fated telegram, full of false optimism, dispatched shortly after the end of the strike, amply demonstrated the severe consequences of independent political appraisal.

Replying to Zinoviev's attack, Tomsky attempted to shift the focus. He argued that the fight for unity of the trade union movement was not plausible without the Anglo-Russian Trade Union Committee: "Your theory is based upon unrealistic expectations of a revolution in Britain. And you are perfectly aware of this fact." Tomsky's assertion provoked an immediate reaction from Trotsky: "And yours depends upon the assumption that it will never take place."[44] The leader of the opposition insisted that remaining with the Anglo-Russian Committee meant that "we cover up the treason of the Trade Union Council, and put the blame for the strike's disruption upon radically minded miners."

Bukharin, whose report was loyal to the views of the majority, focused his attention on whether the Soviet trade unions should leave the Anglo-Russian Committee. His arguments, however, were not devoid of pragmatism. In particular, he pointed towards the specifics of the British workers' movement, claiming that British trade union leaders were more sensitive to pressure from the rank and file than in other countries: "We proceeded from the fact that the pressure on leaders of the British workers' movement is stronger than in other workers' movements. As a result, the center of the world revolution has shifted from central Europe to England."[45]

The representatives of the "majority faction" repeatedly cited historical facts. In the summer of 1917, the Bolsheviks had not abandoned the Soviets, although they were "Menshevik and Socialist-Revolutionary" in their composition. The dissenters, however, expressed their doubts that trade unions could serve as instruments of proletarian power (as had the Russian Soviets) during a "condition of revolution." These conflicting arguments remained within the framework of Russian experience, which was stubbornly applied to foreign Communists. There were almost no references to the opinion of the British Communists at the June 3 Politburo session.

Only Politburo candidate member and majority ally A. A. Andreev gave a more or less consistent account of Moscow's mistakes (while making Trotsky and Zinoviev fully responsible for them): "We have committed a common mistake in that we have exaggerated the significance of the events in Great Britain, and we have overestimated the dimensions of the workers' strike. The reason is that, not being adequately informed, we indulged in wishful thinking."[46] Indeed, under an ideological dictatorship, mistaking the desired for the actual was common in ruling circles, and calling things by their true name meant political suicide.

Mutual accusations among Politburo members reveal the peculiarities of the party regime as well as previously unknown facts and details. Zinoviev singled out the unfortunate role played by D. Z. Manuilsky, delegated to the Comintern Presidium as a representative of the Stalin faction. Zinoviev as head of the Comintern did not hesitate to reject Manuilsky's article on the results of the British strike written for the May issue of the journal *Communist International*, which, as a hostage of the party struggle, was held back from publication.[47]

Even more interesting is the question of the "Russian money," which was excluded from the final version of the session transcript. The violent reaction of Politburo members to the refusal of the TUC to accept financial help was in no small part caused by the fact that previously this had been a normal practice. In the course of the session, Zinoviev noted: "I don't oppose the practice of our proletarian state of bribing the *Temps* or the *Times*; even less I oppose if sometimes we buy the so-called 'workers' leaders' from the trade unions, if it corresponds to the interests of the proletariat."[48] Trotsky, on his part, responded with a sarcastic comment on the eagerness of certain leaders of the English trade unions to cooperate with the Soviet state if it was so good at bribing.

Although Zinoviev's draft resolution did not receive a majority of votes, each of the conflicting sides could interpret the outcome of the Politburo session to its advantage. The dissenters made their alliance clear to the rest of the Politburo and announced their international agenda. All were well aware that June 3 marked the onset of a new stage of internal party conflict. On the next day, the "Russian comrades" failed to appear at the Comintern Presidium meeting. It was necessary for everyone to come to their senses after a heated and lengthy debate and to complete the "program of the majority." No one ever mentioned again the "necessity of more active involvement of the representatives of the foreign parties in Comintern activity." As a result, the British question was silently removed from the agenda.[49]

It was only on June 8 that the Politburo resolution "on the lessons of the British strike" was approved by the Comintern. At its Presidium meeting, Bukharin, in the presence of Zinoviev, delivered his report to the foreign Communists (who had already been informed about "the Kremlin secrets").[50] The representatives of the European Communist parties obediently rubberstamped the Politburo decision. However, one of the participants, the Czech Communist V. Shtern, expressed his support of the Politburo dissenters without referring to them by name. As a result, he was silenced, and blamed for a variety of ideological sins, including "dragging along on the tails of the German ultraleftists."[51] Obviously, the "Russian" method of "ideological destruction of the opposition" had become Comintern practice as well. From that point on, not only manifestation of solidarity with "the Russian opposition" but also defense of similar positions became anathema within the Comintern.

The Developing "United Opposition" Platform

The June 3, 1926 Politburo discussion of results of the British strike marked the début of the "United Opposition." At the June 3 session, it presented its program on international politics. At the June 14 meeting, it focused its attention on internal party problems in the discussion of the report of Moscow Party Committee. On July 5, it criticized party policy in the countryside (the question of agricultural loans).[52] By the eve of the July Central Committee plenum, the "United Opposition" had presented a comprehensive political program that offered alternative solutions to the most pressing problems of domestic and foreign policy.

These Politburo transcripts give researchers a unique opportunity to witness the atmospherics of the heated disputes that marked the sessions of the highest body of the Bolshevik leadership. The outcome was more important than the tone of discussion. The "United Opposition" coalesced around an ideologically pure international platform: British workers had been abandoned by a corrupt trade union leadership, and the chance for a British socialist revolution had been lost. The Bolsheviks, as the representatives of the working class, should throw in their lot directly with the British workers. The Politburo majority, after false starts and hesitations, came down on the side of pragmatism — to continue to cooperate with the British trade union leadership, even though it had refused Russian financial assistance and was suspected of corruption and of doing the bidding of capitalist forces. Although according to ideological criteria the political stance of the majority within the Politburo was inferior to the "platform" of the dissenters, the majority carried with it the power of the party apparatus, which became the decisive factor in the victory over Zinoviev, Kamenev, and Trotsky. As a consequence, the oppositionists had to sit silent as the majority instructed the Communist International on its version of the "lessons of the British strike."

Control of the party apparatus enabled the majority to conceal the proposals of the opposition not only from rank-and-file Communists but also from Central Committee members. On June 18, in a caucus of the Russian Comintern delegation, Trotsky proposed to mobilize all resources in support of the British miners. His memo was transferred to the appropriate subcommittee, where it was buried.[53]

The "United Oppositionists" were ready to resume their struggle at the

Central Committee plenum, which opened on July 14, 1926. A week before, the Politburo added the announcement of its decisions on the results of the British strike to the plenum's agenda.[54] Compared to the Politburo disputes of June 3, the discussion of this question at the plenum did not yield any practical results. The miners were still on strike but the hopes for revolutionary upheaval were dispelled. These events made it much easier for Bukharin, who delivered the main report, to accuse the oppositionists of "radical overestimation of the international situation."[55] Zinoviev reminded the Central Committee that the strike had ruined their attempts to approach the International Federation of Trade-Unions (Amsterdam International), which adopted the "reformist" position. He demanded that this policy be pursued to the end through separation from the Anglo-Russian Committee.

Trotsky offered his own version of the limits of possible collaboration with the reformists, who favored social democracy. Trotsky focused on the principal issue. "The policy of a 'unified front' can be pursued only until the point where opportunists fall into the embrace of class enemies."[56] For the Politburo dissenters the British strike marked a chance to cease collaboration with traitors and, to use Trotsky's words: "to ally with the masses against their leaders." Stalin, supported by the "majority," warned against the perils of omitting necessary stages in the development of the workers' movement.

The resulting Central Committee resolution was entrusted to the Russian delegation to the regular Anglo-Russian Trade Union Committee session with the charge of preventing a break with British trade unionists on the grounds of "common agreement."[57] This stance suited the interests of the British Communists, who preferred to preserve their connections with organized labor.[58]

In the course of the July 1926 Central Committee plenum the "United Opposition" suffered a total defeat and Zinoviev was expelled from the Politburo. Soon thereafter, Stalin decided the time had come to raise the question of Zinoviev's dismissal from his Comintern position. In his typical style, referring to existing "public opinion," Stalin wrote to Molotov: "It seems we will not avoid the question of Grigory's displacement from the Communist International because this issue has been raised by a range of Western parties (England, Germany). . . . It would be to a high degree strange and unnatural if we would go on ignoring this question at the time when all circumstances point towards it, and two of the Western parties have already had their say."[59]

The strike itself, which the miners continued through the end of November 1926, did not provoke further disputes within the Politburo; instead, it was turned into a propaganda campaign. The leadership of the Soviet trade unions repeatedly addressed the "toiling masses" with appeals to donate money "for the strikers." The memoirs of a Swiss worker in a Moscow printing plant reveal that "Under immense psychological pressure from the trade unions, the workers were forced to donate large sums of money 'to England.' In the end, they could console themselves with Soviet press accounts that their contribution that exceeded those of workers from capitalist countries."[60]

This "view from below" coincides with the one "from above." Stalin's letters to his supporters in the Politburo state that "The delegation of English miners should arrive in the USSR soon if it's still not here. We must receive it with all the necessary fanfare and collect as much money for them as possible. Rumor has it the Americans have promised a million dollars. So we should collect two or three millions (in no way less than the Americans). The situation is England is serious and it obliges us to make serious 'sacrifices.' "[61] These instructions suggest that the strike was a pretext for "total mobilization" campaigns, which later became a regular aspect of Soviet life.

Conclusions

The General Strike intensified the struggle within the party leadership. Occurring where and when it did, the strike created an illusion of revolutionary upsurge and provided fertile soil for mutual accusations within the Politburo. Denunciations of the "traitors" from European reformist parties and trade unions were in fact veiled attacks on political opponents within the Politburo. At a time when Bolshevik leaders vowed fidelity to "true Marxism" and assailed each other with quotes from Lenin, the course of events in Europe did not yield much hope for the world proletarian revolution.

The stenograms of the Politburo provide perspective on just a few aspects of the history of internal party struggles that shook the party in the mid-1920s. However, they abundantly demonstrate that those party leaders willing to defy the "majority" had to rely on their own political campaigns and legal rules of party democracy. Stalin's faction, in control of the apparatus and the regional party organizations, preferred "illegal" methods of discrediting their opponents. To study their tactics, other sources are necessary, such as the internal correspondence of members of the Stalinist faction.

The victory over the "United Opposition" manifested itself in the form of absolute intolerance of dissent and transformation of "iron unity" into a fetish of party propaganda. Such steps created a party regime that had little in common with the initial goals and ideals of the Bolshevism. Stalin used this regime to strengthen his personal leadership within the party and the state, which soon entered into one of the most tragic epochs of Soviet history.

Notes

1. RGASPI Fond 17, op. 163, del. 687.
2. RGASPI Fond 17, op. 163, del. 687.
3. RGASPI Fond 17, op. 163, del. 687.
4. RGASPI Fond 17, op. 163, del. 687.
5. "The 'deviationist nature' of Grisha's [Zinoviev's] arguments can result in blackmail in the face of his dismissal, but we shouldn't be afraid of that in any case." Cited in Kosheleva, Lel'chuk, Naumov, Rogovaia, and Khlevniuk, *Pis'ma I. V. Stalina V. M. Molotovu, 1925–1936 gg.: Sbornik dokumentov,* p. 64.
6. Vilkova, *RKP (b) i vnutripartiinaia bor'ba v dvatsatye gody, 1924: Dokumenty i materialy,* introduction.
7. Ibid., p. 129.
8. Feliks Dzerzhinsky (candidate member of the Politburo and head of the OGPU), commenting upon the activity of the Leningrad opposition in his letter to Stalin and Ordzhonikidze of October 5–6, 1925, stressed that a "repetition of Kronstadt, is only now being currently prepared within our party. So the question is not only about the existence of our faction, but about the direct threat to the existence of the party and Soviet power." Graziosi et al., *Bolshevistskoe rukovodstvo: Perepiska, 1912–1927: Sbornik dokumentov,* pp. 309–10.
9. Daniels, *The Conscience of the Revolution: Communist Opposition in Soviet Russia* remains the classic of the history of the struggles within the Bolshevik Party in the 1920s.
10. Vatlin, *Komintern: Pervye desiat let,* pp. 119–41.
11. RGASPI Fond 17, op. 163, del. 682.
12. Kosheleva, Lel'chuk, Naumov, Naumov, Rogovaia, and Khlevniuk, *Pis'ma I. V. Stalina V. M. Molotovu, 1925–1936 gg.: Sbornik dokumentov,* pp. 80–81.
13. RGASPI Fond 17, op. 163, del. 682.
14. *Kommunisticheskii Internatsional v dokumentakh, 1919–1932,* p. 46.
15. Graziosi et al., *Bolshevistskoe rukovodstvo: Perepiska, 1912–1927. Sbornik dokumentov,* pp. 324–25.
16. Ibid., pp. 324–25.
17. The 1959 work by Gurovich, *Vseobschaia stachka v Anglii 1926 g.,* written from a rather orthodox position, remains the best-documented account of the strike in Soviet historiography.
18. RGASPI Fond. 17, op. 163, del. 3, l. 57.
19. RGASPI Fond. 17, op. 163, del. 3, l. 65. This proposal, put forward by Stalin, Molotov, and Dogadov, was accepted by written vote (*opros*) of the rest of the Politburo members on May 7.
20. The Politburo Commission on the British strike was based upon Tomsky's proposal of May 5. Initially it included Stalin, Zinoviev, Molotov, Dogadov, Lozovky, and Chicherin, with Piatnitsky appointed as its secretary. Rykov and Bukharin joined the commission later. On this, see RGASPI Fond 17, op. 163, del. 3, ll. 62, 66. On June 3 Lozovsky stated that the "English committee had sessions on a daily basis. It reviewed all the

important questions, and also all the articles in our newspapers." On this, see RGASPI Fond 17, op. 163, del. 687.

21. RGASPI Fond 17, op. 163, del. 687 (the last remarks of Molotov at the June 3 Politburo session).

22. RGASPI Fond 495, op. 2, del. 71, ll. 30–46.

23. RGASPI Fond 82, op. 2, del. 223, l. 45.

24. Kosheleva, Lel'chuk, Naumov, Naumov, Rogovaia, and Khlevniuk, *Pis'ma I. V. Stalina V. M. Molotovu, 1925–1936 gg.: Sbornik dokumentov*, p. 66.

25. Zhuravlev and Solopov, *Bukharin: Chelovek, politik, ucheny*, pp. 192–93.

26. RGASPI Fond 558, op. 11, del. 197, l. 61. The telegram to Tomsky was sent on May 9. On the next day, Stalin reviewed a Soviet Trade Union Council decree on the TUC's refusal to accept "Russian money." Ibid., p. 71.

27. The telegram, signed by Tomsky and Humboldt, was cited in Zinoviev's report to the Politburo session from June 3. On this, see RGASPI Fond 17, op. 163, del. 687.

28. The latest draft of Zinoviev was also cited in his report. See RGASPI Fond 17, op. 163, del. 687.

29. RGASPI Fond 17, op. 163, del. 3, l. 71.

30. RGASPI Fond 495, op. 2, del. 72, l. 13.

31. RGASPI Fond 495, op. 2, del. 72, l. 26.

32. Vatlin, "Rozdenie politiki edinogo fronta: 'Russkoe izmereniie.' "

33. Firsov, "K voprosu o taktike edinogo fronta v 1921–1924 gg.," pp. 121–22.

34. Trotskii, *Voprosy britanskogo rabochego dvizheniia*, p. 229.

35. This was the term that Trotsky applied at the beginning of the session on June 3. See RGASPI Fond 17, op. 163, del. 687.

36. RGASPI Fond 508, op. 1, del. 27, l. 1.

37. See attachment to the stenogram from June 3. RGASPI Fond 17, op. 163, del. 687.

38. Kosheleva, Lel'chuk, Naumov, Naumov, Rogovaia, and Khlevniuk, *Pis'ma I. V. Stalina V. M. Molotovu, 1925–1936 gg.: Sbornik dokumentov*, pp. 58–59.

39. RGASPI Fond 558, op. 11, del. 197, ll. 72–106 (the draft of Zinoviev's program), l. 92 (Stalin's comment). In his letter to Molotov of June 3 Stalin sent his detailed comments on the draft. He demanded that the Politburo "oppose decisively the policy of Zinoviev and Trotsky, for it leads to the isolation of the Communist parties from the masses and their sacrifice to the dictatorship of the reformists." On this, see Kosheleva, Lel'chuk, Naumov, Naumov, Rogovaia, and Khlevniuk, *Pis'ma I. V. Stalina V. M. Molotovu, 1925–1936 gg: Sbornik dokumentov*, pp. 62–64.

40. Ibid., p. 61.

41. This note was a reaction to Tomsky's proposal to wait for the arrival of the representatives of the British Communist Party in Moscow. It is published as an attachment to the stenogram of the Politburo session. RGASPI Fond 17, op. 163, del. 687.

42. Trotsky's letter is published in an attachment to the stenogram. RGASPI Fond 17, op. 163, del. 687.

43. RGASPI Fond 17, op. 163, del. 687.

44. RGASPI Fond 17, op. 163, del. 687.

45. RGASPI Fond 17, op. 163, del. 687 (the second speech).

46. RGASPI Fond 17, op. 163, del. 687.

47. Instead, a joint issue was published later as no. 54–55, which contained a revision of Manuilsky's article entitled "The British Strike and the Stabilization of Capitalism."

48. RGASPI Fond 17, op. 163, del. 687.

49. RGASPI Fond 495, op. 2, del. 73.

50. RGASPI Fond 495, op. 2, del. 73, ll. 82–92.

51. RGASPI Fond 495, op. 2, del. 73, l. 132.

52. RGASPI Fond 17, op. 163, del. 690, 694.

53. RGASPI Fond 508, op. 1, del. 29, l. 2 (the decision), ll. 20–21 (Trotsky's letter).

54. RGASPI Fond 17, op. 3, del. 573, l. 2.

55. RGASPI Fond 17, op. 3, del. 246, l. 8.

56. RGASPI Fond 17, op. 3, del. 246, l. 36.

57. This session took place on July 30–31, 1926 in Paris. On the fate of the Anglo-Russian Trade Union Committee, see A. Y. Vatlin, *Komintern: Pervye desiat let*, pp. 66–79.

58. RGASPI Fond 495, op. 2, del. 57, l. 205.

59. Letter of August 30, 1926. Lih, Naumov, and Khlevniuk, *Stalin's Letters to Molotov, 1925–1936*, pp. 80–81.

60. The Swiss worker, Deredinger, describes the reaction of the workers on the visit to Moscow of an English miners' choir. Well-fed and well-dressed in comparison with their Soviet comrades in arms, they left an impression of "genuine bourgeoisie." Derendiger, *Erzählungen aus dem Leben: Als Graphiker in Moskau 1910 bis 1938*.

61. Kosheleva, Lel'chuk, Naumov, Naumov, Rogovaia, and Khlevniuk, *Pis'ma I. V. Stalina V. M. Molotovu, 1925–1936 gg.: Sbornik dokumentov*, p. 78.

5

Stalin, Syrtsov, Lominadze: Preparations for the "Second Great Breakthrough"

OLEG KHLEVNIUK

The "antiparty affair" preoccupied Soviet ruling circles from the end of October through the beginning of November 1930. The charge was that party functionaries, headed by S. I. Syrtsov, a candidate Politburo member and the head of the government of the Russian Federation, and V. V. Lominadze, the first secretary of the Transcaucasian Party Committee (which encompassed Azerbaijan, Armenia, and Georgia), had formed an illegal faction. The case of Syrtsov-Lominadze constitutes a puzzling and obscure chapter in the history of power struggles within the Bolshevik Party. This essay uses the verbatim Politburo transcripts and supporting documents from the November 4, 1930 Politburo meeting "About the Factional Work of Syrtsov, Lominadze, and Others" to answer some of the unresolved·issues surrounding the "antiparty affair."[1]

Whereas the internal party conflicts of the 1920s were well documented, primarily due to the efforts of Leon Trotsky, who initially escaped Stalin's vengeance, the frictions of the beginning of the 1930s are known to historians only through a few official publications. Although the Syrtsov-Lominadze affair was largely obscured from public view, those historians who worked with the material available before the opening of the Soviet archives, in particular R. W. Davies, produced works of significant historical value on this subject.[2]

Upon the opening of the archives in the first half of the 1990s, new archival documents became available on the Syrtsov-Lominadze affair. Apart from the Politburo sanctions of Syrtsov and Lominadze, the archive of the Committee of Party Control of the Central Committee contained the personal dossiers of Syrtsov and Lominadze. Also included are the protocols of the interrogations of the participants of the "antiparty faction," conducted by the Central Control Commission and the OGPU. Additionally, transcripts of the remarks of the head of the Central Control Commission, Sergo Ordzhonikidze, on the Syrtsov-Lominadze affair to the joint session of the Politburo and the Presidium of the Central Control Commission on November 4, 1930 were made available along with other private Ordzhonikidze documents.[3] Several works on the Syrtsov-Lominadze case have been published on the basis of these documents.[4]

This essay uses the most authoritative source on the "antiparty affair" — the complete verbatim transcript (stenogram) and the report of the joint session of the Politburo and the Presidium of the Central Control Commission on November 4, 1930 devoted entirely to Syrtsov and Lominadze. The stenogram of the Politburo discussion of November 4, 1930 is the primary source for the study of the Syrtsov-Lominadze affair. Along with the full stenogram, the summary of it, intended for distribution to a wide range of party functionaries, contains the remarks of Stalin, Lominadze, and other "oppositionists," as well as the protocols of their interrogations by the Central Control Commission and the OGPU. The interrogations endow this source with special value and enable us to analyze aspects of the Syrtsov-Lominadze case that had previously been classified.

This essay analyzes the Syrtsov-Lominadze case as an integral part of the broader political processes of Stalin's late 1929–early 1930 "Great Breakthrough" and its subsequent intensification, which we designate as the "Second Great Breakthrough." We focus on three major issues. The first is to pin down the content and concrete circumstances of the Syrtsov-Lominadze affair. Second, we analyze the Syrtsov-Lominadze case as an indicator of the internal party situation as the party elite reacted to the first results of forced collectivization and industrialization. Third, we consider the Syrtsov-Lominadze affair as an integral part of the Stalinist policy of the "Second Great Breakthrough."

As in other political affairs of the Stalinist era, the Syrtsov-Lominadze case was, to use Trotsky's apt characterization of the 1936–38 show trials, "an amalgam," a peculiar combination of real facts and falsifications. Contrary to the show trials, the Syrtsov-Lominadze case was based more on real circumstances than on sheer falsifications. The presence of facts or "near" facts instead of fantasy, therefore, makes an analysis of the apprehensive mood of the party elite during the early phases of the "Great Breakthrough" possible, albeit complicated.

First, an outline of the broader context at the beginning of the 1930s: The Stalinist policy of forced collectivization and destruction of the kulaks as a class plunged the entire country into chaos, resulting in a near civil war in the countryside. In the face of mass peasant revolts in the winter and spring of 1930, Stalin was forced to retreat. Peasants abandoned collective farms on a mass scale, returning to private households. The proportion of collectivized households fell from 56 percent on March 1, 1930 to 24 percent in the summer of 1930.[5] The remaining collective farms remained weak and ineffective, serving as an instrument of resource transfer from countryside to the needs of industrialization. Such policies led to the decay of agriculture. Despite this threat, Stalin continued to increase capital investments in the industrial sector. The economic crisis of the summer and autumn of 1930 was aggravated by the growing ineffectiveness of capital investments, a drastic drop in living standards, declines in labor productivity, and the collapse of the banking system. Against this backdrop, growing criticism of Stalinist policy within the party was inevitable. Stalin's draconic responses to critics (such as Syrtsov) were designed to quell doubts about his policies and to cause those who were undecided to toe to his official party line.

The most highly placed Stalin critic at the center of this story was Sergei Ivanovich Syrtsov (1893–1937), a Bolshevik Party member from 1913, who actively participated in the Revolution of 1917 and the Civil War. At the beginning of 1920s, he held a post in the Communist Party Central Committee. In 1926 he was appointed to the post of the secretary of the Siberia Regional Party Committee. In January 1928, during Stalin's trip to Siberia to oversee grain collections, Syrtsov actively implemented his orders on forced grain extractions. In 1929, Syrtsov became the head of the Council of People's Commissars of the Russian Republic and joined the Politburo as a candidate member. Confronted with the results of Stalinist policies, Syrtsov became critical of the regime. He was fired from his position, expelled from the Politburo and the Central Committee, and transferred to the provinces. In the course of the Great Terror of 1937 he was shot.

The second target of the "antiparty affair" was Vissarion Vissarionovich (Beso) Lominadze (1897–1935), a Bolshevik Party member since 1917. At the beginning of the 1920s, he was a secretary of the Georgian Central Committee; later he worked in the Comintern. In 1930, he was appointed the first secretary of the Trans-Caucasian Party Committee. Within less than a year he was fired and exiled to minor administrative position. In 1935, facing the threat of imminent arrest, Lominadze committed suicide.

As their biographies show, both Syrtsov and Lominadze were rising young stars of the party. Their promotions show that they were supporters of Stalinist policies, far removed from contamination by "Right Deviationist" tendencies. Both represented the kind of young Bolshevik leader that Stalin needed for his socialist transformation.

The chain of circumstances that brought the Syrtsov-Lominadze affair to a head can be reconstructed with the help of the stenogram of the Politburo session of November 4.

According to this record, on October 21, one of Stalin's closest allies, the editor of *Pravda,* L. Z. Mekhlis, was given information on the "factional activity" of Syrtsov and Lominadze during a meeting with the party secretary of the Literature Section of the Institute of Red Professors, B. G. Reznikov.[6] Reznikov's report, sent to Stalin upon Mekhlis' request, contained information about contacts between Syrtsov and his allies in the government of the Russian Republic and the circle of the first secretary of the Caucasus Party Committee, Lominadze, on their common dissatisfaction with Stalin's policies. Reznikov's claim was that both groups had set Stalin's overthrow as their major goal. According to Reznikov's report, Syrtsov felt that "the imminent collapse of the country's economy will cause a crisis in the leadership; to be more precise, in Comrade Stalin (they explicitly stated that by 'the leadership' they meant 'Comrade Stalin'). As a consequence of the panic (similar to what had happened in the spring),[7] [Stalin] will see his own power base shift from under him very rapidly, and the party will finally receive 'proper governance.' After the economic collapse, after the catastrophe, when the oppressed 'classes' let their voices be heard, no apparatus will be strong enough to resist. And Stalin's power rests upon his apparatus."[8] According to Reznikov, Syrtsov and his supporters intended to prepare a pamphlet criticizing Stalin's policy, distribute it among the Central Committee members, and then launch an open attack against him in the course of the upcoming plenum.

A key point was Reznikov's reference to an impending meeting of the Syrtsov and Lominadze groups (Lominadze was at the time in Moscow on business). The Syrtsov group planned to use this joint meeting to prepare a plan of future actions.

What happened next is known from the report of the Central Control Commission delivered by its head, Sergo Ordzhonikidze, at the Politburo session of November 4. He disclosed that Stalin had discussed Reznikov's note with P. P. Postyshev, the secretary of the Central Committee, and with Ordzhonikidze himself (the other Central Committee secretaries, L. M. Kaganovich and V. M. Molotov, were on holiday at the time). On October 22, it was decided to "find out what is happening" from Syrtsov in person. Syrtsov was summoned; however, he appeared in the Central Committee building only four and a half hours later, around half past five. Shortly thereafter, Reznikov also appeared and reported that he, together with Syrtsov, had attended another meeting, which had started at eleven o'clock and had just ended.[9]

In a second memo, Reznikov informed Stalin that during the October 22 meeting, the Syrtsov group had agreed to make preparations for Stalin's overthrow through either legal or illegal measures in close collaboration with the Lominadze group. Additionally, Reznikov reported that Syrtsov had related the details of the Politburo session of October 20 to his allies, an offense against the secrecy requirements of Politburo meetings.[10]

In his denunciation, Reznikov quoted Syrtsov as saying at the meeting: "A large share of party activists, deeply dissatisfied with the current party policy and political regime, still believe a tradition of collective decision making exists in the Politburo, which, on its part, pursues a consistent political line, and that the Central Committee, although having lost its Leninist spirit, remains the real 'Central Committee.' We need to dispel these illusions. The 'Politburo' is a fiction. In reality, all decisions are made behind the backs of Politburo members, by a small group of party insiders, who meet in the Kremlin, or in the former apartment of Klara Zetkin. Some Politburo members, such as Kuibyshev, Voroshilov, Kalinin, and Rudzutak are excluded from the decision-making process; on the other hand, the 'inner circle' includes non-Politburo members, such as Yakovlev, Postyshev, etc."[11]

On the evening of October 22, Syrtsov refused to provide testimony in response to Reznikov's denunciation and demanded to be called by the Central Control Commission. Simultaneously, interrogations of other participants in the meeting (as reported by Reznikov) took place in the Central Control Commission. Those summoned, I. S. Nusinov,[12] V. A. Kavraisky,[13] and A. I. Galperin denied the charges when confronted by Reznikov. They were arrested and transferred to OGPU interrogation.[14]

Between October 22 and the November 4 Politburo meeting, participants in the Syrtsov-Lominadze affair confessed to involvement in a "faction" and to "antiparty activity" after interrogations by the OGPU and Central Control Commission. Their confessions were used as evidence in the joint Politburo and Presidium of the Central Control Commission session of November 4, 1930 on the "faction" created by Syrtsov, Lominadze, and their sympathizers. The Politburo decided to expel Syrtsov and Lominadze from the Central Committee and L. I. Shatskin from the Central Control Commission.[15] A commission was formed to work out a final resolution that included leading figures of the Central Committee and the Central Control Commission, and Stalin himself.[16] The commission confirmed Syrtsov's and Lominadze's expulsion from the

Central Committee and Shatskin's removal from the Central Control Commission. The Politburo resolution was formally approved by the Central Committee on December 1, and published in the press on the next day. Press reports stated that Syrtsov and Lominadze had organized a "Leftist-Rightist" coalition, whose platform coincided with the proposals of the "Right Opposition."

The official story of the unmasking of the Syrtsov-Lominadze group was that its existence became known to the party leadership only on October 21, when Reznikov made his first denunciation to Mekhlis. The Politburo then undertook urgent measures to put an end to the destructive activity of the "deviationists." However, a number of facts cast doubt on the official version. First, Reznikov's report makes clear that the October 22 meeting was planned in advance. Thus, some party official (probably Mekhlis, but hardly without Stalin's approval), upon receiving Reznikov's October 21 report, ordered him to attend the upcoming meeting. It can be inferred from this that attempts to find Syrtsov early in the day on October 22 were a sham. Using Reznikov as an agent provocateur, Stalin deliberately gave the "factionists" the opportunity to aggravate their "crimes."

The rationale for this conclusion becomes clear when the first and the second reports of Reznikov are compared. The first document contained general accusations against Syrtsov and Lominadze; the second, due to unequivocal remarks made by Syrtsov in the course of the October 22 meeting, enhanced the credibility of the charges against him and gave the case a strong factual base.[17]

The crucial role played by Reznikov requires that we focus attention on him and his earlier relationships with the key players. For a considerable period of time Reznikov worked in Siberia with Syrtsov. The latter was then transferred to Moscow and appointed to a high-level government position. After Reznikov's move to Moscow and his subsequent appointment to the Institute of Red Professors, their friendship revived. One of the participants in the Syrtsov case, Kavraisky, upon his arrival in Moscow in May 1930 (according to his testimony during his OGPU interrogation) noted a close friendship between Syrtsov and Reznikov. Moreover, Kavraisky stated that it was Reznikov who provoked Syrtsov to undertake decisive actions. Reznikov proposed to establish contacts with the "Right Opposition" (obviously meaning Bukharin, Tomsky, and others), while other conspirators objected to this plan. During the fateful October 22 meeting, it was Reznikov who proposed recruiting supporters among Central Committee members for the démarche against Politburo policy.[18]

Other attendees confirmed Reznikov's radical stance at the meeting. Under interrogation, Nusinov reported that the October 22 meeting was organized at Reznikov's initiative. Reznikov declared deep dissatisfaction with the group's inactivity and proposed "to get together and decide on future actions." Galperin, in his testimony to the OGPU, insisted that Reznikov set up Syrtsov by asking him blunt and direct questions on the current situation inside the Politburo. Reznikov's provocations were also noted in Syrtsov's testimony to the Central Control Commission.[19]

Such testimony confirms that Reznikov was a key figure in the Syrtsov "faction," or at least that he was regarded as such. No doubt such claims can also be interpreted as attempts to take revenge on Reznikov for his betrayal. Still, the unanimous statements of the accused, gathered under relentless interrogation by the OGPU, appear to confirm the truth of Reznikov's unnatural zeal.

Reznikov's own testimony provides indirect evidence of complicity. It reveals that Reznikov had a number of private discussions on the mistakes of the Stalinist leadership with Syrtsov and Siberian officials, until at some point he "decided to repent." He then informed the secretary of the party organization of the Institute of the Red Professors, a Comrade Vesna, about Syrtsov's "anti-party moods." Vesna, on his part, promised to convey this information "to the top." However, Reznikov's subsequent actions (if his testimony is to be treated seriously) provoke suspicion. While supposedly waiting for feedback from Vesna, Reznikov continued to attend oppositionist gatherings and indulged in dangerous, provocative conversations. Only on October 21, on the eve of the final decisive meeting of the Syrtsov group, did he decide to turn to Mekhlis.[20]

If Reznikov had contacted Mekhlis or other highly placed party functionaries at the time he informed Vesna at the Institute of the Red Professors, then his actions could be easily explained. Driven by fear of discovery, Reznikov could easily betray his friends. Still, if Reznikov had been so apprehensive, why did he continue to aggravate his own situation, regularly attending oppositionist meetings while waiting for word from Vesna? Reznikov could not fail to realize that his own, ostensibly unsuccessful, plea to Vesna could not absolve him if the group were uncovered. If Vesna did not react, Reznikov would have turned to someone higher up (and would have had a perfect opportunity for doing so). Consequently, it can be inferred with a high degree of probability that the version of Vesna's inactivity was invented in order to provide Reznikov with an alibi. Most probably, Reznikov's repetitive contacts with Syrtsov and other oppositionists were part of a special mission assigned him by a high party official, if not by Stalin himself. Not only did he spy on Syrtsov, but he also did his best to provoke the group to launch decisive actions. The question of Vesna's strange inactivity was not even raised in the November 4 session, and Vesna was not involved in the process even as a witness.

Syrtsov himself, as the documents abundantly demonstrate, had concluded that Reznikov was playing the deliberate role of provocateur. During his October 23 interrogation by Ordzhonikidze in the Central Control Commission, Syrtsov made repetitive, almost undisguised, allusions to this point:

> SYRTSOV: You see, some people start shaking with fear from just one question, such as "have you been at that place?" or "have you met with this individual?"
> ORDZHONIKIDZE: You think it's due to the party regime?
> SYRTSOV: I think, Sergo, you should also consider how to make the atmosphere within the party healthier. The insincerity which pervades my behavior and yours destroys the individual and party mentality in such a way, that it's not possible to withstand it any more. We have to do something to get rid of it.
> ORDZHONIKIDZE: So that every Politburo member or a candidate can instigate opposition against the party and its Central Committee?
> SYRTSOV: No. To change the situation where every party member is just a pawn of the state apparatus, and when, in order to obtain information on what he really thinks, the party leadership attaches an informer to every one of them.
> ORDZHONIKIDZE: Aren't you ashamed of what you say?
> SYRTSOV: As to informers, I can share more information, but it is not an issue of primary importance here.[21]

The real role of Reznikov in the Syrtsov-Lominadze affair can only be clarified through access to OGPU operational materials, which are most probably stored in the closed archive of the Federal Security Bureau (FSB).

Despite the high degree of probability of deliberate provocation, the accusations against Syrtsov, Lominadze and their adherents, were in a large degree based on real events. The oppositionists' confessions, available as appendices to the November 4, 1930 stenogram, demonstrate that they had admitted the validity of most of Reznikov's accusations, denying just the interpretation of their actions as "directed against the party and Stalin." However, the sincerity of these statements is highly questionable. Objectively, their acts were "anti-Stalinist." In the case of their success, the party leadership would have been replaced.

Most likely Syrtsov, Lominadze, and their supporters lacked a definite plan of action. They just gathered together, discussed the current agenda, and cautiously recruited new followers. They linked the possibility of more decisive measures to the situation inside the country. In case of an acute political crisis and disorganization of the Stalinist leadership, they did not exclude the possibility of a direct appeal to the Central Committee plenum. In other words, the Syrtsov-Lominadze group conceived of itself as a force which under certain conditions was prepared to form the core of a new government.

Against the background of the later consolidation of Stalin's personal power and the widespread application of terror, the calculations of Syrtsov, Lominadze, and their allies look like incredible political naiveté. But were they really that naïve?

The political experience of Syrtsov, Lominadze, and their allies, along with tens of thousands of other Bolsheviks, was formed under the relative "liberalism" within the Bolshevik party on its way to state power. "Collective leadership," including a prominent role for the Central Committee and party plenums, constituted the pillar of this liberalism. Accordingly, party functionaries from the Central Committee and other leading Soviet institutions enjoyed significant influence in decision making. The bitter power struggles in the Politburo among Lenin's heirs only reinforced their position. Conflicting Soviet party leaders were compelled to seek support among the "party activists" (*partaktiv*). The legitimacy of Stalin's superior position was that he was the most powerful among the party leaders who emerged as the winners of the 1929 Politburo struggle. Still, the fact that, in the five years that had passed since Lenin's death, the balance of power within the Politburo had shifted several times, could hardly convince party functionaries that Stalin's position was unassailable.

The first serious conflict between Stalin and the party bureaucrats erupted after the launch of mass collectivization, accompanied by the "liquidation of the kulaks as a class" campaign. This campaign, coordinated through direct orders from Moscow and complemented by local initiatives, started at the end of 1929. The ensuing bloody violence in the countryside touched millions of peasants. In the face of mass peasant revolts, Stalin was forced to retreat and slow down collectivization and dekulakization. Stalin's March 2, 1930 *Pravda* article "Dizzy with Success" explained away all the "deviations" of collectivization as the fault of overzealous regional administrators. The "Dizzy with Success" article, followed by party directives, resulted in a mass exodus from the collective farms. Party activists, who had endured the immense psychological pressure of several months of collectivization and had ruined the lives of many peasants, now became Stalin's scapegoats.

The reaction of regional party leaders is revealed in Syrtsov's testimony that reflects upon Reznikov's confession. Reznikov, who had taken an active part in the collectivization, was offended by Stalin's article. Claiming that the "activists" had been made scapegoats, Syrtsov claimed that Reznikov stated: "It is better to join the 'Right Opposition' and Trotsky's bloc than remain loyal to such a treacherous regime."[22]

Without doubt, Syrtsov was aware of the proliferation of such views among the party functionaries. He admitted that he personally conceived of Stalin's article "Dizzy with Success" as timely, but erroneous due to Stalin's threats to "make someone responsible for this affair" and his insinuation that some Central Committee and Politburo members had provoked the "excesses."[23]

In the course of his interrogations and his remarks at the November 4 session, Syrtsov openly claimed that the ruling circle, and Stalin personally, were the true instigators of "excesses." Admitting that local administrators had conducted the campaign with unprecedented cruelty, Syrtsov nevertheless correctly pointed to the fact that the full responsibility for the results of collectivization rested on Stalin: "When a politician is launching a campaign, he ought to take into consideration not only the form in which its slogans are cast, but also how they can be transformed in the minds of those who will implement them."[24]

The apparent failure of forced collectivization undermined Stalin's authority and aggravated the dissatisfaction of many party activists with the new Politburo practice of ruthless and immediate suppression of any manifestation of dissatisfaction with or doubts about the legitimacy of the "general line." There was also dissatisfaction with the hasty construction of the Stalin cult proclaiming him the messiah of victorious socialist construction.

The details of the Syrtsov-Lominadze affair disclose that the dissatisfaction of mid-rank party functionaries with Stalinist politics increased significantly in the summer of 1930. Their rising unease was connected with the growing social and economic crisis, and with the disappointing Sixteenth Party Congress of 1930, organized in violation of party rules requiring it to be called in 1929. It was staged as a ceremony of Stalin's glorification and a celebration of his infallibility.

Syrtsov openly proclaimed his dissatisfaction. In his remarks to the Politburo, published as an attachment to the stenogram of the report of the November 4 session, he stated: "Together with my comrades I witnessed with skepticism and bewilderment how the principles of infallibility of central authority and authoritarian rule—incompatible with the tasks of socialist construction—are being implemented.... It appears like a part of a criminal plot, elaborated by a small hidden group, that intends to subvert the power of the party."[25]

Syrtsov's evidence for his accusations was Stalin's (and his accomplices') usurpation of power within the Politburo, ignoring other legitimate Politburo members: "I think the situation is not normal when Politburo decisions are predetermined in advance by a certain group of people. I understand why Rykov is ignored, for he committed 'Rightist' mistakes and is pursuing an erroneous political line. But as far I am informed, other Politburo members (Kuibyshev, Rudzutak, and Kalinin) are also excluded from decision making."[26]

As an alternative to the new wave of repressive tendencies in the intraparty regime and the consolidation of Stalin's power, Syrtsov and his supporters proposed the restoration of the tradition of "collective leadership" and internal party "democracy." To be more precise, they proposed an ideal, semimythic version of party democracy. Syrtsov saw Stalin's violation of "democratic" procedures of decision making through the Central Committee plenums as the major reason for the collectivization and dekulakization catastrophes.

In the course of the November 4 session, Syrtsov repeatedly insisted that Central Committee plenums were superior to the will of the party leader: "I object not to the current government, but to the principle of infallibility of its decisions. . . . I insist that the party as well as plenums have the full right to correct this 'infallible leadership' and we should create appropriate conditions. The doctrine of papal infallibility can pass in other countries, but not in one involved in socialist construction. . . . Hoping at some point that the role of plenums would grow, at least to a small degree, I was confident that at some point I could address all these issues to the Central Committee plenum . . ."[27]

It is certain that in Syrtsov's view, Stalin's drive for unrestricted power and his disregard of the rights of collective bodies of the party (to be more precise, the rights of party functionaries), would have been the most serious accusation in any anti-Stalinist campaign. The November 4 stenogram shows that Stalin himself was also perfectly aware of this fact. Despite a significant growth in his own power, he preferred to play the role of the "loyal leader," always prepared to consider the interests of the party apparatus and Bolshevist "democratic" traditions.

Stalin used as a defense that Syrtsov had not brought his concerns directly to himself. Syrtsov countered as follows:

> SYRTSOV: In one or another form, I tried to articulate all the important questions that had bothered me. I arranged to see Comrade Stalin to discuss them with him.
> STALIN: If you had wished, we could have already discussed it in person twenty times.
> SYRTSOV: You promised me, Comrade Stalin!
> STALIN: You did not want this conversation. If you wanted it, we would have talked for three days.[28]

Stalin's ardent expressions of "liberalism" was so inappropriate that in the course of the correction of the stenogram, the last phrase ("talked for three days") was replaced with the more balanced: "I would have been willing to discuss any question of yours."[29]

Even more telling is that Stalin felt it necessary to defend himself in detail against Syrtsov' accusations of factionalism in the Politburo. Stalin began his November 4 remarks with a denial of private meetings in the Zetkin apartment, claiming that he was only preparing there his report for the Sixteenth Party Congress, ("in safety from phone calls") and having a few private discussions with Politburo members. "In the course of my work there, Molotov, Kalinin, Sergo, Rudzutak, and Mikoyan visited me once at different times. Contrary to what Comrade Syrtsov argues, Kaganovich, Yakovlev, and Postyshev have never been there; no meetings ever took place. Did we, the Politburo members, meet with each other sometimes? Yes, we did, primarily in the Central Committee building. Is this a crime"?[30]

The Politburo session ended, after heated calls for the expulsion of Syrtsov and Lominadze from the party, with the decision to expel them from the Central Committee. Stalin, still acting out his magnanimous role, made an unexpected "reconciliatory" offer:

> STALIN: Listen, can't we relegate them to candidate members of the Central Committee? Won't it work out?
> KOSIOR: This is something new.
> STALIN: Can't we really?

The chairman (Rudzutak) ended this line of discussion. "I think we are not empowered to decide this question."[31]

In the course of editing the final version of the stenogram, these phrases were crossed out.[32] Still, they can be interpreted as testimony to Stalin's desire to play the role of the "loyal leader." It was Stalin's caution and the support of his apparatus that gave him the edge over any competitors in the Politburo.

The policy of appealing to the Central Committee as a referee of internal party issues was actively used in the 1920s. For Stalin's opponents, it seemed the most natural and only possible means of correcting his single-handed usurpation of power in 1930. The Syrtsov-Lominadze affair shows that at least two influential Central Committee members — Syrtsov and Lominadze — wanted to revert to this practice. We will never know how many supporters they had or would have had among Central Committee members. In any case, it is hardly possible that two experienced and well-informed politicians would have indulged in wishful thinking and would be hopelessly "sailing against the stream." They were much better informed than their confessions suggest.

In their expressed hope to appeal to the Central Committee plenum, Syrtsov, Lominadze, and their supporters were well aware that they would have to propose an alternative political program. However, room for maneuver for the "New Oppositionists" was limited by their political views and their previous experience in politics. All of them were more "Leftists" than "moderate centrists." They had been active participants in the ultraleftist turn of the "general line" that Stalin had undertaken in his power struggle with the "Right

Opposition." It was Syrtsov and his allies who had actively supported Stalin during his 1928 trip to Siberia that initiated the infamous "Siberian method" of grain extraction.[33]

Syrtsov and Lominadze had to take into account that the majority of Central Committee members had also been deeply involved in the implementation of the "Great Breakthrough" and had committed excesses (although they hardly conceived of their actions as "crimes") during collectivization and de-kulakization. For this reason alone, most Central Committee members could not be sympathetic to the policies of the "Right Deviation."

These considerations explain why both Syrtsov and Lominadze ardently denied any sympathies for the "Rightists" and stressed their reluctance to turn back to the "Rightist" course. Syrtsov, in referring to the bloody violence in the countryside, euphemistically preferred to call it "overhead costs." As Davies has convincingly argued, the proposals of Syrtsov and Lominadze were radically different from the Bukharin program of 1928–29. They had never suggested "that it was possible to cut back industrialization and restore the market to the point at which the state could offer prices at which the peasant would be willing to part voluntarily with his major foodstuffs."[34] Actually, Syrtsov, Lominadze, and their followers favored continuation in the "Leftist" direction, which had already become a reality, but in more balanced, moderate form, devoid of adventurism and excesses.

The most coherent program of the Syrtsov-Lominadze group was presented in the summer and autumn of 1930 by Syrtsov in the course of several speeches and at the November 4 Politburo session. Referring to the policy of forced industrialization, he noted that "in certain circumstances the rates need to be more moderate; we should reject exaggerated, unrealistic economic plans."[35] Syrtsov also criticized repressive operations against "bourgeois specialists," which created an atmosphere of terror among the nonparty technical intelligentsia. "Afraid of displaying professional enthusiasm, they preoccupy themselves with securing the safety of their positions . . ."[36] Additionally, Syrtsov argued for a more moderate policy in the countryside in the course of future collectivization.

Other archival documents provide more detail on Syrtsov's programmatic statements. The details of the September 16, 1930 Politburo session on Rykov's report on state loans are now known from a letter from Molotov to Stalin (who was on holiday)[37] and from comments made by Molotov and Rykov at the November 4 Politburo session. At this session, Rykov proposed a partial restoration of market economy principles, in particular, to sell some deficit goods, such as sugar, at inflated prices to stabilize state finances. According to Molotov, Syrtsov had supported Rykov "with frantic right-wing opportunist claims that it is not possible to solve acute economic problems with repressive 'OGPU' methods, that 'radical measures are necessary,' and that these matters are difficult to discuss in the 'absence of the party chief,' and so on." Although the majority of the Politburo rejected Rykov's proposals,[38] Syrtsov continued to express the importance of financial stabilization during his interrogations and at the November 4 session.[39]

By and large, the proposals of the Syrtsov and Lominadze group were a moderated version of current left-wing policy. In fact, Stalin himself had already turned in this direction, starting with the rehabilitation of "bourgeois specialists," support for the authority of high-ranking technical personnel, and significant cuts in industrial investment. Stalin's temporary renunciation of radical "total collectivization" and allowance for increases in private peasant households were also moderating factors.[40] Nevertheless, a high price had already been paid by the victims of famine, terror, and economic damage.

We cannot answer the counterfactual question of what would have happened if the Syrtsov-Lominadze group had assumed power. The Syrtsov and Lominadze proposals gained additional credibility by the fact that, in the autumn of 1930, conditions were favorable for correction of the "Great Breakthrough." Despite the devastating effects of Stalinist policy, the harvest of 1930 turned out to be successful due to favorable weather conditions. The threat of a major famine was postponed for the time being. After the Bolsheviks' temporary retreat in the spring of 1930, the percentage of collectivized households remained stable. It is also important to stress that the proposals of the "New Oppositionists," albeit limited in their essence, were particularly appealing to party functionaries. Having survived the stress of the initial period of collectivization, dekulakization, and industrial "breakthroughs," party and state officials had yet to witness achievements or favorable changes. To the contrary, the signs of crisis became more obvious every day. Despite all this, a radical rejection of the current political course did not appeal to party activists, who bore their share of responsibility for the violence of the "Great Breakthrough." Syrtsov's call for a partial correction of the political course and a decrease of tension inside the country and the administrative apparatus coincided with the interests of the party officials. However, the interests of Stalin's Politburo and of party activists were quite different.

In 1930, for Stalin and his allies, even a partial acknowledgement of mistakes and a change in political course were unacceptable. First, it would undermine the position of the Stalin faction that had just increased its influence. Second, Stalin obviously believed that the potential of "total collectivization" and forced industrialization policies had not yet been realized, and the lack of success to date was explained by temporary difficulties and incomplete execution. Third, in 1930, Stalin did not see any alternative to the continuation of the "Great Breakthrough." In sum, having survived extreme difficulties and having ruthlessly suppressed dissent, Stalin was preparing a second edition of the "Great Breakthrough." The relatively successful harvest of 1930 seemed proof of its possibility. Stalin pushed through an ambitious program of state-guided economic development in the autumn 1930, and a new wave of collectivization and dekulakization swept over the countryside.[41]

As he had done at the end of the 1920s, Stalin organized repressive campaigns to support his policies. His overriding objective was suppression of discontent and dissent in the party as well as in the country at large, but also the channeling of social discontent towards fictitious "wreckers," ostensibly responsible for the hardships of everyday life. Along with continuing purge inside the party and mass repressions, the OGPU launched in the summer of 1930 a series of fabricated cases against "wreckers" among technical specialists and leading administrators of state enterprises in Moscow and the provinces. OGPU efforts, directed and controlled by Stalin himself, yielded fabricated materials on a network of closely interrelated "anti-Soviet" organizations (the "Industrial Party," the "All-Union Menshevik Bureau," and so on).[42] Show trials on these cases were accompanied by broad propaganda campaigns.

The Syrtsov-Lominadze affair was just one link in the chain of events that prepared the way for the "Second Great Breakthrough." As the archival documents show, by transforming this affair into a noisy political campaign and attracting so much public attention, Stalin pursued two major goals. First, he sent a message to party officials that even the most insignificant signs of dissent and deviation from the current doctrine would not be tolerated. Second, the Syrtsov-Lominadze affair was used as a pretext for an unrelenting assault on the leaders of the "Right Deviation" and as preparation for the removal of Rykov, the last "Rightist" in the Politburo and the sitting head of government. The "Rykov question" was secretly discussed among the Politburo members in September–October 1930. It was then that the decision was made that Rykov was to be replaced by Molotov.[43]

The official proclamation of these sanctions took place in the course of the November 4 Politburo session. Linking the "Right Deviation," primarily Rykov, with the "New Oppositionists" became a leitmotif of the session. Stalin repeatedly reverted to the accusations of the "Right Opposition" and openly raised the question of Rykov's resignation from his post:

> STALIN: The Central Committee issued a resolution on limiting monetary emissions. It should be kept within certain limits. Why did Comrade Rykov fail to carry out this order?

RYKOV: It was not just me. Rudzutak is also responsible, he is charge of the State Bank.

STALIN: But you are the chair of the Council of People's Commissars, not Rudzutak, so it's your responsibility. Why do we, the "party wolves," travel across the country taking care of grain extractions, of crops, and you behave as though it does not concern you at all?

RYKOV: What about division of labor. Everyone should mind his own business.

STALIN: Why does this bother us, but not you?

RYKOV: I do my best.

STALIN: We can't see it. Really? Your post does not exist for ceremonial purposes, but for implementing party orders on a daily basis. Is this the case now? Unfortunately not. That's the point, that's the reason for our discontent. Such a state of affairs cannot last long.[44]

Such exchanges show that the November 4 session was an important preparatory step towards Rykov's replacement and Stalin's final consolidation of power within the Politburo. The "Rykov question" was finally resolved one and a half months later with his dismissal at the Central Committee plenum on December 21, 1930.

The Syrtsov-Lominadze affair was significant as a benchmark in the development of Stalin's political course and as an indicator of the correlation of forces between Stalin's evolving personal dictatorship and the remnants of "collective leadership." The planned appeal by Syrtsov, Lominadze, and their allies to the Central Committee in the event of further aggravation of the political crisis shows the flux of the political situation in 1930. Although Stalin had already reinforced his position as the supreme party leader, the Politburo members who supported him still possessed a certain political weight. The middle stratum of the party functionaries that constituted a Central Committee majority also retained a certain influence in political affairs.

Coming from the ranks of this "intermediate" stratum, Syrtsov and Lominadze understood the growing tension between the Stalinist leadership and the rest of the party and state functionaries. Their reaction to the devastating consequences of the Stalinist "breakthroughs," attempts to put the blame for excesses on rank-and-file Communists, and the increasing gap between Moscow rhetoric and the reality of the situation was one of increasing anger. From this situation, even the weakest dissent within the party ranks could provide an impetus for an unpredictable chain of events. Syrtsov and his allies had obviously anticipated such a possibility. The ideas of Syrtsov and Lominadze were surely close to many of those party and state officials who had absorbed most of the damage during the implementation of the Stalinist course.

Stalin's management of the Syrtsov-Lominadze affair aimed at suppression of dissent and dissatisfaction within the party and elimination of the threat to his personal power. His attacks against Syrtsov, Lominadze, and the leaders of the "Right Deviation," and the fabricated cases against "terrorist organizations" ostensibly created by the dissident party functionaries can be interpreted as dress rehearsals for the political repressions of 1935–38, during which all of Stalin's opponents were exterminated.

In 1930, the sanctions applied to the dissenting Communists were relatively mild. The stenogram of the November 4 session demonstrates that Stalin was deliberately moderate. Not only did he oppose the "oppositionists'" expulsion from the party, but he proposed to keep them in the Central Committee with relegation in status from member to candidate. Moreover, he found it necessary to provide profuse refutations to the accusations of destroying the unity of the Politburo. Although Stalin's words cannot be taken to reflect his genuine intentions, his position in the Syrtsov-Lominadze affair serves as an indicator of the power balance within the ruling circles. At this stage Stalin had not yet accumulated sufficient personal power to ruthlessly repress and exterminate dissenters. He had to wait another five years before he could launch a punitive strike against a large part of the state and party bureaucracy, signifying the final triumph of his dictatorial power.

Notes

1. RGASPI Fond 17, op. 163, del. 1003.

2. Davies, "The Syrtsov-Lominadze Affair," pp. 29–50. Also see Davies, *Soviet Economy in Turmoil, 1929–1930*, pp. 399–419. These works provide in-depth analysis of the views of Syrtsov and Lominadze and their position relative to other opponents of Stalin's policies.

3. Khlevniuk, Kvashonkin, Kosheleva, and Rogovaia, *Stalinskoe Politbiuro v 30-e gody*, pp. 96–106.

4. Kislitsyn, *Variant Syrtsova (iz istorii formirovaniia antistalinskogo soprotivleniia v sovetskom obschestve v 20–30e gg.*; Hughes, "Patrimonialism and the Stalinist System: The Case of S. I. Syrtsov"; and Khlevniuk, *Politbiuro: Mekhanizmi politicheskoi vlasti v 1930-s gody*, pp. 40–52.

5. Ivnitskii, *Sud'ba raskulachennykh v SSSR*, pp. 24–26.

6. B. G. Reznikov had worked with Syrtsov in Siberia. In 1929–31, he studied in the Institute of Red Professors in Moscow, later on he was employed in the Pravda publishing house. He was arrested during the Great Terror. Information on his subsequent execution or incarceration is not available.

7. What is meant is the unplanned retreat from the forced collectivization policy that took place in spring 1930 under the pressure of the mass antigovernment peasant revolts, resulting in the publication in *Pravda* of Stalin's well-known "Dizzy with Success" edi-

torial. In this work all "deviations" (actually the terror against the peasantry) were explained away as the fault of regional administrators.

8. RGASPI Fond 17, op. 163, del. 1003.

9. RGASPI Fond 17, op. 163, del. 1003.

10. RGASPI Fond 17, op. 163, del. 1003.

11. RGASPI Fond 17, op. 163, del. 1003.

12. I. S. Nusinov (1901–37) had worked with Syrtsov in Siberia; later he was transferred to the Russian Republic state administration in Moscow. After his involvement in
the Syrtsov-Lominadze case was confirmed, he was fired and exiled to a minor administrative position in Kazakhstan. He was shot in 1937.

13. V. A. Kavraisky (1891–1937), also acquainted with Syrtsov from Siberia, was a
section chief in the Siberian Regional Party Committee; in 1930 he became an official of
the Central Committee; he was exiled to Kazakhstan in 1931 and executed in 1937.

14. RGASPI Fond 17, op. 163, del. 1003.

15. L. I Shatskin (1902–37) was a party member from 1917. In the early 1920s, he was
one of the leading figures of Kosovo (Communist Youth Organization). A friend of
Lominadze, after his accusation in participation in the Lominadze group, he was exiled to
a minor administrative post in central Asia. In February 1935 he was arrested and sentenced to five-year camp imprisonment for "counterrevolutionary activity." In 1937, still
in the forced labor camp, he was executed.

16. RGASPI Fond 17, op. 163, del. 1002.

17. RGASPI Fond 17, op. 163, del. 1003.

18. RGASPI Fond 17, op. 163, del. 1003.

19. RGASPI Fond 17, op. 163, del. 1003.

20. RGASPI Fond 17, op. 163, del. 1003.

21. RGASPI Fond 17, op. 163, del. 1003.

22. RGASPI Fond 17, op. 163, del. 1003.

23. RGASPI Fond 17, op. 163, del. 1003.

24. RGASPI Fond 17, op. 163, del. 1002.

25. RGASPI Fond 17, op. 163, del. 1003.

26. RGASPI Fond 17, op. 163, del. 1003.

27. RGASPI Fond 17, op. 163, del. 1003.

28. RGASPI Fond 17, op. 163, del. 1003.

29. RGASPI Fond 17, op. 163, del. 1003.

30. RGASPI Fond 17, op. 163, del. 1002.

31. RGASPI Fond 17, op. 163, del. 1002.

32. RGASPI Fond 17, op. 163, del. 1003.

33. For further details see Danilov et al., *Tragediia Sovetskoi derevni: Kollektivizatsiia i
raskulachivanie*, vol. 1, pp. 152–59.

34. Davies, "The Syrtsov-Lominadze Affair," p. 46.

35. RGASPI Fond 17, op. 163, del. 1002.

36. RGASPI Fond 17, op. 163, del. 1002.

37. RGASPI Fond 558, op. 11, del. 769, ll. 37–40.

38. RGASPI Fond 17, op. 3, del. 797, ll. 1–2.

39. RGASPI Fond 17, op. 163, del. 1003.

40. For more information on various aspects of the policy of "retreat" see Kuromiya, *Stalin's Industrial Revolution: Politics and Workers, 1928–1932;* Fitzpatrick, *Stalin's Peasants: Resistance and Survival in the Russian Village after Collectivization;* Davies, *Crisis and Progress in the Soviet Economy, 1931–1933;* Rees, *Decision-Making in the Stalinist Command Economy, 1932–1937;* and Gregory, *Political Economy of Stalinism: Evidence from the Soviet Secret Archives.*

41. For more information on the second period of collectivization and dekulakization, see Davies and Wheatcroft, *The Years of Hunger: Soviet Agriculture, 1931–1933;* Zelenin, *Tragediia Sovetskoi derevni: Kollektivizatsiia i raskulachivanie*, vol. 3: *1930–1933.*

42. Lih, Naumov, and Khlevniuk, *Stalin's Letters to Molotov, 1925–1936*, pp. 187–223.

43. Khlevniuk, *Politbiuro: Mekhanizmy politicheskoi vlasti v 1930-e gody*, pp. 40–52; Watson, *Molotov: A Biography*, pp. 99–104.

44. RGASPI Fond 17, op. 163, del. 1003.

6

The "Right Opposition" and the "Smirnov-Eismont-Tolmachev Affair"

CHARTERS WYNN

On November 27, 1932 a joint session of the Politburo and the Presidium of the Central Control Commission spent untold hours grilling three "Rightist" Old Bolsheviks: Alexander Smirnov, Mikhail Tomsky, and Alexei Rykov.[1] Much of the questioning in this session reflected the Stalinist leadership's need to hear Smirnov and the leaders of the "Right Opposition," Tomsky especially, repeatedly acknowledge their "mistakes." With Stalin's reputation and party support for the collectivization and industrialization campaigns at a low point, the Politburo was determined to squash those they blamed for "inspiring" discontent within party ranks. It could not tolerate prominent party members criticizing government policies and Stalin's leadership, even in private, small-group discussions. The verbatim transcript (stenogram) of this Politburo session, which is the focus of this essay, captures how vulnerable Stalin and the party leadership felt in the fall of 1932, their hypersensitivity to any criticism, and their need to "unmask" and humiliate the former "Right Oppositionists."[2] Tomsky proved particularly unwilling to kowtow to the Politburo and play his part in the party's self-criticism ritual.

The party leadership interpreted what was labeled the "Antiparty Counter-revolutionary Group of Eismont, Tolmachev, and Others" as a reincarnation of the "Right Opposition" of the late 1920s. All the Stalinist leaders, aware of how fragile their rule still was, viewed party factionalism as the ultimate danger. It is important to emphasize that this Politburo session in November 1932 occurred at a time of extreme crisis. Forced collectivization, dekulakization, and breakneck industrialization resulted in mass hardship and suffering. Months earlier, it was already clear that the criminally high procurement norms imposed on collective farms left death in their wake on a vast scale, with millions succumbing to starvation and disease.[3] The masses of hungry, desperate peasants fleeing to industrial centers brought typhus and other diseases with them.[4] In the cities, food shortages led to a wave of strikes and uprisings.[5] In various places in the country, the political police were apprehending dissident party members who, to give one example, declared that "the mass of workers and peasants were not on the side of the party Central Committee and Stalin but on the side of Bukharin, Tomsky, Rykov, Zinoviev, Uglanov, and Kamenev."[6] The party leadership knew of Trotsky's and the Mensheviks' success at smuggling into the country their newspapers, *Biulleten' oppozitsii* and *Sotsialisticheskii vestnik*. Trotsky had just recently begun to create from abroad a "bloc" inside the Soviet Union of former Zinovievists and Trotskyists with the goal of removing Stalin.[7] Party criticism of Stalin was at a high point, especially among Old Bolsheviks of all political stripes.[8] The party leadership felt no better about newer recruits to the party. Molotov noted at the November 1932 Politburo meeting that many people had entered the party for "opportunistic" reasons and joined "antiparty groups," and "not just in Ukraine and in the northern Caucasus but in other regions as well."[9] As Oleg Naumov and Oleg Khlevniuk argue, "Within the party, the opinion was widespread that [Stalin] was incapable of leading the country out of the crisis or placating the peasantry and that, for these reasons, he had to go."[10]

With Stalin's authority undermined and with such enormous problems confronting the country, the Stalinist leadership genuinely believed that a handful of party leaders airing their discontent might lead to the formation of factional groups that could threaten the party. Critical conversations, even if limited to a narrow circle of high-ranking bureaucrats, were interpreted as evidence of the existence of a "counterrevolutionary group." One member of the Presidium of the Central Control Commission (CCC) stated at this Politburo meeting: "Comrades Rykov, Tomsky, and Smirnov know perfectly well from the experience of the struggle with Trotskyists and Rightists" how antiparty "groups" and then "factions" form from such conversations.[11] J. Arch Getty summarizes well the party's attitude toward internal dissent: "Although they publicly celebrated the victory of their new policies, in their inner councils the Stalinist leaders felt more anxiety than confidence, and they perceived that their position was more fragile than secure."[12]

Consternation about the so-called "Smirnov-Eismont-Tolmachev Group" came on the heels of Stalinist outrage over what was known within party circles as the "Riutin Affair." During the fall of 1932, copies of a seven-page compressed version of Martemian Riutin's 194-page anti-Stalinist treatise, "Stalin and the Crisis of the Proletarian Dictatorship,"[13] had been circulated hand-to-hand within Moscow party circles. This "Appeal" to all party members from the "League of Marxist-Leninists" characterized conditions within the country as "catastrophic" and demanded the party reverse course. The Riutin Platform called in particular for the liquidation of collective farms and a change in the party leadership. Though Riutin censured the leaders of the earlier "Rightist Opposition" for their capitulation at the Sixteenth Party Congress in 1930, he argued "the right wing has proved correct in the economic field."[14] Forced collectivization and breakneck industrialization had indeed led to precisely the economic and political problems that Bukharin, Rykov, Tomsky, and other "Rightists" had predicted and feared. Denouncing Stalin and his clique for their "crimes," the Riutin Platform called on "new forces" within the party and the working class to "destroy Stalin's dictatorship." It mocked Stalin's claim to be Lenin's truest disciple. "To place the name of Lenin alongside the name of Stalin is like placing Mount Elbrus alongside a heap of dung. Lenin was a leader but not a dictator. Stalin, on the contrary, is a dictator but not a leader."[15] It called for removing this "gravedigger of the revolution" from his position as party general secretary.[16] Stalin and his cohort, not surprisingly, were utterly outraged. Years later the Riutin Platform continued to rankle. Stalin ordered Andrei Vyshinsky to use it extensively in his prosecution of Bukharin, Rykov, and others at their show trial in March 1938.[17] They were all accused of participating in the Riutin "plot."[18]

The party leadership felt this scathing attack reflected widespread internal party opposition — the political police had been discovering Riutin-like groups in various industrial cities[19] — even though few could have had an opportunity to read the actual Riutin Platform before the political police arrested Riutin and over twenty of his collaborators in September 1932.[20] Then, on November 8, 1932, the day after the country celebrated the fifteenth anniversary of the Bolshevik seizure of power, Stalin's wife Nadezhda Alliluyeva shot herself. A copy of the Riutin Platform was reportedly found not far from her dead body.[21] "She left me like an enemy!" Stalin bitterly concluded.[22] Robert Daniels characterizes this period as "one of the most desperate of [Stalin's] career."[23] Although usually impressively calm during times of crisis,[24] Stalin was close to losing his nerve. He even offered to resign from the Politburo.[25]

Less than three weeks later, the November 27 Politburo and CCC Presidium session convened. Chaired by Vyacheslav Molotov, the nine members of the Politburo were joined by twenty-one members of the Presidium of the CCC.[26]

The function of the CCC was to maintain party discipline and to investigate and punish corrupt and ideologically dangerous party members. Already by the end of the 1920s the CCC had become an administrative tool of Stalinist policy.

What led to this November 27, 1932 Politburo session was a letter Stalin had received shortly before, on November 19. The Old Bolshevik Central Committee member Maksimilian Savelev had written to Stalin about an informal gathering of party and non–party members on the occasion of the anniversary of the Bolshevik Revolution. Savelev had heard about the party from Nikolai Nikolsky, an old friend and co-worker of Nikolai Eismont. Unbeknownst to Eismont, Nikolsky had become a political police informer.[27] In a second letter Savelev reported additional details and Nikolsky co-signed the letter, explicitly corroborating Savelev's words.[28] The letters, coming from men Stalin characterized as "two very proven and honorable party members," underscored his fears that there was significant opposition to his leadership within the party. The letters stated that while drinking vodka on November 7, a group of people listened as two increasingly intoxicated Old Bolsheviks, Eismont and Vladimir Tolmachev, talked of their opposition to the party leadership and its collectivization campaign.[29] Eismont, who was Commissar for Supply of the RSFSR, and Tolmachev, head of the road transportation administration of the RSFSR, were quoted as talking about the "catastrophic conditions" in Ukraine, Kazakhstan, and the northern Caucasus. They predicted that mass peasant uprisings were in the offing. They were also said to have discussed their desire to see a change in the party leadership, the removal of Stalin in particular. Eismont is quoted as stating: "What's to be done! Either Comrade Stalin, or peasant uprisings." Savelev also informed Stalin that Nikolsky had the feeling at the party that Eismont was trying "to recruit him on the basis of their personal friendship into some sort of Rightist group led by Smirnov."

Almost immediately after Stalin received the first letter from Savelev, the OGPU was on the case. OGPU officers interrogated Nikolsky, Eismont, and Tolmachev, as well as another Old Bolshevik who had been at the party, Vladimir Poponin. They were repeatedly questioned before the OGPU compelled them to sign letters summarizing the discussions, their relationships with each other, and their political views. Before the last of these depositions (*pokazanii*) was even signed, the OGPU turned the testimonies over to the CCC. A few days before the Politburo meeting, on November 24 and 25, Eismont, Tolmachev, and Nikolsky were summoned to a meeting of the CCC Presidium, where Jan Rudzutak, the recently appointed chair of the CCC,[30] then presented the depositions to the Politburo.[31] The members of the Politburo and CCC Presidium who spoke during this meeting did not question the veracity of the letters Stalin received or the depositions the OGPU provided.

The signed depositions provided more detail than the original letters from Savelev about the conversations in Eismont's apartment on November 7. Eismont, who had recently returned from the northern Caucasus as part of a commission led by Lazar Kaganovich and OGPU boss Genrikh Yagoda,[32] which oversaw the crushing of peasant uprisings,[33] admitted he had described conditions in the countryside as grave. Eismont mentioned, for example, the dramatic drop in the number of livestock, and that Ukrainian railroad stations were flooded with starving peasant refugees. He predicted that "in the spring of 1933 there might be armed peasant uprisings in the northern Caucasus" as a result of "Stalin's policies." Eismont added, "If Lenin were alive [today] there would be a reversal of course." Eismont also revealed that he and Tolmachev got together with Smirnov the following day, on November 8.[34] Tolmachev stated in his testimony that they did discuss the contemporary situation at Smirnov's dacha, especially "the extraordinarily harsh agricultural conditions in the northern Caucasus," and that Smirnov "as always" responded by cursing the party leadership's measures. Eismont added that Smirnov's influence predominated among the three of them, but he argued their conversation had an "accidental character." Eismont insisted that they should not be considered a "group" since they did not have a "positive program" and since they did not often meet. In Stalin's addendum to the materials, Stalin wrote that "the group exists, though perhaps only in its infancy." Although no one had mentioned Tomsky in their depositions, Stalin asserted, out of the blue, that Tomsky belonged to the "group."

The Politburo and CCC Presidium members certainly spoke at the November 27, 1932 session as if they believed the testimonies. Indeed the testimony regarding what was said at the social gatherings generally does seem convincing. It seems clear that a number of people did discuss the possibility of replacing Stalin. At Eismont's apartment people threw out various names including Voroshilov, Kalinin, and Smirnov as possible replacements of Stalin. Smirnov was quoted as greeting people at the party with the words, "How is it that Stalin still has not been removed?" The final deposition is a confrontation the OGPU arranged between Eismont and the informant Poponin, during which Eismont agreed he had suggested that in the event of a war the leadership's lack of popular support would come to the surface. But he denied that he had also had speculated about the political mood of General Mikhail Tukhachevsky, who was then Deputy People's Commissar of Military and Naval Affairs.

This last line of testimony in the depositions must have fed one of Stalin's greatest fears. Stalin had already been greatly alarmed by earlier OGPU reports that Tukhachevsky and other top Red Army officers had "Rightist" sympathies. Two years earlier, on September 10, 1930, Stalin wrote to Sergo Ordzhonikidze: "Tukhachevsky, it appears, has been in thrall to anti-Soviet elements among the Right. . . . Apparently the Right is ready to have even a military dictatorship to get rid of the Central Committee."[35] Molotov shared this view, stating many decades later, "Tukhachevsky and his group in the military were connected with Trotskyists and Rightists and were preparing a coup, there is no doubt."[36] Members of the Politburo and CCC Presidium understandably viewed any talk of replacing Stalin with military involvement as extremely alarming.

Historians have long wondered whether Stalin and the party leadership genuinely believed all their public pronouncements about counterrevolutionary terrorist groups. One of the most surprising revelations following the declassification of secret party meetings such as this joint Politburo and CCC Presidium session was that Bolshevik leaders spoke behind closed doors just like they did in more public forums.[37] In B. A. Roizenman's speech at the Politburo meeting, for example, he argued a party leader calling for changes in the party leadership was "an enemy of the party, an enemy of the working class." Politburo and Presidium CCC members apparently genuinely believed that angry, disillusioned party members might take up arms against them. Nikolai Antipov said "sober" discussions among Old Bolsheviks about the necessity of quickly changing the leadership were widespread and would lead party members to consider using terror. Molotov stated terrorism results when Communists call for the removal of party leaders — "it is a single step from this type of vile speeches to Social-Revolutionary acts." Kaganovich asserted that the "Oppositionists" should not be underestimated — they were capable of "terrorist dirty tricks." CCC member Emelian Yaroslavsky was one among many who heartily agreed with the decisions before this session to purge Tolmachev and Eismont from the party and to turn their two cases over to the OGPU, stating "These people who until recently enjoyed the trust of the party" were "like the Riutin group only in a different form. . . . We need not only to purge these people, but arrest them."

Many participants afterwards inserted harsh rhetoric into the official stenogram of the meeting. Anastas Mikoyan inserted that Eismont and Tolmachev espoused a "kulak-terrorist ideology." Stalin, who interpreted the calls for his removal as synonymous with calls for his assassination, added to the stenographic report his support of Mikoyan's assertion that the "Rightists," as well as Trotskyists, were more dangerous than the Civil War counterrevolutionary "White Guardists." Sergei Kirov, Leningrad party boss, likewise inserted that party members espousing views opposing party policy would lead "to the propagation of terror."

While no one, as far as we know, ever actually tried to kill Stalin, he clearly felt vulnerable to assassination. Many historians, following the lead of Nikita Khrushchev, have long suggested Stalin's fear of assassination was simply the product of a disturbed, paranoid mind. In his "secret speech" in 1956, Khrushchev said, "Stalin was a very distrustful man, sickly suspicious [which] created in him a general distrust even toward eminent Party workers whom he had known for years. Everywhere and in everything he saw 'enemies,' 'two-facers' and 'spies.' "[38] A military officer heard Stalin ruminating about his guards, "Each time I take this corridor, I think which one? If this one, he will shoot me in the back, and if it is the one around the corner, he will shoot me from the front. Yes, each time I pass by I get these thoughts."[39] Stalin may have been imagining assassins around every corner, but Walter Laqueur's conclusion that "There were no conspiracies against the regime other than imaginary ones," is obviously wrong.[40] As discussed above, there was considerable opposition to Stalin and his policies in 1932.

In addition to the evidence provided by the Riutin Platform, Stalin had reason to think oppositionists were willing to use force to remove him from power. Trotsky as well as émigré Mensheviks had predicted just that years earlier.[41] Tomsky, for example, told Stalin to his face that workers wanted to murder him. At a party barbecue in Sochi in 1928, Stalin and Tomsky's wife were grilling shashlik together when a "completely loaded" Tomsky walked up and whispered into Stalin's ear, "Soon our workers will start shooting at you, they will."[42] During the period before the November 27, 1932 Politburo meeting, the OGPU arrested party members like I. P. Nechaev in the Donbass, who was quoted as saying that "if he caught sight of Stalin he would shoot him."[43] There is even evidence that Bukharin, Rykov, and Tomsky had, in desperation, decided they had no choice but to kill Stalin, whom they had come to consider the next Genghis Khan. Though it seems far-fetched, the Swiss Communist Jules Humbert-Droz, who supported the "Rightists," recalled Bukharin telling him that "they had decided to use individual terror to get rid of Stalin."[44]

In the face of Stalin's and the party leadership's anxiety, Smirnov requested an opportunity to defend himself when he learned he was to be expelled from the Central Committee based on Eismont's and Tolmachev's depositions. Smirnov, along with the others Stalin suspected of complicity in this "affair" — Tomsky and Rykov in particular — were "invited," apparently at the last minute, to attend a meeting. They apparently had no idea it was going to be such a "high meeting." Once they arrived at the joint Politburo and CCC Presidium session these men, all of whom had seen their health seriously deteriorate over the last couple of years under the onslaught of Stalinist attacks, were confronted with the signed depositions and told the meeting had been convened to evaluate them. Tomsky was stunned: "Today"? Once he regained his wits, Tomsky persuaded the Politburo to give them a full hour to read the "materials."

When the November 27, 1932 session began, members proceeded to denounce and question Smirnov, Tomsky, and Rykov, who gave lengthy speeches in response to this questioning. Their attempts to defend themselves were continually interrupted. It is not clear why Bukharin, the leading figure of the 1928–29 "Rightist Opposition," was not also compelled to appear and be questioned in connection with this "affair."[45]

For most of this session, despite the mass famine stalking the countryside,[46] members of the Politburo and Central Control Commission Presidium members acted as if they had nothing more pressing to do than interrogate these Old Bolsheviks. Stalin was known for dismissing party reports of the famine as "fairytales,"[47] and the Soviet media adamantly denied a famine was occurring — to even mention it made one liable to being labeled a "Right Deviationist" or even a counterrevolutionary.[48] But certain members, Stalin in particular, did feel the need to devote part of this Politburo session to addressing the party's "small difficulties" in the collectivization campaign, as one member characterized what had become by then a horrendous human tragedy. Ordzhonikidze stated that "we don't hide" the fact that the party has had difficulties in implementing collectivization while arguing anyone who thought we wouldn't isn't "a politician but a naïve child." Tomsky and Rykov were told they should recognize that any problems in collectivization and industrialization were "unavoidable," not evidence of an incorrect party policy. The leadership's sensitivity to any criticism from leading "Rightists" no doubt reflected their awareness, as Molotov explicitly stated, that "there is now a considerable number in our party organizations who panic in the face of kulak sabotage of grain collection, who want to slow the pace of industrialization. . . . We can't close our eyes to the fact that in these circumstances a party card can be a weapon." A few of the party leaders who spoke during the Politburo meeting, without discussing rural conditions in any detail, were more candid about the collectivization fiasco. Mikoyan said conditions were "war-like." Stalin frankly compared the contemporary situation to the Civil War years, when there were also serious food shortages and mass peasant, worker, and army unrest.

In Stalin's lengthy speech at the November 27, 1932 Politburo session, he primarily defended the collectivization and industrialization campaigns while finding scapegoats for its problems. What bothered him was not the mass suffering in the famine, but the failure of many in the party to recognize the government's great economic achievements — "our colossal victories." Stalin asked, "Where would we now be without collectivization?" While heralding the economy's "successes" and potential for future growth, Stalin conceded there were problems, but he would not accept any responsibility for the catastrophe. It was the "wreckers" and "rotten elements," or the "Right Deviationists" who spoke out about the "unrealistic" grain procurement quotas, or the starving peasants who were stealing from the collective farms, who were responsible for the problems.[49] A couple weeks after this Politburo meeting, on December 15, 1932, the Politburo established an Agricultural Department within the Central Committee, headed by Kaganovich.[50] At the beginning of 1933 Stalin called for mass repression, a "smashing blow" against *kolkhozniki* who had "turned against the Soviet state."[51]

The primary focus of the November 27 Politburo session was "unmasking" the "Right Oppositionists." The party leaders, Stalin especially, were tormented by the notion that behind the façade of party unity and uncritical support of the leadership, many party members who were expressing support for party policy secretly opposed the leadership and were trying to sabotage party work. As noted above, the Riutin Platform asserted exactly this. The Stalinist leadership believed party members were hiding their true political positions and were organizing groups preparing to attack the party leadership. In the villages, Stalin stated, "they don't come out openly against the collective farms. They express their 'solidarity' with the kolkhozes just like our Right Deviationists express their 'solidarity' with the party's general line." The "Rightists," Stalinists believed, were simply waiting for a more favorable moment to push for a change in party policy. Naum Antselovich denounced these "moldy bureaucrats who at meetings vote for the general line, for the Central Committee resolutions, while words escape their lips such as 'foodstuff crisis,' 'supplies crisis,' '[we've] reached a deadlock.'"

What especially agitated Stalin and the party leadership, and provoked their determined effort to blame Tomsky for the "Smirnov-Eismont-Tolmachev Group," was Tomsky's and Smirnov's failure to attend the joint Central Committee and CCC plenum devoted to the Riutin Platform, held less than two months earlier, from September 28 to October 2, 1932.[52] A number of high-profile former oppositionists who had read the platform, such as Grigory Zinoviev, Lev Kamenev, and Nikolai Uglanov, attended the plenum, where they were called upon to recant. Uglanov, denounced as the guiltiest of the three, after trying to justify himself, broke down and wept.[53] The plenum expelled Riutin's "counterrevolutionary group" from the party, denouncing them "as degenerates who have become enemies of communism and the Soviet regime, as traitors to the party and to the working class, who, under the flag of a spurious 'Marxism-Leninism' have attempted to create a bourgeois-kulak organization for the restoration of capitalism and particularly kulakdom in the USSR."[54] In addition, the plenum adopted another resolution signed by

Stalin, "immediately expelling from the party all who know of the existence of this counterrevolutionary group, in particular those who had read its counter-revolutionary documents and not informed the CCC and CC of the All-Union Communist Party (Bolshevik), as concealers of enemies of the party and the working class." Zinoviev and Kamenev as a result were again expelled from the party and exiled to the Urals.[55]

For Tomsky and Smirnov, both still Central Committee members even though they had been in political disgrace since the end of the 1920s,[56] to go on vacation during the Riutin plenum session was considered by Politburo and CCC Presidium members to be "an act of political protest." They accused Tomsky of "boycotting" the session by going wild boar hunting with Smirnov and Shmidt. Tomsky insisted it was completely "innocent," nothing more than a needed vacation — "I love to hunt while I'm on leave." He argued that his doctor had prescribed that he rest three times a year. Tomsky, who was prone to become seriously ill when under severe stress (perhaps due to years in tsarist prisons and Siberian exile), had suffered a nervous breakdown following the Sixteenth Party Congress.[57] But many questioned how Tomsky could plead he was ill, yet had still gone hunting. Molotov mocked his excuse, adding that Lenin loved to hunt "but he did not miss plenum meetings."

The Politburo and CCC Presidium members demanded to know what Tomsky and Smirnov discussed while they were away. That they shared the same railroad car, lived together, and "drank from the same samovar" during their two-week vacation was viewed with great distrust. Molotov argued, "It is impossible to imagine that during this trip they only strolled and hunted boar." They must have talked about more than "the quality of the wine and the charms of nature," they must have discussed "political issues," Molotov insisted. These interrogations about private conversations unconnected to any oppositional activity convey the tenor of the grilling that occurred at this joint Politburo and CCC Presidium meeting. As with the party at Eismont's apart-ment, the Politburo seemed virtually incapable of distinguishing between such organized opposition as the Riutin group and a couple of party members privately discussing their dissatisfaction with party policy.

Tomsky did not help his case by holding firm to his position that he never talked politics when hunting. As he joked when questioned by party interroga-tors on another occasion about this trip, "If I had been talking about politics, I would have returned empty-handed."[58] Rykov inadvertently undercut Tom-sky's defense by acknowledging during his questioning at this Politburo ses-sion that he of course discussed politics when he got together with Tomsky and other political leaders. Tomsky did not deny that when he got together with Rykov they talked about their "extremely difficult position in the party." Tomsky in the end conceded, "I see now my trip was a big political mistake," but he continued to insist he had not discussed the agricultural crisis or politics while on the hunting trip. Tomsky pointedly asked the Politburo and CCC Presidium members why they thought he would need to go on such a long trip to engage in political discussions. Conceding he often talked in a way that "could be easily distorted," Tomsky insisted it was "laughable" to say Smirnov had proposed replacing Stalin with Voroshilov. But in fact, there is reason to believe Tomsky met with Smirnov and Rykov to discuss the Riutin Platform before he decided to skip out on the Central Committee plenum devoted to the Riutin Affair.[59] In despair over Stalin's catastrophic collectivization campaign, they may have discussed the possibility of a "palace coup."[60]

Tomsky tried to use his sense of humor during the questioning. Tomsky joked that since he was deaf in one ear, coming to the Riutin meeting would have been completely useless unless he was given a front row seat. Tomsky's attempts to fend off attacks with jokes often elicited laughter from Politburo and CCC Presidium members. But while one member characterized Tomsky as "a very witty person as everyone knows," others criticized him for looking for laughs when he responded to serious political issues. Molotov denounced his "rotten jokes." Party leaders were outraged when he characterized the Eismont party as simply "drunks talking about drunken things." Tomsky characterized Eismont as a drunk, "who chatters irresponsibly when drunk, saying whatever comes into his head." Tomsky argued the Politburo and CCC Presidium needed to recognize how alcohol had influenced what Eismont and Tolmachev said at their November 7 party. But CCC Presidium members refused to accept this excuse. Antipov even contested whether Eismont was indeed drunk when he had the conversation with Nikolsky. Andrei Andreev argued it was "ridiculous" for Tomsky and Rykov to portray the "Eismont-Smirnov group as simply a drunken affair." Tomsky felt compelled to add that as much as he would like to drink given how the party was treating him, he had not had a drink in three years.[61]

Most of this Politburo meeting was devoted to Politburo and CCC Presidium members hounding Smirnov and Tomsky, and their futile attempts to rebuff the charges over who said what or who met with whom. Smirnov, who unlike Tomsky was accused of actual membership in the "Eismont-Tolmachev group," was the initial target. He was attacked for allowing young people to hear him criticizing the party leadership for ruining the peasantry, and for shooting peasants for stealing an ear of corn, as well as for his denunciations of Stalin. The son of a poor peasant, who had been with Lenin since the Bolsheviks' earliest days, Smirnov was the Russian Republic's commissar of agriculture during NEP. Smirnov and Tomsky, friends since 1905, had supported one another's attempts to stop the party from abandoning NEP. When Stalin decided in early January 1928 to respond to the grain procurement crisis with "extraordinary" or "emergency" measures, the "very moderate" Smirnov was quickly removed.[62] There was no denying he had vehemently opposed the collectivization campaign, though at this Politburo meeting he tried: "I never spoke against collectivization — I only spoke against some forms of it when I was in the Central Committee." Smirnov's alarm over the impact of collectiv- ization on agriculture — in particular the peasants' slaughtering of livestock and the insufficient fodder and proper care for animals that remained — was twisted into suggesting he favored horses over tractors. At Eismont's party, Smirnov had talked about the appalling condition of the horses in the horse- drawn artillery that had been paraded through Red Square during the anniver- sary celebration earlier that day.

Smirnov tried to defend himself by stating that while he sometimes had different opinions on particular issues and talked too much — "everyone knows I'm crude" — he had never discussed the notion of changing members of the party leadership, Stalin in particular. On November 8, Smirnov argued, they had not discussed anything of substance, certainly "never talked about removing Stalin." They simply chatted, for no more than an hour, while play- ing billiards and drinking some tea. Smirnov's responses to the intense ques- tioning were hardly convincing.

Smirnov had been under a cloud for his "Rightist" support in 1928 of Nikolai Uglanov's leadership of the Moscow party organization as well as of Tomsky's leadership of the trade unions when they came under Stalinist at- tack. The party leadership also dredged up various past grievances against him. Even though Smirnov had suffered a massive heart attack, Kirov attacked him for going abroad to receive medical care during "the brutal class struggle" with the kulaks. During the Politburo meeting Smirnov could only fall back on pointing out to the Politburo and CCC Presidium members that when he had led Narkomzem (the People's Commissariat of Agriculture) "for six years the party said I was correct." Why, Smirnov repeatedly asked the Politburo and CCC Presidium members, do you trust Tolmachev and Eismont more than me, stating at one point to Kaganovich: "You don't believe one word of mine but you believe them 100 percent." Towards the end of the session Smirnov did concede he had discussed conditions in the northern Caucasus with Eis- mont on November 8, although he still insisted he did not say a word about Stalin.

If Smirnov's attempts to defend himself were unconvincing, the Politburo and CCC Presidium's determination to inflate comments at a social gathering into some sort of Smirnov-led counterrevolutionary organization was obviously ludicrous. Smirnov, Eismont, and Tolmachev had not even seen each other more than a few times over the previous couple of years. Smirnov stated that while he had been close friends with Eismont and Tolmachev for twenty years, for the past two years he had been very ill and therefore had rarely socialized with them. Throughout the session, Smirnov denied he was part of, much less led, any "group" with Eismont and Tolmachev. Without contradicting this, Kirov still responded "if not today, then tomorrow" such a group would have been organized.

Various Politburo and CCC Presidium members argued that Tomsky, and Rykov to a much lesser extent, shouldered the "primary responsibility" for the "Rightist" oppositional activity of the early 1930s — "they arm the party's enemies, inspiring all those elements within the party who are vacillating or directly disagree with party policy." That Tomsky and Rykov had not attended the social gatherings in question was apparently irrelevant. More important in the minds of the Politburo and CCC Presidium members was that Smirnov's conversation with Eismont and Tolmachev took place shortly after he returned from his vacation with Tomsky. This was sufficient evidence for Stalin and other members of the leadership, who were determined to draw a direct connection between the Riutin Platform, the "Smirnov-Eismont-Tolmachev group," and the leaders of the earlier "Rightist Opposition." In Mikoyan's words: "Tomsky was primarily responsible for the Smirnov affair. . . . This group doesn't begin or end with Eismont, Tolmachev, and Smirnov." Stalin suggested that Tomsky's and Rykov's belief that the collectivization and the industrialization campaigns had "failed" inspired Smirnov, Eismont, and Tolmachev.

Tomsky—the sole authentic former worker on the Politburo during the 1920s — was the primary target of this meeting. Despite his short, stocky appearance, large nose, and bad teeth and hearing, Tomsky possessed considerable personal charm and during the 1920s had been popular not only within the trade unions but within the party leadership as well. Bukharin considered him "a morally pure comrade."[63] Though he had his fair share of critics, Tomsky won respect across the political spectrum. The Menshevik émigré newspaper, *Sotsialisticheskii vestnik*, described him as "the most colorful and splendid figure among the Bolshevik leaders."[64] His long-time adversary Leon Trotsky "thought highly of Tomsky's character and caustic, sarcastic mind."[65] His geniality and biting wit, scarce qualities among Politburo members during the 1920s, have been depicted by some as reflecting a lack of forcefulness.[66] But while he was a Politburo member and head of the trade unions Tomsky generally did not shy away from a fight, even with Lenin, who described him as "subtle, firm, and stubborn."[67] Tomsky spoke bluntly — he could speak the "masses'" language[68]—and participated with fervor in political discussions. During the fight over whether to abandon NEP, Molotov thought Tomsky was "venomous."[69]

Tomsky dismissed the charge at the Politburo meeting that he had organized a "group" with Smirnov and Shmidt or anyone else as an "enormous fantasy. . . . It is completely unfounded." He explained that he often disagreed with Smirnov and Shmidt on policies, though they each still valued their friendship. Smirnov, according to Tomsky, was not even interested in broad political questions. He was an agronomist, Tomsky argued, more interested in such questions as the depth fields should be plowed, crop rotation, and cattle breeding than big political issues. Tomsky, like Smirnov, tried to defend himself against the baseless accusations by insisting he barely knew Eismont and Tolmachev and by dismissing the political significance of what they had admitted in their depositions. Tomsky claimed that outside official meetings, he had met Tolmachev only twice at large social gatherings and had never had a political discussion with either him or Eismont. Tomsky explained that since he had expressed his political opinions at party congresses his views were well known, but he had never given Tolmachev and Eismont any reason to use his name in oppositional activities. To suggest otherwise was "absolute nonsense." Party leaders were not appeased by Tomsky's attempts to counter these or other charges. Molotov dismissed it as the talk of a "cunning lawyer," arguing that "for Bolsheviks the antiparty facts of Tomsky's deviation have already been established." The Stalinist "logic" that any oppositional attitudes equaled conspiratorial terrorist activity would of course be central to the Great Terror a few years later.

Tomsky's and Rykov's primary offense was of course their earlier opposition to Stalinist policies, in 1928–29. "As we all know Tomsky is a party member who actively participated in a grave delinquency against the party," Rudzutak stated. Tomsky and Rykov had joined with Bukharin to try to prevent the abandonment of NEP following Stalin's insistence in early 1928 that the coercive economic policies toward the peasantry be more than a stopgap measure. It was not enough that Tomsky and Rykov had stopped their oppositional activity. They were taken to task for their public silence over the past two years. Politburo and CCC Presidium members questioned their failure to speak up in defense of Stalinist policies. Tomsky was asked, for example, why he did not write an article in the press criticizing the "Riutin Platform." Andreev suggested Tomsky and Rykov were lying low until they believed the party would be forced to reverse course. Tomsky was accused of bragging of his as well as Rykov's and Bukharin's "secret reserve" of oppositionists. Tomsky fired back, asking why, if the party considered "Tomsky an insufficiently trustworthy person" it kept him in all his positions of authority. Since 1931 Tomsky had successfully headed the State Publishing House (OGIZ), a prestigious and important position but one without political influence.[70] Tomsky's various objections were dismissed as "whining."

During this Politburo and CCC Presidium session Tomsky, Rykov, and Smirnov tried to maintain some dignity while admitting their "mistakes" and contesting some of the accusations. But it was obviously difficult. Tomsky, who was prone to become highly emotional, found especially frustrating the repeated charges that he was insincere in his speeches. Angry at being accused of party disloyalty, Tomsky exclaimed that there was no defense against the charge that "you don't say what you think, you don't vote like you think." Why are my statements "never enough," an exasperated Tomsky asked time and again. "If I say 10–15 words . . . I'm asked why did you not say 20." Declaring that Tomsky's speeches were "insufficient," Valerian Kuibyshev stated towards the end of the meeting: "Tomsky, Rykov, and Shmidt need to understand our psychology, our demands toward them." Kaganovich and others told Tomsky that he had evaded the central issues and that he had not talked sufficiently about his mistakes. Kaganovich questioned whether Tomsky and Rykov had truly "disarmed."

Tomsky had come to know this humiliating ritual all too well during the previous two years. At the Sixteenth Party Congress in 1930, Tomsky had also expressed his resentment at the calls for his repentance, sarcastically declaring that "it only remained to him to put on a hair shirt and go seek penance in the Gobi Desert, living on locusts and wild honey." He demanded, "Permit us to work and not merely to repent."[71] At the November 1932 Politburo meeting, Tomsky expressed astonishment that his fellow party members on the Politburo and CCC Presidium — with many of whom he had worked closely during the 1920s — would not accept his explanations; that they would attack so harshly someone who, as Tomsky described himself, had devoted his life to the party for nearly thirty years.

It is easy to feel sympathy for Tomsky. But keep in mind that he eagerly took part in the nasty personal attacks that had long characterized intraparty debates. When he was aligned in the leadership with Stalin, Tomsky did not hesitate to treat the so-called "United Opposition" in a similar fashion to the way he was treated at the November 27, 1932 Politburo meeting. As Jay Sorenson argued, Tomsky "was not merely a victim of Stalin's intrigue, he was also a victim of his own policies, and of the party dictatorship that he helped to build."[72] At the October 8, 1926 Politburo session (the stenogram of it is also included in this book),[73] Tomsky played a leading role in the grilling of Kamenev, Zinoviev, and Trotsky. He accused them of violating party discipline and not speaking sincerely. Tomsky attacked Trotsky for his "impermissible," non-Bolshevik methods. Tomsky stated "we aren't demanding anything special from you, only the most elementary Bolshevik demands." Tomsky had long shared the Bolshevik unwillingness to tolerate any dissent within their ranks. In words that would come back to haunt him, he joked in November 1927 that "under the dictatorship of the proletariat, two, three or four parties may exist, but on the single condition that one of them is in power and the others in prison."[74] Robert Daniels' analysis of Tomsky's and the leadership's treatment of the "United Opposition" could apply even more aptly to the November 1932 Politburo meeting's treatment of Tomsky and Smirnov: "Why the leadership had to respond with such vehemence cannot be explained by the organized political strength of the Opposition, which was of little consequence. It was rather the issues raised by the Opposition, the threat of acute political embarrassment which such criticism carried with it, that drove the leadership to such extremes."[75]

The attacks in this November 1932 Politburo and CCC Presidium session were preparations for the more public performance that would come shortly afterwards at the Central Committee plenum in early January 1933.[76] The Stalinist leadership demanded the "Rightists" capitulate unconditionally in this larger forum. Smirnov, after he was attacked for wanting to replace Stalin with Tomsky and Rykov, complied. He stated in his plenum speech, "I would like to resolutely and categorically disavow the vile, counterrevolutionary words concerning Comrade Stalin ascribed to me. . . . who could possibly remove Comrade Stalin? I think that only someone drunk out of his mind or insane could ever say such a thing." Smirnov agreed with his attackers that "One must not discuss anything behind the party's back. In view of our present situation, this is a political act, and a political act behind the party's back is manifestly an antiparty action."[77] Bukharin, who was summoned to speak at the Central Committee plenum, obligingly lambasted Tomsky and Rykov for their "extremely serious and grave political error." Demanding "the utmost ruthlessness," Bukharin declared that "such factions must be hacked off without the slightest mercy, without [our] being in the slightest troubled by any sentimental considerations concerning the past, concerning personal friendship, relationships. . . . These are all totally abstract formulations, which cannot serve the interests of an army that is storming the fortress of the enemy."[78] Tomsky was more stubborn and loyal to his friends and fellow former oppositionists. Performing with more dignity than the others, Tomsky continued to defend Smirnov. As one speaker stated, "We expect Tomsky to tell us unequivocally his attitude toward Smirnov and the faction headed by him. . . . Even the kind of negative opinion, as expressed by Comrade Rykov toward the faction headed by Smirnov, is lacking in the case of Tomsky."[79] Despite knowing the outrage that he would again provoke, Tomsky made light of the charges. Ivan Akulov, for example, predictably expressed disgust that "Even today, at this critical juncture . . . Comrade Tomsky is making jokes, but he really shouldn't."[80] Kliment Voroshilov proclaimed: "I believe Comrade Bukharin a hundred times more than Rykov and a thousand times more than Tomsky."[81] Summarizing the Politburo's and the CCC Presidium's contention that Tomsky's self-criticism was completely insufficient, Matvei Shkiriatov stated, "There is not a single Bolshevik word in what Tomsky says when he speaks from this podium."[82]

In the end, the Central Committee plenum approved the decision of the November 1932 Politburo meeting to remove Eismont and Tolmachev, to expel Smirnov from the Central Committee, and to reprimand Tomsky, Rykov, and Shmidt. In the typically short resolution, prepared by Stalin and Rudzutak,[83] the Central Committee attacked the three for giving "antiparty elements grounds for counting on the support of the former leaders of the Right Opposition" and threatened them with "severe measures" if they continued to do so.[84] The repercussions of this resolution spread widely, as Khlevniuk and Naumov have noted: "These dramatic events in Moscow sent smaller shock waves throughout the country. Provincial GPU officers who received the relevant decrees on these cases concocted their own local 'counterrevolutionary groups.'"[85] The purging of hundreds of thousands of party members followed.

This stenographic transcript highlights the party leadership's extraordinary sensitivity, years before the Great Terror, to even the most private criticism of the collectivization campaign and Stalin's leadership of the party. In this secret arena of a Politburo meeting, as in the more public ones we have long been familiar with, the Stalinists were able to exploit the ingrained Bolshevik culture of party discipline. Rather than focus on correcting the enormous problems in the country, the Politburo and CCC Presidium used the discovery of some private, oppositional activity to renew their attack on the Old Bolshevik, former "Rightist" leaders — Tomsky and Rykov. All the members of the party leadership joined in the attack.

Notes

I am grateful to Joan Neuberger and Hiroaki Kuromiya for their comments on my paper.

1. To a much lesser extent another "Rightist" Old Bolshevik, Vasily Shmidt, was interrogated at this Politburo session. Shmidt served as commissar of labor from 1923, after a stint under Tomsky on the Trade Union Central Committee (VTsSPS). Shmidt was removed from the post in late 1928 following Tomsky's fall from grace.

2. The transcript is from the Politburo meeting of November 27, 1932 "About the Group of Smirnov, Eismont, and Others," from RGASPI Fond 17, op. 163, del. 1011. All quotations from this meeting are from this stenogram.

3. Conquest, *The Harvest of Sorrow: Soviet Collectivization and the Terror-Famine*, p. 243.

4. In 1932–33 there were over 1.1 million registered cases of typhus and more than half a million cases of typhoid fever. On this, see: Khlevniuk, *Politbiuro: Mekhanismy politicheskoi vlasti v 1930-e gody*, p. 60; Fitzpatrick, "The Great Departure: Rural-Urban Migration in the Soviet Union, 1929–33," pp. 28–33.

5. *Sotsialisticheskii vestnik*, July 23, 1932, November 26, 1932; cited in Filtzer, *Soviet Workers and Stalinist Industrialization: The Formation of Modern Soviet Production Relations, 1928–1941*, pp. 83–84; Khlevniuk, *1937: Stalin, NKVD i sovetskoe obshchestvo*, pp. 10–11; Rossman, "A Workers' Strike in Stalin's Russia: The Vichuga Uprising of April 1932," pp. 44–83.

6. Quoted in Kuromiya, *Freedom and Terror in the Donbas: A Ukrainian-Russian Borderland, 1870s–1990s*, p. 177.

7. Kuromiya, *Stalin: Profiles in Power*, p. 106; Rogovin, *Vlast' i oppozitsii*, p. 236.

8. Service, *Stalin: A Biography*, p. 286; Broue, "Party Opposition to Stalin (1930–1932) and the First Moscow Trial," p. 104.

9. Getty and Naumov agree that opposition to Stalin's polities was also widespread among second-and third-rank oppositionists. See Getty and Naumov, *The Road to Terror: Stalin and the Self-Destruction of the Bolsheviks, 1932–1939*, p. 52.

10. Lih, Naumov, and Khlevniuk, *Stalin's Letters to Molotov, 1925–1936*, p. 225.

11. RGASPI Fond 17, op. 163, del. 1011. Henceforth, quotations from this Politburo stenogram will not be noted separately unless to identify their location, such as in a specific appendix, or to add clarification.

12. Getty and Naumov, *The Road to Terror: Stalin and the Self-Destruction of the Bolsheviks, 1932–1939*, p. 15.

13. Reprinted in Iakovlev, *Reabilitatsiia: Politicheskie protsessy 30–50-kh godov*, pp. 334–443.

14. Quoted in Conquest, *The Great Terror: A Reassessment*, p. 24.

15. Quoted in Getty and Naumov, *The Road to Terror: Stalin and the Self-Destruction of the Bolsheviks, 1932–1939*, pp. 54–58.

16. "O dele tak nazyvaemogo 'soiuza marksistov-lenintsev,' " *Izvestiia TsK KPSS*, No. 6, June 1989, p. 105.

17. See Tucker and Cohen, *The Great Purge Trial*: Tomsky shot himself after Zinoviev and Kamenev testified in the 1936 Moscow show trial that he along with Bukharin and Rykov were part of their terrorist organization.

18. Ibid., p. 348; Conquest, *The Great Terror: A Reassessment*, p. 23.

19. Kuromiya, *Freedom and Terror in the Donbas: A Ukrainian-Russian Borderland, 1870s-1990s*, p. 177.

20. Rogovin, *Vlast' i oppozitsii*, p. 290.

21. According to Stalin's personal bodyguard, N. S. Vlasik: Montefiore, *Stalin: The Court of the Red Tsar*, p. 20.

22. Quoted ibid., p. 108.

23. Daniels, *The Conscience of the Revolution: Communist Opposition in Soviet Russia*, p. 380.

24. Stalin's paralyzed reaction during the initial days following the German launching of Operation Barbarossa stands as the obvious counterexample.

25. Daniels, *The Conscience of the Revolution: Communist Opposition in Soviet Russia*, p. 380; Deutscher, *Stalin: A Political Biography*, p. 332. Stalin, however, shortly afterwards "gathered the reins of power even more firmly in his own hands": Davies, Ilic, and Khlevnyuk, "The Politburo and Economic Policy Making," p. 109.

26. Attendance figures from RGASPI Fond 17, op. 163, del. 1011, Appendix 1. A dozen of the CCC Presidium members did not speak during the meeting.

27. *Neizvestnaia Rossiia,* no. 1, 1992, p. 66.

28. M. Savelev reported to Stalin what he heard from the engineer I. Nikolsky, who attended the party. RGASPI Fond 17, op. 163, del. 1011.

29. Eismont joined the party in 1907, Tolmachev in 1904.

30. Khlevniuk, *Politbiuro: Mekhanismy politicheskoi vlasti v 1930-e gody,* p. 67.

31. The depositions are included as appendices to the transcripts of the Politburo meeting. RGASPI Fond 17, op. 163, del. 1011.

32. Yagoda's official position at this time was deputy chair of the OGPU under the sick Vyacheslav Menzhinsky.

33. Kaganovich cruelly oversaw mass executions and deported whole villages. Montefiore, *Stalin: The Court of the Red Tsar,* pp. 14, 64; Medvedev, *All Stalin's Men,* p. 119.

34. Smirnov, Eismont, and Tolmachev had earlier worked together in the northern Caucasus. On this, see *Neizvestnaia Rossiia,* no. 1, 1992.

35. Quoted in Rayfield, *Stalin: The Tyrant and Those Who Killed for Him,* p. 236.

36. Molotov, *Molotov Remembers: Inside Kremlin Politics, Conversations with Felix Chuev,* p. 280. The NKVD arrested and executed Tukhachevsky in June 1937.

37. As Getty and Naumov concluded, "Their hidden transcripts differed little from their public ones": *The Road to Terror: Stalin and the Self-Destruction of the Bolsheviks, 1932–1939,* p. 22.

38. Talbott, *Khrushchev Remembers,* p. 585.

39. Quoted in Konstantin Simonov, *Glazami cheloveka moego pokoleniia,* pp. 332–33.

40. Laqueur, *Stalin: The Glasnost Revelations,* p. 61.

41. Deutscher, *The Prophet Unarmed: Trotsky, 1921–1928,* p. 428; *Sotsialisticheskii vestnik,* July 23, 1928, p. 15 reported that it had learned from a member of the Bolshevik "old guard" that a coup against Stalin was in the offing.

42. Related by Bukharin to Kamenev during their clandestine meeting on July 11, 1928, quoted in Deutscher, *The Prophet Unarmed: Trotsky, 1921–1928,* p. 442. In his suicide note Tomsky wrote "Don't take seriously what I blurted out then — I have been deeply repenting this ever since": Gorelov, *Tsugtsvant Mikhaila Tomskogo,* p. 234.

43. Kuromiya, *Freedom and Terror in the Donbas: A Ukrainian-Russian Borderland, 1870s–1990s,* p. 177.

44. Humbert-Droz, *De Lénine à Staline: Dix ans au service de l'Internationale communiste, 1921–1931,* pp. 379–80.

45. This seems especially puzzling since Bukharin reportedly regularly visited Stalin's wife before she killed herself, during which they talked about Stalin's disastrous agricul-

tural policies according to Larina, *This I Cannot Forget: The Memoirs of Nikolai Bukharin's Widow,* p. 141; Medvedev, *Nikolai Bukharin: The Last Years,* p. 39.

46. It is generally now agreed that about 7–8 million men, women, and children lost their lives in the 1932–33 famine.

47. Montefiore, *Stalin: The Court of the Red Tsar,* p. 84.

48. Kuromiya, *Freedom and Terror in the Donbas: A Ukrainian-Russian Borderland, 1870s–1990s,* p. 169; to speak of it even in starving villages, according to Conquest, "became an offense bringing ten-year sentences, or sometimes death." On this, see Conquest, *Stalin: Breaker of Nations,* p. 165.

49. For background on the regime's attack on party members reluctant to force peasants to fulfill procurement norms in starving villages and the regime's notoriously vicious August 7, 1932 Law on the Protection of Socialist Property, see Khlevniuk, *1937: Stalin, NKVD, i sovetskoe obshchestvo,* pp. 21–23; Davies, Khlevniuk, and Rees, *The Stalin-Kaganovich Correspondence 1931–1936,* p. 180; Rayfield, *Stalin: The Tyrant and Those Who Killed for Him,* p. 111; Viola, *The Best Sons of the Fatherland: Workers in the Vanguard of Soviet Collectivization,* p. 198.

50. Khlevniuk, *Politbiuro: Mekhanizmy politicheskoi vlasti v 1930-e gody,* p. 68; Medvedev, *All Stalin's Men,* p. 118.

51. Quoted in Lewin, *The Making of the Soviet System: Essays in the Social History of Interwar Russia,* p. 155.

52. Historians have long argued that at a Politburo meeting around this time Stalin demanded that Riutin be shot because his platform could inspire acts of terrorism, but that Stalin's desire to institute the death penalty for oppositional activity was blocked by a moderate bloc of Politburo members led by Kirov. See Conquest, *Stalin and the Kirov Murder:* Getty has convincingly called into question the sources used for this account in "The Politics of Repression Revisited," pp. 42–44; E. A. Rees agrees with Getty and questions "whether politically Stalin could at that time have presented such a demand to his colleagues": Rees, "Stalin as Leader 1924–1937: From Oligarch to Dictator," p. 45.

53. "'Delo M. N. Riutina' v sud'be G. E. Zinovieva i L. B. Kameneva, Oktiabr' 1932," *Istoricheskii arkhiv,* no. 1, 2006, pp. 73, 80.

54. "O dele tak nazyvaemogo 'soiuza marksistov-lenintsev,'" *Izvestiia TsK KPSS,* no. 6, June 1989, p. 107.

55. Iakovlev, *Reabilitatsiia: Politicheskie protsessy 30–50-kh godov,* pp. 95–96, 151.

56. Tomsky and Rykov had been removed from the Politburo in 1930, but the defeated "Rightists" were treated much more leniently than the Trotskyists, presumably because they did not go public with their opposition and were more willing to recant.

57. Also see RGASPI Fond 593, op. 1, del. 2; "'Pust' kazhdyi otvechaet za sebia' (Materialy partiinoi chistki M. P. Tomskogo)," p. 104.

58. Ibid., p. 112.

59. *Voprosy istorii,* no. 2, 1993 reprinted in Getty, *The Road to Terror: Stalin and the Self-Destruction of the Bolsheviks, 1932–1939,* pp. 401–2.

60. Testimony of Mikhail Chernov in Tucker and Cohen, *The Great Purge Trial,* p. 105. Numerous historians, including Robert Conquest and J. Arch Getty, who have studied the purge trials agree there was usually a "kernel of truth" in the testimonies.

61. Tomsky followed a simple diet on doctor's orders and had indeed sworn off drinking alcohol: Citrine, *A Trade Unionist Looks at Russia,* p. 132.

62. Lewin, *Russian Peasants and Soviet Power: A Study of Collectivization,* p. 230; Heinzen, *Inventing a Soviet Countryside,* pp. 193–95.

63. Larina, *This I Cannot Forget: The Memoirs of Nikolai Bukharin's Widow,* p. 288.

64. *Sotsialisticheskii vestnik,* August 30, 1936, p. 11.

65. Trotskii, *Portrety revoliutsionerov,* p. 228.

66. See, for example, Ulam, *Stalin: The Man and His Era,* p. 257; Sorenson, *The Life and Death of Soviet Trade Unionism, 1917–1928.*

67. Lenin, *Collected Works,* p. 297. Though he can be criticized for doing Lenin's bidding against the "Workers' Opposition," Tomsky led the trade unionists' successful opposition to Leon Trotsky's effort to militarize labor, while fighting, unsuccessfully, against Lenin's push for one-man management. In 1921 the Central Committee accused Tomsky of leading a virtual trade union revolt against the party's attempt to curtail union autonomy, which led to his temporary exile to Central Asia.

68. Trotskii, *Portrety revoliutsionerov,* p. 228; Molotov, *Molotov Remembers: Inside Kremlin Politics: Conversations with Felix Chuev,* p. 119.

69. Ibid., p. 182.

70. Walter McLennan Citrine, who met with him in his OGIZ office, recalled, "Tomsky was very proud of his present position" where he had some thirty-six thousand employees working under him: *A Trade Unionist Looks at Russia,* p. 132. But OGIZ offered no respite from political attacks. In August 1933, the party cell at the OGIZ headquarters subjected Tomsky to further interrogations: see " 'Pust' kazhdyi otvechaet za sebia' (Materialy partiinoi chistki M. P. Tomskogo)."

71. *Shestnadtsaty s"ezd VKP(b): Stenograficheskii otchet,* pp. 146–47.

72. Sorenson, *The Life and Death of Soviet Trade Unionism, 1917–1928,* pp. 242–43.

73. RGASPI Fond 17, op. 1613. del. 167.

74. *Pravda,* November 19, 1927; quoted in Serge, *Russia Twenty Years After,* p. 92.

75. Daniels, *The Conscience of the Revolution: Communist Opposition in Soviet Russia,* p. 287.

76. Many of the speeches at the Central Committee plenum are translated and reprinted in Getty, *The Road to Terror: Stalin and the Self-Destruction of the Bolsheviks, 1932–1939.*

77. Quoted ibid., pp. 76–77.

78. Ibid., p. 96.

79. Ibid., p. 81.

80. Ibid., p. 80.

81. Ibid., p. 100.

82. Ibid., p. 86.

83. Avtorkhanov, *Stalin and the Soviet Communist Party: A Study in the Technology of Power,* p. 194.

84. Egorova and Bogoliubova, *Kommunisticheskaia partiia Sovietskogo Soiuza v rezoliutsiiakh i resheniiakh s"ezdov, konferentsii i plenumov TsK,* vol. 2, p. 742.

85. Lih, Naumov, and Khlevniuk, *Stalin's Letters to Molotov, 1925–1936,* p. 226.

PART III

Discourse, Ideology, and Propaganda

7

The Way They Talked Then: The Discourse of Politics in the Soviet Party Politburo in the Late 1920s

ROBERT SERVICE

The Soviet Politburo in the late 1920s was the agency for the most important discussions and decisions about domestic and foreign policy. Its institutional ascendancy in the state order was consolidated almost instantaneously at the point when the central party apparatus was reorganized in early 1919, and the Central Committee devolved powers between its meetings to the Politburo and Orgburo. The Politburo was by far and away the more important of the new internal adjuncts of the Central Committee. It was established at a time of civil war and several of its members could not always be in Moscow. This was no obstacle to its dominance. Lenin consulted the other members by telephone and telegraph to arrive at agreed decisions.[1] The scope of its practical authority was huge. In the interim between Central Committee meetings it was the Politburo which fixed policy in international relations, politics, public security, culture, and the economy. Questions of military strategy were settled by its members. The appointment of personnel to the main posts was done at its meetings. The Politburo, furthermore, gave direction and supervision to every principal state agency: the Council of People's Commissars, the Red Army, the Cheka (the secret police), and the trade unions.[2]

This structure of power was modified in practice when Lenin fell mortally ill. Such was the fear of Leon Trotsky among the other Politburo members that they started to hold discussions and agree decisions before coming to the Politburo itself. Trotsky objected that the Politburo was being turned into an agency for rubberstamping policies previously elaborated in his absence.[3] He had a point even though he exaggerated the decline in the capacity of Politburo members to change official decisions by intervening at the Politburo itself. The basic structure, in any case, remained in place, and it was chiefly at the Politburo where decisions continued to need to be confirmed.

The Politburo transcripts (stenograms), newly made available, make it possible to examine several fundamental historical hypotheses about the workings of the Soviet political system in the 1920s. Many Politburo items, especially agendas and minutes, were published in Moscow from the late 1980s onwards. But the stenograms, which offer a verbatim record of the proceedings, have until now been off limits to scholars. I intend to investigate the important joint meeting of the Politburo and the Central Control Commission Presidium of September 8, 1927 as a means of ascertaining the ways in which our more general understanding may be corrected or sharpened by such records. This was a period of intense factional conflict. The dominant group in the central party leadership was headed by Stalin and Nikolai Bukharin. Against them were ranged Trotsky, Grigory Zinoviev, and Lev Kamenev. Trotsky had led the Left Opposition continuously since 1923 — and Zinoviev and Kamenev had been his enemies in the early years. Trotsky argued that the New Economic Policy as implemented by the Politburo majority was turning against the objectives of the October Revolution. Then in 1925 Zinoviev and Kamenev formed what became known as the Leningrad Opposition and, like Trotsky, criticized the Stalin-Bukharin group for showing insufficient radicalism. The Left Opposition and the Leningrad Opposition coalesced in 1926 in the United Opposition, which was firmly defeated by Stalin and Bukharin in the last months of 1927.

The history of the rise and fall of the United Opposition need not detain us here. What we want to examine is the discourse of Politburo meetings. One conventional assumption is immediately dispelled: this is that the words spoken at the Politburo remained entirely secret. The idea has been that each decision-making body in the party kept its proceedings confidential and refused to relay them to any bodies at lower levels. Thus the Politburo was supposedly already the innermost cave of political mystery that it undoubtedly was by the 1930s. In fact the stenogram of September 8, 1927 shows that hundreds of party officials outside the central party apparatus were made privy to full records of the proceedings.[4] They included secretaries of Provincial Committees (*gubkomy*). This is surprising and important in itself. But the list of addressees also included the chief secretary of the Komsomol, the leading political commissars in the armed forces, the People's Commissars, the USSR ambassadors, the leaders of trade unions, the secretary of the Society of Old Bolsheviks, and the party cells of the Communist Universities. The further specification was that the addressees were to "acquaint" their own leading comrades with the general contents of the "conspiratorial stenograms." Far from wanting the rest of the Bolshevik political elite to remain in ignorance of the course of Politburo debates, the ascendant leadership was eager to distribute detailed information.[5]

The stenograms of other meetings had different distribution lists; some went to only a few party leaders or were not distributed at all,[6] but most were distributed for the purpose of informing the most authoritative officials at the party's lower echelons about important current business. Needless to stress, there were severe warnings against disseminating such information beyond the range of the designated addressees. The Politburo majority placed strict limits on freedom of distribution. In the highly charged political atmosphere of 1926 and 1927 it would have been undesirable to reveal the disputes in the Kremlin to party members who could not be trusted to keep a secret. The Soviet regime always sensed danger in its international isolation and its weak support in the country. From such a perspective it is impressive that sterner measures were not yet taken to secure the absolute confidentiality of Politburo discussions.

Stalin and Bukharin were not behaving out of a commitment to universal glasnost. Their motives can only be guessed at. It would seem that they acted in line with party tradition. They also wished to appear fair-minded and open about their maneuvers against the United Opposition. But perhaps there was a further factor at work. The usual interpretation of Bolshevik politics in the 1920s has postulated that the factional conflicts were brought to an end predominantly by bureaucratic procedures. Thus Stalin, who had access to all the principal levers in the central party apparatus, merely had to pack the Politburo with his supporters and relay his orders down the hierarchy of the territorially laddered edifice of the party as a whole. Recently, however, the case has been made that Stalin and his allies had to work hard politically to ensure victory.[7] This involved putting their arguments in the strongest fashion to the rest of the Bolshevik elite at central and local levels. It is now clear from the stenograms under consideration that the Politburo majority believed that the detailed verbal record of its debates would contribute to this end. In the process a lot of dirty linen would be exposed. But the judgment must have been that the verdict of those acquainted with the proceedings would go in favor of the ascendant leaders.

The proceedings in the Politburo in 1926–27 were in several respects similar to sessions held by other bodies of the central party leadership in those years: the Central Committee, the Central Control Commission, and the Party Congress. The Party Congress debates were published quickly after they happened, and Central Committee and Central Control Commission records have been made accessible to visitors to the central party archives in Moscow. This is one of the reasons why the Politburo has been assumed to have been the impenetrable fortress of the supreme party leadership. As we now can see, the Politburo did not keep its proceedings entirely secret from important leaders at central and noncentral levels of the party.

It is equally obvious that Trotsky, Zinoviev, and Kamenev were stretching the truth when they claimed that they were given scant time to put their case at the Politburo. This can be exemplified by two earlier occasions. Kamenev had spoken twice at great length at the brief Politburo meeting of October 8, 1926. The Politburo meeting on October 11, 1926 had been six times longer. Kamenev had again led the United Opposition in putting its case; Ivar Smilga, Kamenev, Grigory Sokol'nikov, Zinoviev, and Trotsky followed him with their own arguments—and it must be remembered that Smilga (deputy chair of Supreme Economic Council) and Sokol'nikov (finance minister) were not even Politburo members.[8] Something similar happened at the joint meeting of the Politburo and the Central Control Commission Presidium on September 8, 1927. Zinoviev led on that occasion for the United Opposition; he was followed by his allies Nikolai Muralov and Trotsky.[9] Muralov, a firm Trotskyist, belonged to neither the Politburo nor the Central Control Commission. The United Opposition had been equally vociferous at the various Central Committee and Central Control Commission various meetings in 1926–27. At all these bodies the ascendant central leadership was orally assailed by their oppositionist enemies who both denied the charges laid against them and took the opportunity to explain their political platform. It is not the bureaucratic clampdown that catches the eye about the Bolshevik disputes of the period but the political latitude offered to the United Opposition to say what it wished at the highest levels of the party.

This does not mean that the ascendant party leaders were behaving altruistically. If Stalin and Bukharin wanted to keep their existing support and win over the doubters, they had to be seen to have acted with a degree of fairness towards the United Opposition. In other arenas they acted differently. The central party newspaper *Pravda* was simultaneously restricting the United Opposition's access to its pages. Trotsky, Zinoviev, and Kamenev had to consign their writings mainly to clandestine presses manned by their sympathizers. In the provinces, the supporters of the official leadership operated a strict censorship; they also sacked oppositionists—and they put the word around the party's less enlightened members that the United Opposition was headed by Jews who were about to get their come-uppance.[10] The struggle between the ascendant leaders and their factional enemies was a brutal one behind the scenes. Stalin, supported by Bukharin, was playing a clever, complicated game. It was triumphantly successful.

Stalin and Bukharin also made a point of staying within the framework of Marxism-Leninism whenever they spoke. This applied as much to their Politburo contributions as to anything else. At open political meetings such discourse was only to be expected. The USSR was a state committed to Lenin's variant of Marxism; the supreme objective was the attainment of a fully communist society by the route of a proletarian dictatorship. Without a continued overt commitment to the founding ideology, the entire state order was put at risk (as the fate of Gorbachev and perestroika was to show in the late 1980s).

There has always been room for speculation about how the supreme leaders talked among themselves. A little of this has already emerged through Stalin's published correspondence with Vyacheslav Molotov and Lazar Kaganovich.[11] The memoirs of both Molotov and Kaganovich point in the same direction.[12] Now we can affirm that Politburo members at their formal sessions spoke in the same fashion. They did not confine their case to merely pragmatic arguments. Nor did they want to be regarded simply as personal rivals for supreme power and victory over their factional adversaries. They asserted their Marxist-Leninist credentials and frequently resorted to justification by "Leninist" doctrine and "Leninist" precedent. Each side claimed to be standing on a platform of Leninism and to represent ideas that Lenin, if he had lived longer, would have favored.[13]

Yet they were not philosopher-kings calmly examining the pros and contras in their disputation. Anger was seldom very far from the surface. The bad-tempered and unpredictable nature of the debates is in the exchange between Trotsky and Stalin's ally and fellow Georgian Abel Enukidze at the September 8, 1927 joint meeting of the Politburo and the Central Control Commission Presidium. Trotsky in a fit of pique declared: "But in 1917 you had been arguing against the Bolsheviks at the time when I pulled you into the party." He was speaking with pride about his activity in the months before the October Revolution. Among his achievements he liked to list the way he had brought other antiwar Marxists into the ranks of Bolshevism by his own example. The so-called Interdistricters (*mezhraiontsy*) were a case in point. In picking on Enukidze, Trotsky was hoping to pull rank as a Bolshevik proven in the fire of revolutionary challenge. The problem was that Trotsky had been a well-known anti-Bolshevik before returning to Russia in May 1917. Worse still, Enukidze was a veteran Bolshevik; indeed he was one of those few Georgian Marxists who had opted for Bolshevism rather than Menshevism.[14] He jabbed back at his accuser: "Are you living in a dream or something, Comrade Trotsky?"[15] Trotsky stupidly refused to give way and said, "No, I'm not dreaming: I pulled you into the party in 1917."

Enukidze had had quite enough by that point in the proceedings. As a respected member of the Central Control Commission Presidium he would not tolerate condescension from the likes of Trotsky: "Look here, I've been in the party since its formation, and was a Bolshevik fourteen years earlier than you. If you refuse to budge from your point, I'm going to call you before a party court for saying something that's untrue; I'll show you that you're either confusing me with someone else or else you've simply dreamed up what you're saying about me." Trotsky would still not back down; he insisted: "You were there with Eliava." Enukidze retorted: "That never happened, and I never had a conversation with you in that period." "Untrue," said Trotsky. "I said to you: come along with us." At this moment there was an intervention by Molotov (who was conducting himself with considerable — and highly effective — restraint despite every temptation): "[Trotsky] mixed him up with some Menshevik or other." By this stage Enukidze was thoroughly annoyed at what he regarded as a stain on his personal honor as a man and a Bolshevik: "This is untrue, Comrade Trotsky, and once again I ask it to be recorded in the stenogram that I'm summoning Trotsky to a party court. Nothing like this ever happened, and I'm amazed by what Comrade Trotsky is saying."

The majority of the plenum's participants were on Enukidze's side: "We know, we know!" By now he had the meeting in the palm of his hand: "I affirm, comrades, at this joint session that beginning with the February Revolution I never said a single word to him. We came across each other at meetings and gatherings but not a single conversation took place between us. When Comrade Trotsky was released from prison after the July Days he gave a speech in the Tauride Palace at a gathering of the Bolshevik fraction. Comrades asked him to talk about Lenin, and I was sincerely delighted and I welcomed the fact that he'd joined; but I was not personally acquainted with him at that time. He's surely mixed things up in telling this lie about me." It was only then that Trotsky owned up to his mistake. But this was far too little and too late to assuage the feelings of Enukidze, who asked his accuser:

"So how come you stayed silent for these past ten years? That's not good. When people said things about you I always tried to think [for myself]; but now that you've said such a thing today, I'm going to believe everything about you and I say this: you are a dead man after all this." Called to order, Enukidze then started his attack on the entire political standpoint of the Opposition.

For sheer personal effrontery, Trotsky's behavior took some beating. Historians with the exception of out-and-out Trotskyites have long accepted that he had an arrogance about him. But by and large the assumption has been that he was devoid of any outward aggressiveness. Supposedly when he offended the sensibilities of other Bolsheviks, he did this involuntarily. Trotsky's treatment of Enukidze behind the doors of the central party leadership shows us another side of his character and comportment. Quite explosively and unproductively he let loose his temper on a fellow Bolshevik leader who was generally known for his equable temperament. The spectacle of the face-to-face dispute between Enukidze and his tormentor must have convinced the waverers that Trotsky was an impossible person.

Of course, Enukidze was no political innocent. He was one of Stalin's cronies and a close friend of his Alliluev in-laws; and it was Enukidze who controlled the organization and finances of the Kremlin precinct.[16] He had already made up his mind fundamentally about Trotsky. Enukidze was already an enemy of the Opposition. No doubt he was genuinely insulted by Trotsky's intervention at the plenum; but he had long been likely to take offense at the behavior of Trotsky: the spat between them at the joint meeting was therefore not an entire surprise. Trotsky, moreover, ought not to be judged too harshly. Immense pressures were being exerted upon Trotsky in the late 1920s. He was being comprehensively vilified in the official press on a daily basis. His associates were losing their jobs. The history books were being rewritten. Such respect as he had enjoyed in Lenin's lifetime had been systematically challenged. He could no longer realistically expect to win any debate in the central party leadership: his faction was being trounced in the factional struggle. He himself was not in the best of health. He knew he would walk out of the joint session as the principal loser. In such a situation any politician, however self-controlled, might have lost his temper. In previous years he had not been easily goaded into making a fool of himself (although intemperate outbursts had not been completely unknown). He was fighting for his place in public life and in history. He was on the point of losing everything — and Trotsky, the co-leader of the Bolshevik seizure of power in the October Revolution, was understandably at his wits' end.

Even so, this episode demonstrates that his prime enemies — Stalin and Molotov — had qualities that he lacked. Obviously they knew the cards were stacked in their favor. They comported themselves with what might be called a militant moderation. They had brought the man to the political scaffold. Yet they refrained from tying the rope round his neck. To their delight, Trotsky did this for himself. There was almost a sadistic aspect to the detached comportment of Stalin and Molotov. It cannot be known what they would have done if the discussion at the plenum had developed less favorably for them. But evidently they had gauged the atmosphere in the leadership correctly; and they certainly came out well from the episode. Criticized by Trotsky's supporters as being brainless and unpersuasive, they had shown that Trotsky himself had feet of clay when the audience in front of him was not already on his side.

There was a definite growing tendency in the central leadership to treat the dispute between the ascendant leadership and the Opposition in personal terms. Stalin led one faction, Trotsky the other. This was a tendency recognized within each faction. Enukidze, for example, objected to the Opposition's castigation of the Politburo's failure to understand that "the Stalinist path" (*stalinskii put'*) was leading in practice to the retardation of "the development of the productive forces" of the country.[17] Stalin was at last acquiring the prestige and authority of an adjective: this was one of the great accolades for any Bolshevik politician. Enukidze, bruised by Trotsky and loyal to his clique, declared that "everyone is talking about the softness of the Central Committee"; he picked out Stalin and Molotov as the promoters of this gentleness. Bukharin was not mentioned. In Western historical writing there has been a strong wish, albeit not a universal one (and certainly not one shared by this author) to represent Bukharin as a realistic contender for the supreme leadership in the struggle for the political succession to Lenin. Bukharin was undoubtedly a prominent figure in Soviet public life. He had joined the Politburo as a candidate member in 1919 and as a full member in 1924. He edited *Pravda*. He had a massive impact on Bolshevik discussions on social, economic, and cultural questions throughout the 1920s. He was widely loved in the party; Lenin had called him its "golden" son — and even the Opposition's leaders turned to him when they wanted to appeal against the worst excesses of the polemics they had to endure.[18]

But both factions by then knew who the potential supreme bosses really were: Trotsky and Stalin. (Lenin had been unusual in guessing this early on, in his testament of 1922–23; but his judgment was widely shared by the end of the decade.) There have always been grounds for wondering how much substance inhered in Bukharin's attempt to stand up to Stalin in 1928–29.[19] His arrangements to oppose the plundering of the peasantry attracted few allies. Whereas Trotsky had helped to lead a Left Opposition and a United Opposition, Bukharin was outmatched on every point of play. The Stalin group signaled this when they referred to Bukharin and the Rightists not as an "opposition" but as a mere "deviation." This was not a terminological triviality. Bukharin had simply not succeeded in assembling anything near to the number of followers that could have mounted a serious challenge to the "Stalinists." (I use quotation marks since they as yet lacked the ideological and behavioral definition of later years.) We can now surely add that the weakness of Bukharin was not suddenly discovered by leading party figures when Bukharin and Stalin clashed at the end of the decade. It was already part of their conventional wisdom. Bukharin was no champion: he was not even a plausible contender.

Not that Bukharin was without his uses for Stalin. He was a popular speaker; he had intellectual credentials of higher prestige than anyone's in the party apart from those of Trotsky himself. Such supporters as Bukharin had at the uppermost level of the party were more than willing to take up the struggle against the Opposition in 1926–27. They feared that the New Economic Policy would be destroyed — and with it the October Revolution — by Trotsky and his friends. Nikolai Uglanov, secretary of the Moscow city party organization, was one of them. Stalin said against Zinoviev, Trotsky's confederate in the United Opposition, that "we don't want to turn the party into a discussion club."[20] This was a pretty mild remark at that time. It expressed the sort of sentiment that most Bolsheviks would have subscribed to. But Uglanov went a lot further. Talking directly to Zinoviev, he declaimed impromptu: "Come on, don't worry! At any gathering we'll be able to give proof of your demagogy." He tackled Trotsky's ally Nikolai Muralov head on and did not eschew descending into personal abuse: "Now let's look at Comrade Muralov's speech. Here we have a democrat who plays the part of a 'poor peasant' from an agricultural academy . . ." Uglanov included Zinoviev in his attacks: "Stop engaging in demagogy, Comrade Zinoviev."

Others lined themselves up in Uglanov's support. Among them was Nikolai Antipov. Having heard the Opposition charging the ascendant leadership with behaving improperly, he asked how it had come about that important secret documents had fallen into the hands of oppositionists at every level of the party. Lenin's testament was a case in point. According to Antipov, the Opposition was utterly unworthy of the party's trust.[21] Both Bukharin and Stalin interjected brief comments; they wanted to make sure that the appropriate lessons were learned by the rest of the plenum's participants. Within a couple of years both Uglanov and Antipov would lose their posts along with Bukharin. In 1927 they still belonged to a victorious oligarchy and evidently were doing what they thought to be their political duty. Almost certainly they assumed their place in the leadership was secure. To their lethal cost they were about to learn that that they were being used by Stalin and his inner group. Unlike Bukharin, neither Uglanov nor Antipov were prominent intellectuals; they were basically Leninists who thought that Bukharin had the right idea about how best to defend and enhance the interests of the October Revolution. They assumed, ill-guardedly and unusually, that Bukharin was the Politburo member who was about to acquire the leadership mantle of Lenin.

Late in this factional struggle Trotsky decided to play rough by trying to split the ascendant party leadership. The historiography for decades in the West and for the decade and a half since the collapse of "Soviet power" in Russia itself has depicted him as a politician who had no clue about how to divide and rule his enemies. He has been thought to have lacked all guile and underhandedness. Now it would scarcely be demonstrable that he was successful in his political cunning. But this is far from meaning that he was entirely straightforward in his contributions to the current debates.

Trotsky's verbal exchange with Politburo member Jan Rudzutak shows this. It came at a delicate moment at the plenum. Rudzutak was well known as the rising party official in 1920 who had, to general surprise, supplied a form of words which Lenin had adopted in his struggle against Trotsky in the "trade union controversy."[22] He and Trotsky were therefore old adversaries. Rudzutak taunted Trotsky at the joint plenum on 8 September 1927: "Comrade Trotsky, I know that you possess an intelligent head, but it's been left to a real scoundrel."[23] This riled Trotsky, who retorted with sarcasm: "Your wit is already well known to the entire USSR more than your administrative talents which are spoken about in the People's Commissariat of Communication and absolutely everywhere, and even Stalin in quiet little corners talks about your administrative talents."

For once Trotsky caught Stalin off balance, and Stalin blurted out to Trotsky: "You saw that in your sleep!" Rudzutak, Stalin's ally at the time, continued: "I know you, Comrade Trotsky. You specialize in slandering people. I think that your talent in this respect is no less famous than my wit. I reckon we can award you a diploma as an experienced, qualified slanderer. There is no kind of slander you couldn't have dreamed up. You've forgotten the famous telephone which Stalin allegedly installed in your apartment. You've been like a little boy or a schoolboy telling fibs and you've omitted to carry out a technical investigation [*proverki*]. It's you who does the slandering in every corner. Stalin could not have had a more eager helper. (Rudzutak was shot by Stalin's NKVD in 1938.)

Rudzutak was in no mood to hold back and designated Trotsky's foreign sympathizers Ruth Fischer and Arcady Maslow as "unequivocal counter-revolutionaries." This was extreme language. The penalty for treason to the Soviet state and, by extension, to the cause of world revolution was death. Fischer and Maslow were not citizens of the USSR but adherents of the Opposition in the Comintern. Oppositionists were not yet being killed for their political activity in the Soviet Union. Fischer and Maslow, moreover, were beyond the OGPU's reach — the agency of state security did not at this point go beyond the borders and assassinate communists. Not yet. But a dangerous statement had been made by Rudzutak. Those who opposed the ascendant party leadership in the country were being declared traitors.

Yet Trotsky and Zinoviev could still catch the mood of the party even if they lacked the votes at crucial gatherings. They knew how to get under the skin of the majority which was ganging up on them. Zinoviev, who had not yet recanted his hostility to Stalin, announced: "Whatever you say, you've made a series of terrible mistakes [*tiazhëlykh oshibok*]; and the party silently voted against you on the Chinese question." This was a reference to the policy of collaboration with the Kuomintang imposed on the Chinese Communist Party only to be revoked in 1927 by a sudden insistence that the Chinese Communist Party should regard all nationalists, including the Kuomintang, as enemies to be politically and physically attacked. This resulted in the obliteration of the Communist Party organization in Shanghai and elsewhere in China. Zinoviev and Trotsky criticized this debacle in severe terms. A caveat needs to be entered here. Both Zinoviev and Trotsky had approved and encouraged "adventurist" revolutionary actions in Bulgaria and Germany earlier in the decade; they liked to draw a veil over their recommendations when later they reviewed and explained them. Although the party in 1927 was Stalin's for the taking, he needed to explain his policies with care; his monopoly of the levers of the party's administrative apparatus by itself was not adequate for the rise of himself and his clique to political supremacy.[24] Certain weak points persisted, and Zinoviev was trying to expose them.

The "Stalinists" struck back. Trade commissar and candidate Politburo member Anastas Mikoyan, went as far as demanding that the minutes — and indeed the full stenograms — of central party gatherings should be read out at meetings of the party at lower levels. He declared that "the distribution of stenograms of the Central Committee plenum is one of the most important instruments binding the Central Committee with the entire party and one of the most important methods of internal party democracy."[25] As it happened, Zinoviev had no objection to this. Indeed he wanted the distribution to be hurried up: he indicated that sometimes the printed version took as long as three months to appear. But despite what the Opposition claimed at the time and subsequently, the leaders and adherents of the Stalin clique were not trying to stop local leaders knowing what went on at the top of the party — or at least what went on in formal party sessions at the top — any more than previously.

Then, late in the proceedings, Bukharin asked to speak. He was verbally savage, castigating the Opposition's "unprecedented hypocrisy" and its "departure from Leninism." He charged the adversaries of the ascendant leadership with having "deceived the party."[26] Zinoviev got worked up and yelled out at Bukharin. Trotsky did the same. Here for the first time the shorthand secretaries failed to catch their words for posterity: possibly the shouting was difficult to understand or perhaps the edited script was censored.[27] Bukharin, far from being the softy of the leadership, ruthlessly assaulted Zinoviev and Trotsky; he concisely and sharply rehearsed those many occasions when they had fallen into conflict with Lenin. He dwelled on their inconsistencies since the October Revolution. He asked them directly to explain this history. Were they previously lying? Or were they lying now? And Bukharin rejected the accusation that the ascendant party leadership was guilty of "Bonapartism." It was his contention that the party as a whole and not an individual ruled the Soviet Union. He did not need to add that if any single person was thought to have aspirations to supreme individual leadership it was less himself or Stalin than Trotsky: the idea was being suggested widely and ceaselessly in the party.

Trotsky pulled out all the stops, introducing the charge that Bukharin in the course of the Brest-Litovsk dispute in early 1918 had wanted to arrest Lenin for advocating the signing of a separate peace with the Central Powers. This was a potentially devastating attack; in fact it was subsequently to be used by Stalin when he moved against Bukharin and had him shot in 1938. Bukharin was good at thinking on his feet. He jabbed back at Trotsky, declaring that it had been the Left Socialist-Revolutionaries and not any Bolsheviks who had proposed the taking of Lenin into custody. Bukharin also maintained that a prolonged political controversy such as had occurred over Brest-Litovsk would be a "crime" against the party.

Thus it is clear from the September 8, 1927 stenogram that the public discussion of party history, in *Pravda* and at party congresses, was not merely a device to mobilize the support of the "party masses." Participants in the joint plenum of the Party Politburo and the Party Central Control Commission Presidium were like dogs fighting over a bone. Unless the participants either were feigning their emotions or were unaware of the way they were playing around with Bolshevik party history, their disputes were an authentic expression of internal party factionalism. Speakers seem to have meant what they said to a greater or lesser extent. Trotsky was a master of the annals of the Red Army. He reminded listeners about how he and Lenin had removed Stalin from the Southern Front in the Civil War for his "incorrect policy." Stalin interrupted this speech. But Trotsky had come along well prepared: he told the plenum that Lenin had told his deputy that Stalin behaved capriciously. Trotsky proclaimed: "This really happened! [*Eto bylo!*]" Stalin again interrupted, but to no great purpose. The meeting continued to crackle with personal conflict. Trotsky and Stalin were putting themselves up against each other. Sometimes the historic significance of the moment gave them the psychological shivers. But they had to go on fighting. The stakes were high: the winner would be able to impose himself as unchallengeable leader of the entire party.

Stalin and his faction came out on top. There was nothing inevitable about this. But Trotsky was a poor tactician and an ill-advised strategist. He disastrously underestimated Stalin. He catastrophically overestimated his status and authority. He was not helped by the fact that he was Jewish. He was impeded by bouts of severe illness. He had not always been a Bolshevik, and this too was held against him. Many genuinely supposed that he was aiming to be the military dictator — the Napoleon Bonaparte — of the October Revolution.

What is sharply revealed by this short but very full stenogram of the Party Politburo and the Central Control Commission Presidium is that so much of what was said in wider circles was said in more or less the same language and with the same force in the innermost recesses of the central party leadership. What the central leaders proclaimed while standing on top of the Lenin Mausoleum was not very different from what they said to each other in their public exchanges. We can now also see that the factional struggle at the party's apex, so far from being secluded in the recesses of the Kremlin precinct, was brought to wide attention of the central and local elite of the Bolshevik party. Trotsky, after being deported from the USSR in 1929, collected material to claim that he was a victim of the "Stalinist school of historical falsification." His chief accusation was that Stalin in the period of the NEP — and subsequently — had restricted both public and confidential political deliberations, had alone engaged in intolerable methods of debate, had relied more or less exclusively on bureaucratic modalities, and had turned the central party leadership into a replay-apparatus for his contributions to the dispute between the ascendant leadership and the Opposition. Trotsky in his last years as well as posthumously has molded global opinion about the history of the USSR. His literary elegance as well as the manner of his death have lessened the critical attention that might otherwise have been accorded to the Opposition.[28] Undoubtedly he wrote well. Without question he was *sans pareil* as a glamorous communist leader until Fidel and Che led the revolutionary seizure of power in Cuba in 1959. But he was no saint. Nor did he supply the ungainsayable case for far-left revolution in his lifetime.

Who could deny that Trotsky was a sincere and intellectually powerful enemy of Stalin? He himself told the world as much in his brilliant autobiography.[29] The stenogram of the Party Politburo and Party Central Control Commission Presidium holds to a somewhat different narrative. And it undermines the legend, frequently accepted by noncommunist and even anticommunist historians, that the Opposition lost the factional battle mainly because it lacked the organizational resources of the ascendant party leadership. This has always been implausible. It is good to be able to demonstrate the case on a documentary basis from the Politburo archive.

Notes

The author thanks the Hoover Institution for the chance to work as a visiting fellow from 2004 in its archives on Soviet history.

1. Service, *The Bolshevik Party in Revolution: A Study in Organisational Change*, pp. 124–25.

2. Ibid., pp. 125 and 175–78.

3. Trotskii, *Moia zhizn': Opyt biografii*, vol. 2, chaps. 40–42.

4. RGASPI Fond 17, op. 3, del. 705.

5. RGASPI Fond 17, op. 3, del. 700.

6. See Paul Gregory's introductory chapter in this volume.

7. See Tucker, *Stalin as Revolutionary 1879–1929: A Study in History and Personality*; Service, *The Bolshevik Party in Revolution: A Study in Organisational Change*; and Service, *Stalin: A Biography*.

8. RGASPI Fond 17, op. 3, del. 700.

9. RGASPI Fond 17, op. 3, del. 705.

10. Trotsky to Bukharin, March 4, 1926: Hoover Institution Archives, Trotsky Collection, box 9, folder 48, p. 2.

11. Kosheleva, Lel'chuk, Naumov, Naumov, Rogovaia, and Khlevniuk, *Pis'ma I. V. Stalina V. M. Molotovu, 1925–1936 gg.: Sbornik dokumentov*; Khlevniuk, Davies, Rees, and Rogovaia, *Stalin i Kaganovich: Perepiska, 1931–1936 gg.*

12. Chuev, *Molotov: Poluderzhavnyi vlastelin*; Kaganovich, *Pamiatnye zapiski*.

13. RGASPI Fond 17, op. 3, del. 705.

14. Jones, *Socialism in Georgian Colors: The European Road to Social Democracy, 1883–1917*, pp. 220–21 and 272–73.

15. The exchange between Trotsky and Enukidze is found in RGASPI Fond 17, op. 3, del. 705.

16. Service, *Stalin: A Biography*, pp. 292–93.

17. RGASPI Fond 17, op. 3, del. 705.

18. For the pro-Bukharin case see Cohen, *Bukharin and the Bolshevik Revolution: A Political Biography, 1888–1938*.

19. Merridale, *Moscow Politics and the Rise of Stalin*, chap. 2.

20. RGASPI Fond 17, op. 3, del. 705.

21. RGASPI Fond 17, op. 3, del. 705.

22. Daniels, *The Conscience of the Revolution: Communist Opposition in Soviet Russia*, chap. 5.

23. RGASPI Fond 17, op. 3, del. 705.

24. Service, *Stalin: A Biography*, pp. 5–10.

25. RGASPI Fond 17, op. 3, del. 705.

26. RGASPI Fond 17, op. 3, del. 705.

26. The first rather than the second hypothesis is surely the correct one.

27. Service, *Stalin: A Biography*, p. 4.

28. Trotskii, *Moia zhizn': Opyt biografii*, vols. 1–2.

8

Making the Unthinkable Thinkable: Language Microhistory of Politburo Meetings

LEONA TOKER

The meetings of the Politburo held on October 8 and 11, 1926 and September 9, 1927 officially addressed the "party discipline" that was being subverted, as it were, by the United Opposition (Lev Trotsky, Lev Kamenev, Grigory Zinoviev, Grigory Sokol'nikov, Nikolai Muralov, and others). This essay studies the lexical tug-of-war at these meetings. It follows developments in the use of one syntactic structure and of two words at the meetings of October 8 and 11, 1926 and, in less detail, a broader range of stylistic phenomena that characterize the meeting of September 8, 1927. The essay demonstrates the overlap and the difference between the official agenda of the meetings and the actual goals pursued by their participants.

The language microhistory of the meetings that took place in October 1926 is dominated by struggles for the semantic value of words. That of the meeting of September 1927 is largely shaped by a pattern of reversals — both sides to the conflict accuse each other of the same mortal sins, until the abuse is drastically escalated by Stalin, signaling to his adherents a change of attitude that anticipates and helps to prepare a transition from verbal to physical violence against the Left Opposition.[1]

Vocabulary was, indeed, one of the fields in which the battle between Stalin's "ruling collectives" and the opposition was waged. Stalin's ear for semantic subtleties had already once saved him at a moment of crisis. In his "Letter to the Congress" (December 1922–January 1923) Lenin had recommended that Stalin, who was "too rude" and who had "amassed immeasurable power" as general secretary, be replaced by someone "more tolerant, loyal, more considerate to comrades, and less capricious."[2] When this text was read aloud on May 21, 1924, at a meeting of the Central Committee and heads of local party organizations, Stalin, in his usual version of *nolo episcopari,* offered to resign so that the search for someone "more polite" could begin.[3] Capitalizing on Lenin's miscalculated choice of words, he managed to divert the meeting's attention from the charge of disloyalty. One of his trusting friends, A. P. Smirnov (who was to change his mind in 1932 and be duly executed in February 1938), then defused the tension by declaring that a proletarian party is not to be frightened by rudeness. In the absence of a well-prepared and determined opposition, the ploy worked: objections against Stalin were moved from the ethical plane to that of manners.

The formula "rude and disloyal," joining items from different parts of Lenin's so-called "testament," entered Trotsky's vocabulary — and was used, for instance, in the letters of the opposition to the Politburo in October 1926, as a reminder of Lenin's having been right.

I

There were two dueling processes in the Soviet Communist Party in the twenties. One was the self-organization of an internal opposition based on the resentment of the hijacking of the revolution by Stalin's bureaucracy and "metaphysical police,"[4] as well as on the workers' discontent with their economic condition, no longer compensated for by their sense of participation in the power-forces ruling the country ("What did we fight for?"). The second process was Stalin's steady consolidation of his hold on the party apparatus. By indefatigable work with cadres — calculated appointments ("recommendations") of Regional Committee secretaries (usually from frondeurs against Trotsky or Zinoviev) and the resulting upward answerability, as well as through perks, personal patronage, and ad hoc "insinuations, obloquy, and stage-whisper"[5] — Stalin's tentacles were creeping from the center into party cells. At larger meetings his adherents made efficient use of "activists," loudmouthed upwardly mobile party recruits; Stalinist nominees among the secretaries maneuvered the wording of resolutions.[6] The clandestine meetings of opposition supporters were traced and disrupted by hooligans.

Starting with the Twelfth Congress (1923), most of the delegates were the general secretary's men. From 1925, most of the larger official party gatherings (in particular the Fourteenth Congress) were already pervaded by a claque that would greet Stalin's speeches with admiring ovations. By 1926 Stalin had practically won the race: his hecklers could successfully subvert the public speeches of opposition leaders, puncturing their most fiery rhetoric and reducing it to ludicrous incongruity.

By October 1926 Kamenev (demoted to a candidate-member) and Trotsky faced a new deployment of forces in the Politburo, which already included most of the grandees of Stalin's inner circle (Vyacheslav Molotov, Kliment Voroshilov, and Mikhail Kalinin), as well as the future "Right Deviation"— Nikolai Bukharin, Aleksei Rykov, Mikhail Tomsky, and Nikolai Uglanov.[7] At Politburo discussions of intraparty discipline the Left Opposition was attacked on the basis of the resolutions against factional activities adopted at the Tenth Congress in 1921—as if a half-hearted experiment in intraparty democracy in 1923 had never happened. Stalin's struggle against opposition leaders addressed not their policies (most of which he would adopt, under modified names, within two years) but their status and their psychological hold on the minds of fellow Marxists. Such a struggle necessitated shifts in discourse at meetings and in publications.

October 1926 and September 1927 marked different stages in this struggle. At the Politburo meeting of September 9, 1927, a prelude to Zinoviev's and Trotsky's expulsion from the party, the language used is radically harsher. In October 1926 the ruling faction still seems to be making efforts to restrain its animosity—mainly because its immediate objective is to coerce the opposition not only into proclaiming the cessation of their "factional" activities but also into recanting. Characteristically, they still occasionally address Kamenev and Trotsky (not Zinoviev) by the respectful—or else mock-ceremonious—name-and-patronymic (Lev Borisovich, Lev Davydovich), which does not occur in the transcript of September 9, 1927.

Isaac Deutscher believes that the idea of the opposition's (namely Trotsky's) recanting was first suggested, with "fatal recklessness," by Zinoviev himself, still a member of the ruling triumvirate, at the Thirteenth Congress of 1924.[8] At the time the idea was shocking even to that assemblage of delegates, and Nadezhda Krupskaya's [Lenin's wife] protest against this "psychologically impossible" demand received applause.[9] But the seed had been planted; its sprouts would eventually intertwine with the OGPU-NKVD pursuit of false confessions; it would bloom luxuriously at the show trials of the thirties, including the trials of Kamenev and Zinoviev. One of these sprouts emerged at the Politburo meetings of October 1926, when the opposition leaders were called on to cooperate in their own gradual destruction: they were required not only to relinquish dissemination of their ideas but also to publicly admit their errors and to denounce supporters on the far left, who had actually made a move towards the creation of a new party, as well as Comintern members recently expelled from the German Communist Party.[10] Unable to gauge their residual sway among the party's rank and file and unsure of the possibility of promptly "liquidating" their political base, Stalin sought to demoralize the United Opposition by having its leaders discredit themselves.[11] After Kamenev understood the intent of the 1926 meetings, his agenda changed from pursuing freedom of discussion to containing damage. He conceded that the "six-point" countermemorandum of October 6 prepared by Bukharin, Rykov, and Tomsky (rather than the opposition's memorandum) should serve as the basis for the Politburo resolution. He then found himself struggling against the additional two points pressed on October 11 — recantation and disowning associates. Eventually, this failed too, as did the attempts to extract a promise that surrender would put a definitive end to "the episode."

The transcripts of the October 8 and 11, 1926 meetings read like a text with hyperlinks to preceding documents.[12] The subject of the actual political and economic content of the opposition's platform is almost taboo. On the agenda is "The Situation within the Party," a metapolitical issue: the resolution to be adopted has to state how the opposition must atone for the "factional activity" of publicizing their "platform" among the rank and file — which was regarded as qualitatively different from commenting on separate political issues.

One of the immediate linguistic effects of this agenda is the repeated reference to "documents," "formulations," "public statements," and "proposals" rather than to their content. The dominant syntactic construction is "that which we propose/have written," e.g. in Kamenev's opening statement on October 8:

Мы сформулировали в точных выражениях **то, что** мы хотели бы сказать Центральному комитету и **то, что** в той или иной форме должно быть сказано от нашего имени всей партии.[13]	We have formulated in precise expressions *that which* we would like to say to the Central Committee and *that which*, in one form or another, must be said to the whole party on our behalf.

The "that which" construction, sometimes supplemented by vague lexical references with a similar deictic function,[14] helps to keep the material referred to both *in* the present discussion and *out* of it. The pattern is particularly characteristic of the speeches of the oppositionists, probably because the content of the texts discussed (including their own memoranda) remains distasteful to them. Sokol'nikov, for instance, overstates the offer of the opposition's "open" (explicit) declaration about toeing the party line, while evading, by way of oral shorthand, the contents of this and other documents:

А второй гарантией является **то, что** ведь мы согласны открыто перед партией сказать, что вот мы за **такой-то** модус установления нормальных отношений в партии. Сказав это открыто перед партией, мы не можем аннулировать **те заявления, которые** мы открыто перед партией делаем. . . . И **то, что** скорее всего поведет нас сейчас на путь окончательного решения, это есть, во-первых, признание **того, что** в основу кладутся эти шесть пунктов, которые вы предложили, и что мы совместно с вами редактируем свой ответ **на эти** шесть пунктов.

And the second guarantee is *the fact that* we actually agree to say openly before the party that we are in favor of *such-and-such* a mode of establishing normal relations in the party. Having said that openly before the party, we shall be unable to annul *those* declarations *which* we make openly before the party. . . . And *that which* will most certainly lead us to the road of a final solution[15] is, first, our admission of *the fact that* these six points that you have suggested are to form the basis and that jointly with you we are editing our response to *these* six points.

Stalin first uses this deictic construction likewise in reference to what is distasteful to him, namely Krupskaya's position: "When she was picked to pieces throughout Russia, she explained herself *in such a way that* things became worse; she made worse *that which* she had said."[16] This is syntactically echoed by Rykov: "Krupskaya is believed not to have meant *that which* she said."

A. A. Solts, head of the Central Control Commission ("the conscience of the party"), uses the infectious syntactic euphemism with the tone of a governess: "If you consider *that which* you have been doing as harmful, stop doing it." Voroshilov, however, counters the implication that the opposition's current compliance will end the episode: we cannot, as it were, keep these matters secret from the party:

я считаю **то, что** нам предлагает сейчас оппозиция, это хуже **того, что** у нас было до сих пор в самые острые дни, в самые острые моменты борьбы Центрального комитета с оппозицией. . . . А если оглянуться на **то, что** мы пережили за эти дни, так **вышесказанное**-подтверждается целиком и полностью.[17] . . . **те** предложения, **которые** были внесены, все **то, о чем** здесь говорили, само собой

I consider *that which* the opposition proposes to us now as worse than *that which* we have known in the most acute days, the most acute moments of the Central Committee's struggle with the opposition. . . . And if we recall *that which* we have lived through in the recent days, then the *above* is wholly and fully confirmed. . . . it is self-evident *that* those proposals *which* have been submitted, all *that which* has been

разумеется, должно быть на конференции доложено. Все вопросы внутрипартийного положения, все **то, что** происходило, все эти разговоры, заседания, должны быть также доложены.

said here, must be reported at the conference. All the issues of the intraparty situation, all *that which* has been taking place, and all *these* conversations and sessions must also be reported.

By the time the floor is given to another Stalin ally from the Control Commission, Emelian Yaroslavsky, the construction *that which* has become politically correct. The safety of its use overrules logical or stylistic strictures:

Ведь вы, тов. Каменев и тов. Троцкий, голосовали в свое время **за то, что** если Шляпников или Медведев позволят себе в дальнейшем **то, что** они позволили на X и XI съездах, мы обязаны их исключить.

Haven't you, Comrade Kamenev and Comrade Trotsky, once voted *in favor of that* if in the future Shliapnikov and Medvedev [two supporters of the United Opposition] allow themselves *the kind of* behavior *that* they allowed themselves at the Xth and XIth Congresses, we shall be obliged to expel them.

The pattern recurs with an almost neurotic involution, in Kamenev's opening statement three days later, at the meeting of October 11, to which the proceedings have been adjourned:

Если в **этих вопросах** и были разногласия, то скорее мы высказывались **за то, что** ведется недостаточная борьба с уклоном в правую сторону, а совсем не **за то, что** мы разделяем взгляды, высказанные Медведевым и Оссовским.

Even if there was a difference of opinion on *these matters*, *what* we voiced was rather *that* there was not enough struggle against the right deviation and not at all *that* we concur in the views voiced by Medvedev and Ossovsky.

Acquiring a life of its own, the *that which* structure starts creeping in even where not called for. Below I have enclosed superfluous words in figure brackets:

Сольц: Так что я не знаю, как понять {то}, что {заявлял} Лев Борисович {, что он} согласен принять эти предложения в основу.

Solts: Thus I do not know how to understand **that** {which} Lev Borisovich {stated that he} agrees to accept these proposals as a basis.

The bureaucrat Molotov uses the pedantically precise "the fact that" (*to, chto*) instead of the more colloquially easy "what":

Вы забываете {то} **что** Центральный комитет как выразитель воли и руководитель "целого" — партии	You forget {**the fact**} **that** there is the Central Committee expressing the will and directing the "whole" — the party

In some utterances of Tomsky and Kamenev, such a deictic superfluity helps to distance the speaker from "that which" he reports, as if a more economical sentence structure might have left a space for the suspicion of the speaker's concurrence.

The overwrought syntax sometimes betrays insecurity. Thus Jan Rudzutak, "recently promoted to the full membership lost by Zinoviev,"[18] on the hypothetical possibility of the Leningrad workers' support of Zinoviev and his group:

Это значило бы то, что у нас внутрипартийная борьба не только бы *еще более обострилась,* а это означает, что дело могло действительно кончиться вторым Кронштадтом.	*This* would mean *the fact that* the intraparty struggle among us *would not only grow even sharper,* and this means that the matter might indeed have ended in a second Kronstadt.

The repetition "would mean . . . means" (*znachilo by . . . oznachaet*) marks Rudzutak's inept use of Stalin's tested rhetorical device of gradation or "cumulative chain"[19]: from the Leningrad workers' support for Zinoviev (a separate incident) to the intensification of the intraparty struggle (a general condition) to an all-out rebellion, for which Kronstadt, the site of the disenchanted revolutionary sailors' armed rebellion against the Bolshevik regime in 1921, is both a metaphor and a metonymy.

Rudzutak is uneasy with such stencils. His "indeed" (*deistvitel'no*) denotes concurring, but he gets confused between references to semantics ("this means that") and causality ("might have ended in"); symptomatically, the "not only but also" construction is aborted in midsentence. The italicized phrase indicates Rudzutak's correcting the original transcript: the struggle in the party is already intense, so he must add, for the sake of political correctness, that it would have intensified *further* — concerned with preempting the accusation of insufficient vigilance, he has no attention to spare for the syntactical or logical consistency of his troubled support of Stalin. The latter, sensitive to stylistic nuance, is all the time engaging in a tacit "hermeneutics of the soul"[20] of each speaker, an attempt to read and piece together the signs of his hidden (class-) consciousness. At the September 1927 meeting, Stalin will actually claim knowing Trotsky's and Muralov's "souls."[21] In 1938 Rudzutak will be executed; the underlying reasons of his fall, by contrast to the spurious official charges, will remain shrouded in mystery.

More confidently in line with Stalin on October 11, 1926, is the head of the Council of Peoples' Commissars Aleksei Rykov:

Что же вы хотите получить, кроме мира, еще какие-то особые права за все **то, что** вы проделывали после XIV съезда? Нет, слуга покорный. Документ, который тов. Каменев защищал, является насквозь фальшивым.	So what do you want to get, in addition to peace, some other special rights for *all that which* you have been contriving after the XIVth Congress? No, pardon me. *The document that* Comrade Kamenev has been defending is thoroughly false.

In what sounds like genuine animosity against the left faction, still using the "hyperlinks," Rykov facilitates a transition from the discourse of procedural metapolitics to that of personal insult—the irony of "special rights," an allusion to the privileged status of the three top Jews (Trotsky, Kamenev, and Zinoviev) in the revolutionary movement, is reinforced by the ironic oxymoron of a categorical "Net" joined to an old-time verbal bow, *sluga pokornyi* ("[your] obedient servant"—in the sense of "pardon me"). Rykov also implicitly turns Kamenev and his associates into rogues by using the word *prodelyvali*, related to *prodelka* ("trick," "mischief"), instead of the neutral *delali* ("did").

With the benefit of hindsight the transcripts of these two meetings may be read as a paradigm of ways in which the freedom of thought can be given up, from faked or reluctant minimal surrender to zealous maximal surrender. They may also be read as a theater of one spectator—Stalin. A decade later this relatively reticent judge, for whom the correction of the transcripts might have doubled as mnemonic recapitulation, forced most of the actors into the ultimate disgrace of playing the roles of repentant traitors. Was the retention of the modicum of role-distance at the Politburo debates a capital offense? Perhaps as a symptom rather than as an act—if, that is, Stalin needed such subtleties.

However that may be, the grating *that, which* (*to, chto*) construction adopted by most of the speakers in October 1926 suggests their need for a procedural anchor to contain the passions that might send the discussion drifting away from the rulers' goal of coercing the oppositionists into self-abnegation and the opposition's groping for a less humiliating compromise. It also suggests the contagiousness of a language stencil within the framework of a single political event.

Use of a stencil adopted through group dynamics puts a speaker on what at the moment seems to be the safe side. Circumstances can turn a neutral word into a badge of the side taken. At the October 8 and 11 meetings of the Politburo, such a word is "elementary." It rings like a keynote in the Bukharin-Rykov-Tomsky memorandum, composed, revised, and reread in preparation for the meetings. During the meetings it seems to exempt the listeners from thinking, to stunt their reason. Having been used several times in the same context without encountering criticism, it acquires the safety of political correctness. It can no longer be *controverted*—the most that the opposite side can do is *subvert* it.

Indeed, at the beginning of the meeting, Kamenev attempts to appropriate the word "elementary" but in the meaning of "minimal" rather than in the meaning of "basic" or "the simplest":

наше обращение [меньшинства] не вызвало со стороны большинства никаких шагов, хотя бы самых **элементарных,** которые бы показали, что есть некоторое желание создать действительно обстановку спокойного обсуждения наших предложений.	Our [the minority's] appeal failed to elicit any steps on the part of the majority, not even the most *elementary* steps, that would show that there is some wish to create conditions for a calm discussion of our proposals.

Molotov plays along with this usage for a while, reinforcing it by the synonym "minimal" and at the same time laying the ground for a distinction between the shades of meaning:

В этом документе я не вижу даже **минимального,** даже **элементарного** желания отмежеваться от ренегатской идеологии некоторых элементов ВКП и в Коминтерне	In this document I do not see even a *minimal,* even an *elementary* desire to disown the renegade ideology of certain elements in the VKP and the Comintern

Yet Tomsky, one of the signatories of the majority resolution draft, promptly reverts to the use of "elementary" as "basic," "the simplest," "natural":

. . . документ наш представлял . . . самые **элементарные,** разумные и безусловно неоспоримо справедливые требования, направленные к оппозиции, бесспорные и **элементарные** требования для того, чтобы в пределах одной партии установить нормальную работу	. . . our document presented the opposition with the most *elementary,* reasonable and doubtlessly unquestionably just demands, indisputable and *elementary* demands for the establishment of normal work in the framework of a single party

In official discourse, an abundance of positive adjectives (an epithet attached to every noun) is usually a sign of lip-service to the goals of the specific media genre;[22] and the same is true of an abundance of adverbs. Here "demands" are modified by "elementary" (twice), "reasonable," "just," and "indisputable," while "just" is modified by "unquestionably," in its turn modified by "doubtlessly" (note also the use of the adjective "normal" about which more later). Tomsky, a no-nonsense trade union leader, will commit suicide to avoid arrest in 1936. Here he takes care to use the badge-word "elementary" in the safe meaning — except, to his own peril, when referring to the views of the United Opposition, in indirect speech:

Мы, веря в **минимум** искренности оппозиции, выдвинули предложения, о которых они сами говорят, как об **элементарных** приемлемых требованиях	*Believing in the **minimum** of sincerity [i.e., minimal sincerity] of the opposition we have raised proposals which they themselves describe as elementary acceptable demands*

Half-aware of the reference to "minimal," Tomsky uses "minimum of" in the insertion that he makes (italicized) when editing the transcript. His problem is sincerity with himself.

Once relaunched, the use of "elementary" as "basic," "natural," "self-understandable" acquires its own momentum. In Rudzutak's use, it enhances the tone of reproach that can already be sensed in Tomsky, adding to it notes of irritation:

Взамен чего они согласны подчиниться **элементарным** условиям, которые являются обязательными для всякого члена партии: подчиниться решениям съезда, не нарушать партийной дисциплины, не создавать своей фракции. За выполнение этих *элементарных обязанностей членов партии* они выставляют целую программу, предъявляют свои требования.	In return for what do they agree to obey the *elementary* conditions that are mandatory for any member of the party: to obey the decisions of the congress, not to breach party discipline, not to form their own faction. In return for carrying out these *elementary duties of members of the party* they submit a whole program, present their own demands.

The superfluous expression "elementary duties of members of the party" is added in the process of editing the transcript: political correctness seems to demand it.

When he offers his interpretation of the stance of the opposition, Rudzutak conflates the two meanings of "elementary" ("minimal" and "basic"); ungrammatically switching to the first person plural of mock direct speech in order to reduce Kamenev's rhetoric to a bargaining position, he ascribes this confusion to the latter. According to Rudzutak, the opposition says:

Мы выполним **элементарные** условия дисциплины, которые необходимы и обязательны для всех членов партии, а вы нам за это дайте то-то и то-то	We shall fulfill the *elementary* conditions that are necessary and mandatory for all the members of the party, and in return you give us this and that

The pose of introducing clarity, however, is belied by the indefiniteness of the deictic reference to the opposition's demands ("give us this and that"), as if Kamenev et al. were demanding a reward. In fact, as it appears from Kamenev's responses, all that the opposition is asking for is to be left alone, to have the Politburo call off the public "baiting" (*travlia*) of its members. Oppositionist Grigory Piatakov hints that this is not a negotiating bid but the "elementary right" (i.e., the minimal right) of every member of the party. Like a judo wrestler, Rudzutak attempts to turn the force of this remark against Piatakov himself, sinning against syntax by a midsentence switch to the first person plural (in reference to the opposition) and projecting on his adversary the logical fog into which he gets himself, especially since the first person plural of the end of the sentence ("our heads") already refers to the his own faction:

Если эта программа есть **элементарное** право всякого члена партии, тогда так же смешно выставлять эти требования, как смешно заявлять, что мы подчиняемся решению съезда, решению ЦК и прочее, потому что этими **элементарными** правами партии пользуются все члены партии и в этом отношении ни вам, т. Пятаков, и никому другому не удастся нам голову затуманивать.	If this program is the *elementary* right of every member of the party, then it is equally ludicrous to present these demands as it is to proclaim that we submit to the decision of the congress, the decision of the CC, and so on, because these *elementary* rights are enjoyed by all the members of the party and in this respect neither you, Comrade Piatakov, nor anyone else will manage to fog up our heads.

Partly recovering from this confusion, Rudzutak goes on to defuse the concept of the "elementary" ("minimal") rights of the members, replacing it by the notion of their "elementary" ("natural," "basic") duties to party discipline:

Речь идет лишь о том, чтобы выполнить постановления партии,	At issue is only the carrying out of the resolutions of the party, the

выполнить **элементарное требование партийной дисциплины.**	carrying out of the *elementary* demands of party discipline.

The repetition of the word "elementary" is here in tune with the type of Engelsian doublethink ("freedom is the recognition of necessity") which identifies "intraparty democracy" with "party discipline."

Majority representative Kliment Voroshilov rephrases Rudzutak's interpretation of Kamenev's "bid," further vulgarizing it by the use of the scornful diminutive "little platform":

Как правильно отметил здесь т. Рудзутак, мы, мол, хотим подчиниться всем **элементарным** требованиям, которые у нас существуют для каждого члена партии, а за это платформочку нашу примите.	As was correctly noted by Comrade Rudzutak, we, they say, want to submit to all the *elementary* demands that exist for every member of our party, and in return you accept this little platform of ours.

Voroshilov here puts his own faction's usage of "elementary" (for duties instead of rights) into the mouth of the oppositionists. He congratulates himself with "we are not simpletons either" (*my tozhe ne lykom shyty*).[23] But while editing the stenogram, Voroshilov develops Rudzutak's insinuation that Kamenev has been delegated to defend the opposition's cause because he is such an expert trickster.[24] He seems to have understood that gang-baiting the aristocrats is the order of the day. At the meeting he anticipates the invective that would be unleashed at the party conference, yet in post factum editing he hides his *Schadenfreude* behind the restatement of "elementary demands":

Извините, пожалуйста, конференция является таким представительным органом партии, который должен знать и обязан знать все, что делается в партии. *Конференция должна узнать*, это **элементарное** требование внутрипартийной демократии, почему ЦК допустил такую слабость, долготерпение, что сразу же не поставил вас на *должное* место.	Excuse me please, the conference is such a representative organ of the party that it must know and has to know everything that is going on in the party. *The conference must be informed, this is an **elementary** demand of intraparty democracy,* why the CC has been so soft, so long-suffering, why it has not put you in your *due* place at once.

The sarcastic "Excuse me please" is a sample of this baiting: on the surface a polite paraphrase for a simple "No," it is actually a mock-ceremonious addition of insult to injury.

The others pick up the cue: Rykov will use "elementary" four times, Molotov four times, at one point as the superlative (*elementarneishee* — "the most basic"), Tomsky six more times, Kalinin three times. Fighting back, Zinoviev insists on the "elementary rights of the minority," but Kamenev notes, more to the point, that the two demands added to Bukharin's initial six-point memorandum — that the opposition proclaim its activities "detrimental (*vrednye*) and dangerous to the party" and publicly renounce its associates in the Comintern — are not "elementary" at all.

In general, however, the members of the opposition attempt to counter the harping on their "elementary" duties by demanding "normal" party relationships. The word *normal* had been launched in the opposition's October 4, 5, and 8 letters to the Politburo. The latter, a counterproposal to Bukharin's six-point document, offered to call on adherents to cease the struggle for their views in forms that "transgress the frame of *normal* party life" yet insisted on the opposition's right to defend their views "in the *normal* way." Kamenev repeats these formulations at the meeting three or four times. Admitting that Zinoviev's recent address to the workers in Leningrad could be seen as the last "splash" of "nonnormal" intraparty relationships, he offers to limit the expression of the minority's views to "a normal way" of doing things.

Molotov and Tomsky then deny that Kamenev's "document" can contribute to "normal" working conditions in the Central Committee; Tomsky characterizes it as of a "quite teeth-shattering kind" (*ves'ma zubodrobitel'nogo kharaktera*) — another metaphor that will be literalized in the NKVD interrogation rooms. It is the main body of the Politburo, Tomsky suggests, that has been bending over backwards for the sake of reestablishing "normal" party work.

Kamenev moves to reappropriate the word, by stating that the cessation of the ("not normal") activities which clash with the party regulations would be in "normal" good order and that thereafter it will be necessary to preserve "the normal" conditions for the minority; he offers to go a step beyond this concession in order to end disagreements about the party's organizational "norms." He insists on the need to "liquidate" (another word that gains momentum in the discussion) the current "nonnormal" situation, implicitly accusing both sides of the divide — his own side because "the existence of factions is nonnormal and detrimental," and Stalin's for seeking to preclude freedom of opinion in any form and thus departing from the norms of democratic procedure. He calls for "normal" conditions in the party three more times, and alludes to the "normal" past state of affairs when discussion of different political options in advance of the party congresses used to be possible. The word "normal" is used in the same meaning by Kamenev's supporters Sokol'nikov (once) and

Smilga (three times). Zinoviev refuses to play up to the pretense that the treatment of the opposition and the undemocratic way in which the Fourteenth Party Congress was "prepared" are "normal" party functioning. Conceding the demand that the minority should accept the decisions of the majority, he denies (five times, and not unjustifiably) the "normality" of the current "baiting" of the opposition. Whether bluffing or still confident of his clout, he suggests that it is not "normal" to prefer massive accusations against people who are, nevertheless, not expelled from the Central Committee. This abnormality Stalin will indeed soon correct.

For Rykov normality would lie in the opposition's announcement of their total acceptance of the Bukharin memorandum. In a later speech, however, Rykov reserves the word "normal" for interpretive reformulations of the stance of the opposition — he has, as it were, already ceded the word to the opposition. Tomsky uses it once, likewise in reference to the need to establish "normal relationships in the party." These two speakers, perhaps already earmarked as the next "deviation," have not yet understood that, under the present circumstances, the word itself, pitting as it does connotations of cultural tradition versus natural ("elementary") forces, has ceased to be politically correct.

What helps to convince the opposition to publish a statement which, though not a reproduction of Bukharin's eight points, amounts to capitulation is Stalin's ceding a little ground. Stalin, whose policymaking frequently took the shape of editorial emendations, suggests the replacement of the adjective "harmful" (*vrednye*) for the opposition's activities by the adjective "erroneous" (*oshibochnye*): it is easier to admit error than sabotage. Zinoviev and Kamenev will later be forced into graver admissions; in the meantime, Stalin still dances his own peculiar tango — two steps forward, one step back.

After a few more revisions, counterrevisions, and further discussions of statements and counterstatements, the opposition's statement was published on October 16, 1926, a week before Trotsky and Kamenev would be expelled from the Politburo.

II

Verbal battles took uglier shapes at the Politburo meeting of September 9, 1927.[25] Trotsky, Zinoviev, and their adherents had again attempted to gain support by open criticism: the defeat of Stalin's policies in China and the carnage of Chinese communists by Chiang Kai-shek had seemed to offer their last fighting chance. At the meeting they demand that a broad discussion of their critique of the party policies (their "platform") should start three months in advance of the Fifteenth Congress. Yet the draft of the Politburo resolution, this time bearing signs of Stalin's own style, denies this request and attacks the oppositionists in a manner expected to set the tone for their demolition at the congress. The meeting serves as a prelude to Trotsky's and Zinoviev's expulsion from the Central Committee (October 1927) and from the party (November 1927).[26] The agenda of *coercion* that dominated the meetings of the previous year is now replaced by that of *suppression* and *humiliation*.

The content of the opposition's concrete criticism of party policies is again barred from the debate — references to not talking "about real business" (*po sushchestvu*) are made six times, mainly by the opposition.[27] Stalin, about to adopt a much more brutal version of the Left Opposition's policies, must first depose its leaders.

The meeting starts with a reading of the draft resolution which provides keywords for the discussion. When he takes the floor, Bukharin accuses the opposition of having "cheated," that is, of not having abided by its promise to cease factional activity (made in the statement of October 16, 1926, and reiterated at the April Plenum of 1927). Carried away, Bukharin, whose animosity towards the United Opposition is still a matter of genuine though not untroubled political disagreement, overdoes his rhetoric by introducing the motif of criminality: "Rogues always shout 'Stop the thief.'" He thus helps Stalin to revise the discourse concerning Lenin's associate Trotsky and his own former fellow triumvirs, Zinoviev and Kamenev, demoting them from the status of living legends to that of obnoxious, petty, despicable saboteurs. What used to be unthinkable — their expulsion and ultimate "liquidation" — is now gradually being made thinkable, in widening circles.[28]

One of the less dramatic yet psychologically significant changes in the tone of the two meetings is the higher frequency of references to "the party." If at the October 1926 meetings the noun "party" was used once in approximately 73 words, at the meeting of September 9, 1927, the ratio is one to about 45 words. This word applies mainly to the Communist Party of the Soviet Union; in reference to the German Communist Party the word *kompartiia* rather than *partiia* is used — except, symptomatically, in mentioning *the* expulsion of Trotsky's supporters Arcady Maslow and Ruth Fischer "from the party" (*iz partii*). Among the 442 cases of the use of this noun (not counting references to "the new party" that the opposition is accused of trying to create), in 61 cases it is modified by "our" (*nasha partiia, u nas v partii*): the ruling faction has already mentally expelled Trotsky and Zinoviev. "The party" undergoes a new kind of sanctification by a taboo on replacing the noun "party" by a third-person pronoun, especially, perhaps, since that pronoun would have been feminine. There is, of course, no problem about using the pronoun "she" in application to the opposition. By contrast, the ruling faction at times seem to savor replacing the word "party" by the first-person "we."[29] The speech of Kaganovich strictly observes this morphology though it sometimes fails in syntax:

Сейчас оппозиция срывает это решение, она вносит платформу, требует ее опубликования и начать сейчас же лихорадочную дискуссию, которая бы сбила **партию** с правильной подготовки **партии** к съезду. . . . Тов. Муралов . . . всегда упрекал **партию** в том, что **мы** якобы не освещаем жизнь **партии** перед всей **партийной** массой . . . [П]артия не хочет такой дискуссии, которую вы **партии** навязываете. . . . [К]огда это было в **нашей партии**, перед каким съездом партии, хотя бы раз за всю революцию кто в **нашей партии** выступал . . . оппозиции, которая бы выдвигала свои предложения, свою платформу, буквально по всем вопросам **партийной** практики и политики. . . . Никогда этого в **нашей партии** не было. И мне думается, что этого не потому не было, что это случайность в **нашей партии**, а потому, что это законно, нормально, единственно возможно для **нашей партии**, если мы не предполагаем, что **партия** находится накануне раскола, если не предполагать, что нужна новая платформа для построения новой партии.

Now the opposition subverts this decision, it (she) introduces a platform, demands its (her) publication and to immediately begin a feverish discussion that would divert the *party* from a correct preparation of the *party* for the Congress. . . . Comrade Muralov . . . has always reproached the *party* that *we*, as it were, do not elucidate the life of the *party* for the whole of the body of the *party*. . . . The *party* is not interested in the kind of discussion that you wish to impose on the *party*. . . . [W]hen was it in *our party*, before which congress of the *party*, at least one in the whole course of the revolution, that anyone in *our party* should speak out . . . opposition, which should present its suggestions, its platform, literally about all the issues of *party* practice and politics. . . . Never did it happen in *our party*. And I think that it did not happen not because this is accidental in *our party*, but because it is legitimate, normal, the only way possible for *our party*, if only we do not assume that *the party* is on the eve of a split, do not assume that a new platform is needed for the construction of a new *party*.

The cumulative effect of such language is to emphasize the opposition's self-alienation from Stalin's faction ("our party") — as if their expulsion would only formalize a de facto state of affairs. When Mikoyan says (twice) that "the party has grown," the implication is not that its ranks have grown numerically but that the apparatus has matured sufficiently for a psychological self-liberation from its inspirational/incendiary father figures.[30]

The resolution draft places the motif of the Trotskyites' alienation on a moral and class basis. Characterizing the opposition as "ideological-political bankrupts" and "unprincipled demagogues," it claims that, in view of its "ideological poverty," the opposition has resorted to the tactics of falsification (*podtasovyvanie*), gossip, and slander. The label "gossip" is used by Stalin as a gag when no other is at hand: when Zinoviev accuses him (correctly) of having insisted on trusting Chiang Kai-shek, Stalin counters with "It pleases you to gossip, Comrade Zinoviev." Yet the main semantic battlefields of the meeting are "falsification" and "slander."

The word *podtasovyvanie* for "falsification" derives from "to shuffle" (*tasovat'*) and implies fraudulent card play, slipping in one card instead of another. Zinoviev employs words with related meanings — *fokus* ("a card trick," or "a magician's trick"), *shtuchki* ("underhand capriciousness"), *moshennichestvo* ("petty fraud"), to suggest that his adversaries are tampering with data. One of the techniques of *podtasovyvanie* is diffusion of issues by means of half-truths. For example, the resolution draft states that only when threatened by expulsion did the opposition back down at the recent plenum: according to Zinoviev, this misrepresentation was adopted when there was no time left for his adherents to protest it. Half-truths are supplemented by rhetorical misquotations, as when the memorandum alludes to Trotsky's theory of the permanent revolution by imputing to him a theory of "a permanent 'ruin' " of the revolution.

At the meeting the ruling faction gets considerable mileage out of a tactic that will gain further momentum in Soviet official discourse — namely, the dismissal of hard facts as "not characteristic." When Zinoviev complains that members of the opposition have been deported in advance of the Congress, Yaroslavsky counters this first by denying that this is a typical procedure and then by the more inventive claim that the party often has to transfer its members from job to job — being affiliated with the opposition should not make any of them untouchable.

One of the coarser methods of falsification is kindergarten reversal: what side A says about side B is turned around by the latter and applied to side A ("you are one yourself").[31] Such reversals gift-wrap specific lexical items while modifying their meaning, so that the word is emptied of its semantic core and filled with an altered content. When the opposition accuses the ruling faction of "Bonapartism" — in the sense of the ruling minority's imposing its policies on the majority — Antipov, Bukharin, and Stalin respond in kind: it is the oppositionists who are guilty of Bonapartism. But now this word is used in the sense of a flashy rise to glory or seizure of power — as if Trotsky's recent speech at the Yaroslavl railway station had been meant to be his Toulon. Accordingly, a battle is waged over the meaning of the word *naviazat'* ("to impose, or force something on someone"), used four times by the opposition and six times by the ruling faction: after Zinoviev accuses that faction of having created the conditions under which a party secretary can impose any resolution on his organization, it accuses the opposition of imposing a useless discussion and its own plan of preparation for the congress on the majority of the Central Committee. Eventually, Antipov escalates "to force" into "to rape" (*iznasilovat'*): the opposition is accused of *violating* the party's will. Yet Stalin is, apparently, displeased with the semantics that can undermine the sense of the party's might; he therefore switches to his tested device of "unanswerable irrelevancy"[32]—a majority is, by definition, not Bonapartism:

Бонапартизм есть попытка меньшинства навязать большинству свою волю путем насилия. Кто, кроме чудаков, может утверждать, что большинство нашей партии навязывает себе самому свою же собственную волю путем насилия? Не глупо ли это? Если вообще возможна попытка бонапартизма в нашей стране, то она может исходить лишь со стороны оппозиции, так как она представляет ничтожное меньшинство и, по всей вероятности, ни одного делегата не будет иметь на партийном съезде . . .

Bonapartism is an attempt of the minority to impose its will on the majority by way of violence. Only cranks can assert that the majority in our party imposes its own will on itself by violence. Is this not stupid? If a Bonapartist attempt is possible in our country, it can only be generated by the opposition because it represents a paltry minority, and will most probably not have a single delegate at the party congress . . .

The ways in which the majority has been achieved are probably on everyone's mind but cannot be shaped into an outright accusation; the most Trotsky can do at this point is interject a sarcastic "Obviously."

A similar expropriation of the opponent's vocabulary takes place when Zinoviev objects to conducting the congress and the party conference *nakhrapom* ("with insolent high-handedness"). Turning the tables, Bukharin applies the same image-bearing word to the opposition's breaking its promise to cease factional activity.

The ruling faction is on the alert for possibilities to catch opposition spokesmen in their own verbal traps. Thus Nikolai Muralov slips into prefacing a complaint that he has been brought to this meeting under false pretenses (he had thought that the content of the "platform" would be discussed — *po sush-*

chestvu) with a spuriously apologetic "to confess frankly," which elicits Kalinin's sarcastic "How sincere you are!" But Muralov commits his most painful gaffe when he speaks about women nursing babies at party meetings, so that the babies imbibe hatred of the opposition "with mother's milk." Anastas Mikoyan reinterprets this anecdote: the party must be proud of the politically active working women who have no one to leave their babies with and so bring them along to meetings. It does not help Muralov to explain that the woman in question was the wife of a professor of the Agriculture Academy (who, implicitly, could afford help); at the end of the meeting he tries a different tack: what one needs is not such pro forma readings of conference transcripts, disturbed by babies' crying, but genuine discussions. By this point, however, Muralov has lost the hermeneutic contest over the image that he himself tossed into the fray.

A reinterpretation is particularly successful if it turns a serious matter, such as deliberate disruptions of party cell meetings, into a joke — no one dares or has the energy to protest against Stalin's and his coterie's contemptuous misuse of comic relief:

Антипов: Один ленинградский оппозиционер (Левин) бросил мне реплику ... что в Мариинском театре ... большинство сорвало собрание тем, что потушили свет. ... я тогда этому оппозиционеру ответил, что, вероятно, у него просто в глазах потемнело от того, что собрали на таком собрании только 5 голосов.
Бухарин: Это на том же собрании. (*Смех*).
Антипов: Я говорю, что у них в глазах потемнело, потому что они собрали только 5 подписей.
Сталин: Это при свете они столько собрали?
Антипов: Да, именно при свете собрали. Мы ушли с тов. Бухариным последними, никакого света не было потушено.

Antipov: One Leningrad oppositionist (Levin) threw a remark at me . . . that at the Maryinsky theater the majority disrupted the meeting by switching off the light. . . . I then replied to the oppositionist that his eyesight must have failed him because they collected only 5 votes at such a meeting.
Bukharin: Indeed, at that same meeting. (Laughter).
Antipov: I am saying that their eyesight must have failed them because they collected only 5 signatures.
Stalin: And did they collect that many while the lights were on?
Antipov: Yes, exactly, while the lights were on. Comrade Bukharin and I were the last to leave; the lights had not been turned off.

The touches of *Schadenfreude* in this banter are reminiscent of the episodic camaraderie among Hitler's SS, whose derisive cruelty to their helpless victims escalated in a process of group dynamics which also served psychological consolidation.[33] A year later and, in particular, eleven years later, Bukharin would be on the wrong side of such camaraderie.

Kindergarten reversals go ad hominem. The resolution draft charges the oppositionists with slander; Zinoviev counters that the opposition has itself been slandered, calling the draft *skloka* ("malicious squabble") and studding his speech with terms like "fairy tale" and "hypocrisy." Much of the meeting passes in such accusations and counteraccusations: the word "slander" and its derivatives are used 25 times.

Recriminations are exchanged concerning current or recent jobs: Is Rudzutak a poor administrator? Does the oppositionist Safarov perform poorly in his post? Is Zinoviev taking too many rest-cure absences? Such discourse descends from the empyrean heights of party discipline to what Rudzutak calls the level of "a kitchen anecdote." The barbs coming from Stalin's side are particularly venomous: this is no longer about attempts to discredit adversaries; it is about settling scores.

The easiest target is Zinoviev. His erstwhile fiery rhetoric, known to produce an almost demoniac and doubtlessly enviable effect on large audiences, was reduced to farcical failure already at the Fifteenth Conference in 1926; his jack-in-the-box resilience was irritating; his erratic zigzags were well on the way to earn him disrespect.[34] In October 1926 Zinoviev jotted down notes for a speech,[35] which he actually uses a year later, on September 9, 1927. By now his assessment of the situation is outdated, but the verbal play (*klevetat'*— *oklevetat'*) is probably judged too good to dispense with:

Самое плохое, что вы хотите с нами сделать, это попытаться оклеветать нас, а этого-то вам и не удастся сдалать. **Клеветать** на нас еще можно, но **оклеветать** нас уже нельзя.[36] Рабочие знают уже, чего, мы хотим. И даже значительная часть рабочих за границей знает уже об этом.	The worst that you want to do to us is to attempt to slanderously discredit us, and this you will not manage to do. You can still *slander* us, but you can no longer *discredit* us. The workers know what we want. And even a considerable part of workers abroad knows it.

His 1926 notes, which include a reminder to demand that the meetings be stenographed (a bid for a wider audience), show Zinoviev's awareness that Stalin may do other "bad things" — "expulsion, arrest, physical violence." In 1927 his claim that it is impossible to discredit the opposition is made while the discrediting is snowballing full speed. Stalin will call his bluff later; at present, his rhetoric is maliciously punctured by Uglanov: "A coward, and pretends to be a courageous man." Several years previously Zinoviev had removed Uglanov from the Leningrad party apparatus, kicking him upstairs; now the day of reckoning with the former benefactor has arrived. Uglanov, the only one of those present to sink at times to low colloquial style ("you've failed, and now you're trying to sell us a bill of goods," he says to Muralov), will be arrested as part of the "Right Deviation" in 1932, released, rearrested, and finally killed in 1937 without being brought to a show trial.

In the meantime, Rudzutak, the chairman of the meeting, does not call Uglanov to order. On the part of Stalin and his yes-men invective is deliberate. The tone has been set by the resolution draft which claims, among other things, that the opposition leaders are conceited defeatist intellectuals (*intelligenty*) unconnected with the life of the masses — by implication, because of their class roots. The epithets that modify "intellectuals" range from stigma to insult: "self-alienated (*otorvavshiesia*) from the party/from the proletariat/from life/from the Comintern," "whimpering," "frightened by difficulties," "disoriented," "backward-looking," "blinded by factionalism," etc. The idea of freedom of discussion is reduced to love of palaver; arbitrary rule is elevated to the status of real creative work. At the beginning of the meeting Molotov refuses, as it were, to disrupt the established order of the preparation for the Congress at the "whim" (*po prikhoti*) of fickle prima donnas; for the sake of their "windbag platform," adds Kaganovich. The opposition's arguments are further qualified as garishly clamorous (*kriklivye*); the tag used for their statements is not "say" but the less dignified "scream" (*krichat'*).

Sweeping under the carpet the fact that Trotsky and Zinoviev have been ousted from their most important positions, Uglanov harps on their idleness — these are irresponsible flâneurs with too much time on their hands:

. . . свободные безработные люди, как тт. Зиновьев, Троцкий и другие, которые шляются свободно и ничечо не делают. Мы отвечаем за дело, мы не безответственная оппозиция, мы отвечаем перед партией, перед государством за работу и т.д., а потому и сроки ограничены. Мы не хотим уподобиться вашей роли ничеяо не делающих, шляющихся из конца в конец, а нам нужно в начале хозяйственного года намеченную партией хозяйственную политику	. . . free nonworking people like Zinoviev, Trotsky, and the others, who loaf about at leisure and don't do anything. We are responsible for getting the job done, we are not an irresponsible opposition, we are accountable to the party, to the state for the work, and so on, and therefore our timelines are limited. We do not wish to become like you in your role of idlers who loaf up and down; at the beginning of the economic year we have to implement in practice the economic

практически проводить. Вы ничего не делаете, вы можете заниматься чесанием языков, мы занимаемся делом и на эту удочку не поддадимся.

policy delineated by the party. You are not doing anything, you can employ yourselves in tongue-wagging; we are doing the real work and will not swallow this bait.

They want, says Uglanov, an ample dressing gown and soft shoes, which we are not going to give them. Stalin picks up the motif of the opposition's idleness with a consciously vulgar sarcasm: he turns its criticism into "fantasy," its platform into "brochure," and the debates with it into "a little squabble":

Может быть, для оппозиции положительная работа представляет излишнюю роскошь, но мы не можем так смотреть на творческую работу партии. Мы не можем далее создавать вредную иллюзию, что партия превратилась у нас в дискуссионный клуб, что партия неустойчива и т.д. . . . . А то, **извольте радоваться**, пришла **фантазия** оппозиционерам написать большую **брошюру**, отвечай обязательно на эту **брошюру**, чтобы вся эта **драчка** стала достоянием заграницы и чтобы это создало впечатление слабости в нашей стране.

Perhaps for the opposition positive work is a superfluous luxury, but we cannot regard the creative work of the party in that light. We cannot continue to create the harmful illusion that our party has turned into a discussion club, that the party is unstable, etc. . . . And then, *may it please you*, the oppositionists got the *fantasy* to write a thick *brochure*, and we are demanded to answer this *brochure*, so that all this *little squabble* might become accessible abroad and create the impression of weakness in our country.

Thus Zinoviev and Trotsky have been transformed from useless to downright harmful figures. Their interference with "real work" is also persistently dwelled on by Rykov and Tomsky in their roles of hardworking proletarian administrators. When interrupted by Trotsky, Rudzutak lowers the stylistic register of the meeting's discourse by — symptomatically — calling him a fool (it takes brains to be a real fool): no one dares to voice a doubt about the intelligence of, for instance, Kalinin, whose blunders sometimes provoke laughter; by contrast, in respect to Trotsky, Zinoviev, and Muralov, this is already an open season:

Троцкий: Да разве я могу опровергать всю клевету против меня? Где? Каким путем? Издадим всю переписку с Лениным, она у меня подобрана.
Сталин: Я вам не мешал, не мешайте и мне.

Trotsky: How can I deny all the slander against me? Where? By what means? Let us publish all my correspondence with Lenin; I have it prepared.
Stalin: I did not disturb you, do not disturb me.

Троцкий: Вы всегда имеете предзаключительное слово.	*Trotsky.* You always take the penultimate word.
Сталин: Вы говорите неправду, потому что вы жалкий трус, боящийся правды.	*Stalin:* You are telling untruths, because you are a pathetic coward, afraid of the truth.
Троцкий: Вы ставите себя в смешное положение.	*Trotsky:* You are putting yourself in a ridiculous position.
Муралов: Это ложь, спросите Красную армию.	*Muralov:* This is a lie — ask the Red Army.
Сталин: Подождите, тов. Муралов, получите и вы ответ. Я знаю всю вашу душу.	*Stalin:* Wait, comrade Muralov, you will get your answer too. I know your whole soul.
Муралов: Какую душу?	*Muralov:* What soul?
Сталин: Фарисейскую.	*Stalin:* That of a Pharisee.

Muralov, a larger-than-life hero of the Civil War, is thus verbally ground to dust — using "Pharisee" for "hypocrite," the former seminarist Stalin claims insight into his "soul," as if all his previous achievements were just a matter of appearances.

At times the attacks on the opposition take on anti-Semitic overtones. In view of the internationalist claims of the Communist Party, overt anti-Semitism is still inadmissible; indeed the remarks in question are sufficiently ambiguous for the speakers to deny anti-Semitic purport if reproached. Uglanov, for instance, repeatedly uses *ne ierikhontes'* (for "you are making much noise") — a reference to the walls of Jericho falling from the clangor of the Israelites' trumpets but possibly also to the vulgar idiom describing a large (Jewish?) nose which is "like a trumpet of Jericho." Molotov interjects that Trotsky's methods of struggle befit a person from a "provincial township" (*meshchanskogo gorodka*), though Trotsky had actually come from a farmstead rather than from a *shtetl*. The opposition leaders are accused of wishing to look like a bunch of Messiahs. When his speech is interrupted by Trotsky's hint at his non-Bolshevik past, the obnoxious Yaroslavsky, himself a Jew and one who, not noticing a change in the wind, had been writing panegyrics on Trotsky up to 1923, strikes back by equivocally invoking the latter's "Menshevik breed." Zinoviev cannot make an open charge of anti-Semitism but he has sensed it and implies as much when on two occasions he characterizes the baiting of the opposition as *chernosotennaia travlia*, alluding to the anti-Semitic hoodlum violence of the Black Hundreds.

Trotsky's being mocked as a would-be prophet ("He is always predicting") at one point combines with the presentation of the opposition's criticism of the party as a self-fulfilling prophesy. Things are not as bad as you say, claims Enukidze; you want it all to be (or look) that bad, he resumes, so that you can come as knights on a white horse and fix it . . .[37] But the party does not need being rescued by you:

На все это партия вам ответит, что **без вас** она прекрасно понимает, как обстоит дело во всех областях, перечисленных вами, **без вас** вся партия и ее руководящие органы верят, что несмотря на многие трудности и недочеты, дело наше безусловно поправимое и прочное, и все трудности будут устранены **без вас**, сколько бы вы не **мешали**.	To all this the party will answer that *without you* it perfectly understands the state of affairs in all spheres, *without you* the party and its guiding institutions believe that despite many difficulties and oversights our enterprise is doubtlessly remediable and stable, and all the difficulties will be removed *without you*, no matter how much *you interfere*.

In this utterance, the repetition of "without you," its meaning varying from "without your telling us," through "except for you," to "without your help," combined with an insinuation of sabotage, paves the psychological way for repressions against the oppositionists. Enukidze does not realize that such invective, vapid and floating, can just as well be applied, if need be, to himself. Likewise naïvely, he admits "difficulties and oversights," and the need for remedies. He makes the additional mistake of quoting the opposition's critical remarks at great length: in Stalin's mental ledger these items are no doubt accumulating to Enukidze's debit.[38] Meantime, Enukidze continues the trend of subverting the opposition leaders' towering stature; he represents them as expendable—and worse. Like Bukharin and other future spokesmen of the "Right Deviation," he does not realize that a precedent is being set: if one living legend can be thus demoted, why not another?

Gradually, the metaphors used by the "ruling collective" become more violent. Uglanov, for instance, talks about "a Menshevik cock with a bloody mug." The quiet Molotov, whose long-distance sadism will eventually appear in his scribbling on the lists of the accused, interjects the ominous "There'll be worse." Uglanov picks up the cue and promises the opposition an additional thrashing: "Yes, there'll be worse, we'll try to add, so that they slap you more strongly." Response to opposition is described in terms of hitting (*potrepliut*) or spanking (*nashlepaiut*); and Stalin mentions that at present it is the opposition whom "Lenin's testament" is "killing."

As Trotsky has predicted, Stalin takes the floor as the penultimate speaker, aiming at an escalation. At a key moment of his speech, he uses the strongest and most insulting language of all. He does so in response to Trotsky's references to his Civil War record: throughout the public discourse of the period, the ad hominem parts of reciprocal accusations pertained to the biographical past of the participants—who had joined the party when and who opposed Lenin's policies on what occasions. Much is said at the meeting that would suffice for depositions against those present soon after 1934. Passions are allowed to explode on the question who was transferred from place to place, owing to incompetence, during the Civil War—Stalin, as Trotsky recalls, or Trotsky himself, in accordance with Stalin's revision of the conduct of the creator of the Red Army. Stalin may really be angered by Trotsky's bringing up the Civil War (the victory in it being at the time undoubtedly credited to the latter) but it seems more likely that he has been biding his time for a chance to unleash a contemptuous verbal fury that must not look unprovoked.

Сталин: жалкий вы человек, лишенный элементарного чувства правды, трус и банкрот, нахал и наглец, позволяющий себе говорить вещи, совершенно не соответствующие действительности. Вот вам мой ответ.

Троцкий: Вот он весь: груб и нелоялен. [Кто это: "вождь" или лошадиный барышник].

Сталин: В отношении Троцкого никогда у меня лояльности не будет, ибо[39] он не лоялен к партии.

Троцкий: Ленин говорил не о *вашем отношении ко мне*, он вообще вашу душу определил, *взвесил вас на ладони и сказал, груб и нелоялен.*

Сталин: жалкий вы человек, трус, нахал и наглец, чего вам никогда не простят рабочие.

Троцкий: Бессилие ваше обнаруживает ругань ваша.

Сталин: На вашу ругань вам отвечаю руганью, которую вы заслужили, чтобы вы знали свое место в партии и чтобы вам было известно, что рабочие потреплют вас за такие вещи.

Stalin: You are a pathetic person, deprived of an elementary sense of truth, a coward and a bankrupt, impudent and brazen; you allow yourself to say things that have no correspondence with reality. That's my reply to you.

Trotsky: That's how he is: rude and disloyal. [What is he: a "leader" or a horse dealer].

Stalin. In relation to Trotsky I shall never be loyal for he is not loyal to the party.

Trotsky: Lenin *spoke not of your relation to me*, he defined your soul in general, *weighted you on his palm and said, rude and disloyal.*

Stalin: You are a pathetic person, a coward, impudent and brazen, which the workers will never forgive you.

Trotsky: Your abuse reveals your impotence.

Stalin: I reply with abuse to your abuse; you have earned this, so that you should know your place in the party, and know that that the workers will thrash you for such things.

The history of kindergarten reversals is here difficult to trace. In exile, Trotsky would write about Krupskaya's having reported to him Lenin's words about

Stalin's "lack of elementary honesty."[40] Whether echoes of that opinion had also reached Stalin, his remark that the "pathetic" Trotsky lacks "an elementary sense of truth" is a springboard for a tautological and self-contradictory torrent of insults: coward, bankrupt, brazen insolent man — the language of the earlier speakers must have struck Stalin as still too inhibited for the present purposes. The best that Trotsky can do in the ensuing exchange of one-liners is use his favorite formulaic allusion ("rude and disloyal") to Lenin's "Letter to the Congress," as well as a horse-trader metaphor (which is later removed from the transcript, possibly as an ethnic slur); Stalin retorts with a kindergarten reversal and with further browbeating which Trotsky cannot match. Challenging a fellow communist to a duel is out of the question, and what intellectuals like Trotsky and Zinoviev do not understand is that the spirit of the Politburo has already been infected by the principles of the criminal underground: unless one strikes out against an imputation immediately and with all one's might, the imputation begins to stick, and no later denials can be sufficiently effective. True, when the meeting is about to be concluded, the participants are given the floor for brief "personal" issues — which is when Trotsky, Muralov, and Zinoviev attempt — too little, too late — to parry some of the slander. In the meantime Trotsky responds to Stalin's vituperation by a characteristically generous gesture: when Stalin's time runs out, he offers to give him another five minutes (or perhaps enough rope). Stalin makes use of the extra time to lower the pitch and return from ad hominem to ad hoc matters, but he also inserts the motif of "madness," or rather "rabies" into the witch's brew: "the platform of the opposition is the platform of a complete ideological and political bankruptcy of rabid (*vzbesiv-shikhsia*) petit-bourgeois intellectuals." This word choice might remind the hearers that gods first make mad those whom they wish to destroy, but the sheer valence of *vzbesivshikhsia* anticipates (and in a sense prepares) the future references to the accused at show trials as mad dogs, making their execution almost a logical necessity. Where verbal abuse begins physical abuse is likely to follow.

The last to take the floor is Yaroslavsky. Few are likely to be listening to his prepared speech by now. The tension is allowed to subside, and towards the end, as usual, Stalin asks for minor editorial emendations to the draft of the resolution. In October Trotsky and Zinoviev will be expelled from the Central Committee; and on November 12 they will be expelled from the party. A month later the Fifteenth Party Congress will call for a Five Year Plan and adopt a decision about the creation of collective farms, thus beginning to act on a version of the policies of Stalin's ousted rivals.[41] Worse would, indeed, follow.

Thus, whereas at the meetings of October 1926 Stalin's role was mainly that of a scorekeeping observer, at the meeting of September 9, 1927, a time when, as he hinted to Muralov, he had completed his study of the "souls" of his entourage, his role largely turned into that of a conscious performer who set the tone for about forty people present (members and candidate members of the Politburo and of the Central Committee, members of the Presidium of the Central Control Commission, secretaries, and stenographers), some of whom could be fully expected to further disseminate the new style of reference to the heroes of the recent past. Things that had seemed unthinkable three or four years before were, with a little histrionic help, becoming thinkable. One may wonder whether Stalin resented those for whose edification he was putting on the show. Indeed, no such exertions were needed in an entourage made up entirely of his own people such as Molotov, Voroshilov, Mikoyan, and Kaganovich: tyrants tend to develop a taste for being obeyed at a single word to the wise.

By contrast to the meetings of October 1926, during which Stalin's faction sought — for the most part successfully — to force the opposition to sign a self-disgracing document, the meeting of September 9, 1927 seemed to end almost where it began — its conclusion predetermined, its resolution-draft accepted with Stalin's microscopic emendations. And yet that meeting was not just a matter of going through the motions of debate; it was also a stage in and a signal for a shift in the discourse relating to Trotsky and his supporters. Though Stalin represented the political discussion demanded by the oppositionists as a harmful waste of time, he turned the still necessary evil of a metapolitical arguing session to a definite though not quantifiable advantage.

Notes

I thank Dimitry Segal and Tzachi Zamir for useful consultations. I am grateful to H. M. Daleski and Zephyra Porat for constructive criticism of drafts of this paper.

1. Indeed, four months later Trotsky, passively resisting his exile to Alma Ata, was physically carried downstairs from a Moscow apartment and taken to the railway. His aids were subjected to much worse mistreatment even at this point, ten years before most of his supporters lost their lives.

2. Lenin, "Letter to the Congress," pp. 345, 346.

3. See Rogovin, *A byla li alternativa? "Trotskizm": Vzgliad cherez gody,* pp. 171–74.

4. Nabokov, *Pnin,* p. 35.

5. Deutscher, *The Prophet Unarmed: Trotsky, 1921–1929,* p. 123.

6. According to Boris Bazhanov, even when votes in local cells went in favor of the opposition, Stalin's man in *Pravda* arranged "accidental" reversals in the reports of the ballot count; see Bazhanov, *Vospominaniia byvshego sekretaria Stalina,* p. 63.

7. Zinoviev had been expelled from the Politburo in July 1926 as the authority behind the attempts made by Deputy Defense Commissar Lashevich to spread the platform of

the opposition in the army. He was summoned to the meetings that started on October 4, but October 7 found him in Leningrad, breaking the injunction against "factional activity" by addressing the workers of the Putilov factory. Cynically mocked in absentia for missing the Politburo meeting on October 8 under the pretext of his father's illness, he attended the meeting of October 11.

8. See Deutscher, *The Prophet Unarmed: Trotsky, 1921–1929*, p. 138.

9. *Trinadtsatyi s"ezd RKP(b): Stenograficheskii otchet*, pp. 236–37.

10. This issue created an aporia in the motivations of the opposition: "the logic of the situation drove the opposition into the role of a separate party. Every step . . . in that direction filled its leaders with remorse and horror. Every such step was retracted and recanted, only to be followed by another that was again to be regretted and retraced. Such an attitude appeared as insincere and dishonest in the eyes of most Bolsheviks; and it could not but dishearten the adherents of the opposition." Deutscher, *Stalin: A Political Biography*, p. 308.

11. In his triumphant October 13 letter to Ordzhonikidze (RGASPI Fond 74, op. 1, del. 98), Molotov exults in having forced the opposition to sign "a little document" which will keep them "covered with shit by their own exertions" for two or three years.

12. RGASPI Fond 17, op. 163, del. 700.

13. Here and throughout, unless otherwise noted, the boldface is added by the author. Except for speakers' names in dialogue, italic passages indicate material added by the speakers in revising the stenograms.

14. "Deixis" is a complex of linguistic markers of the situation within which an utterance is made — in particular, its personal, temporal, or spatial aspects, indicated by pronouns (*I/ you, this/that*) or adverbial modifiers (*here/there; now/yesterday*). The construction "that which" is deictic in so far as it points to an issue of common knowledge under the current circumstances.

15. The "final solution" of Sokol'nikov's (Hirsch Brilliant's) own case was his murder by prison cell-mates at the instigation of the NKVD in 1939.

16. "Когда по России ее разнесли, она разъяснила **так, что** хуже стало, ухудшила **то, что** она сказала." With an eye to history, someone, probably Stalin, eventually edited out this sentence from the transcript.

17. The German calque "целиком и полностью" ("ganz und voll") was a widespread postrevolutionary neologism; see Selishchev, *Iazyk revoliutsionnoi epokhi: Iz nabliudenii nad russkim iazykom poslednikh let 1917–1926*, p. 38.

18. Conquest, *The Great Terror: A Reassessment*, p. 12.

19. Vaiskopf, *Pisatel' Stalin*, pp. 98–106.

20. Halfin, *Terror in My Soul: Communist Autobiographies on Trial*, p. 7.

21. Bazhanov, *Vospominaniia byvshego sekretaria Stalina*, pp. 96–98, claims that Stalin's aide Tovstukha was, since at least the Thirteenth Congress, with the help of a graphologist compiling lists of voters who had struck Stalin off the list of the candidates for the Central Committee and substituted another name instead.

22. See Naidich, *Sled na peske: Ocherki o russkom iazykovom uzuse*, p. 50.

23. Apparently, Voroshilov's IQ was significantly lower than that of his fellow grandees. On this, see Montefiore, *Stalin: The Court of the Red Tsar*, p. 54.

24. Kamenev does not deserve this compliment, no matter how left-handed. On an

earlier occasion he slipped into offering a "truce" rather than "peace," which was seized upon by Uglanov and others. On the way in which Stalin "made a meal" of Kamenev's other stylistic slip — "nepman Russia" instead of "NEP Russia" see Service, *Stalin: A Biography*, p. 228.

25. RGASPI Fond 17, op. 163, del. 705.

26. Kamenev is meantime serving as an ambassador to Mussolini's Italy. Soon, on his return, he will have a fatal secret consultation with Bukharin (July 11, 1928).

27. Broad debate has already been preempted by what Zinoviev calls "the calendar trick": in accordance with the resolutions of the Tenth Congress, the theses for the Congress must be published "*no later* than a month" before the Congress (scheduled for November). But the demand that they be first presented to the plenum of the Central Committee (scheduled for October 20, 1927) meant that they could not be published much *earlier*. Hence, the countertheses of the opposition also had to wait until shortly before the Congress.

28. The possibility of harsh reprisals against Trotsky had been suggested by Zinoviev while still a member of the triumvirate; at the time (December 1924), Stalin made a public statement that this was "inconceivable"; see Deutscher, *Stalin: A Political Biography*, p. 297. At the Politburo meeting of October 11, 1926, expelling the opposition leaders from the party was referred to as unnecessary ("до поры, до времени" ['so far"] interjected Voroshilov) — what was inconceivable to some was already an option for others.

29. On Stalin's hybrids of *l'état c'est moi* and the *pluralis majestatis*, see Vaiskopf, *Pisatel' Stalin*, pp. 69–75.

30. Cf. Trotsky on the spirit of burgher complacency established in the ruling circles in 1923–24, "the self-liberation of a philistine in the Bolshevik," *Moia zhizn': Opyt biografii*, vol. 2, p. 245. The "family romance" of the Russian Revolution still remains to be written; on Trotsky's own case see Weisskopf (Vaiskopf), "Leon Trotsky's Family Romance."

31. With Stalin's added hyperbolization of the charges to stun his audiences, this will develop into what Trotsky will call "the Stalin reflex"; see Trotskii, *Portrety revoliutsionerov*, p. 63.

32. Ulam, *Stalin: The Man and His Era*, p. 227.

33. Cf. Sofsky, *The Order of Terror: The Concentration Camp*, pp. 103–4.

34. In his 1926 letters to Molotov Stalin first still refers to Zinoviev by the diminutive "Grisha," then goes over to "Grigory," and then to his last name; see Kosheleva, Lel'chuk, Naumov, Naumov, Rogovaia, and Khlevniuk. *Pis'ma I. V. Stalina V. M. Molotovu, 1925–1936 gg.: Sbornik dokumentov*, pp. 55, 62, 80, and 90. At the Politburo meeting no first names are used, but the adversaries are still addressed with the honorific "Comrade" before their names.

35. RGASPI Fond 324, op. 2, del. 26.

36. Boldface in the transcript.

37. Robert C. Tucker notes that the "Bolshevik political community felt no need of a savior-leader in the mid-twenties because it was not, basically, in a state of distress"; see *Stalin as Revolutionary 1879–1929: A Study in History and Personality*, p. 393. Stalin, however, kept using the threat of foreign intervention as a rhetorical ploy, while Trotsky was genuinely concerned about the bureaucratic degeneration of revolutionary forces.

38. This is not to deny the likelihood of more personal reasons for Enukidze's execution in 1938; see Ilizarov, *Tainaia zhizn' Stalina: Po materialam ego biblioteki i arkhiva*, pp. 336–49.

39. The use of the word *ibo* (of Church-Slavonic origin and bureaucratic currency), approximately equivalent to "for" used instead of "because," had spread in post-revolutionary language. "These days there is no Soviet official without *ibo*," Selishchev, *Iazyk revoliutsionnoi epokhi: Iz nabliudenii nad russkim iazykom poslednikh let 1917–1926*, p. 61.

40. Trotskii, *Portrety revoliutsionerov*, p. 90.

41. If before 1921 party discipline meant that the minority would cooperate in implementing the decisions taken by the majority without losing its status in the party, and if later the exponents of the minority opinions would be set aside, in 1927 the people set aside are the ones whose ideas would be taken over by the faction that cast them out.

9

The Short Course of the History of the All-Union Communist Party: *The Distorted Mirror of Party Propaganda*

RUSTEM NUREEV

The Politburo sessions of October 11 and 12, 1938, which were devoted to the publication of the *Short Course of the History of the All-Union Communist Party (Bolsheviks),* took place at a time when the official end of the Great Terror lay one month ahead. The party had already been purged from top to bottom as a new and younger party leadership replaced the Old Bolsheviks who had perished in the purges. The *Short Course* was written by and approved by a committee of the Central Committee, but Stalin was its principal author. Between 1938 and 1953, over 42 million copies of the *Short Course* were issued, in 301 printings and 67 languages. The *Short Course* was regarded throughout the communist world as the most authoritative source on Soviet Marxism until de-Stalinization began in 1956.

This essay addresses Stalin's revision of party history after the Great Terror of the 1930s, his intended goals and implementation plans, and his reorientation of propaganda towards the Soviet intelligentsia. We show how a new "party history" was born along with a "renewed" party that reemerged after the Great Terror, and how Stalin used depersonalized history to blot out the memory of other Old Bolsheviks as a convenient foundation for his own "cult of personality." We also discuss the strengths and weaknesses of party propaganda, where demands for total submission of the individual to the state coincided with the growing alienation of the population from official ideology.

The session of the Politburo on October 11 and 12, 1938 was called "On the Question of Party Propaganda in the Press Associated with the Publication of the *Short Course of the History of the All-Union Communist Party*."[1] The main report was presented by Andrei Zhdanov, soon to be promoted to full membership in the Politburo and already Stalin's main advisor on propaganda and cultural matters. Zhdanov's report was followed by lengthy discussion that included nineteen invited representatives of Regional Party Committees from various cities in Russia, Ukraine, and Belorussia.

The invited participants must have been overwhelmed by the "honor" of a personal meeting with Stalin. Most were in charge of local propaganda, such as the Gorky representative, a Comrade Troshin, who bravely responded to Molotov's call for comments on Zhdanov's presentation:

> MOLOTOV: Comrade Troshin has the floor.
> TROSHIN: Comrade Zhdanov in his report . . .
> STALIN [interrupting]: Excuse me, where do you work?
> TROSHIN: In Gorky province, Comrade Stalin.
> MOLOTOV: Propaganda work?
> TROSHIN: Yes, I am head of the party propaganda department of the Gorky Party Committee.

The tone of these invited officials was deferential to Stalin, and most of the discussion was in the form of exchanges between Stalin and attending local party officials. There were also prepared remarks by Stalin that were separately included.

Given the almost complete turnover of regional party officials as a result of the purges, most local officials were new appointees or relatively new to the job. A Comrade Antropov from the Orel Party Committee, who headed a propaganda department of forty, reported to Stalin that "if you take the case of editors, then we have 99 percent new cadres."

The Great Terror had not yet been officially halted; so we can imagine that the local party officials approached this meeting with Stalin with considerable trepidation. Attendees treated Stalin as an oracle, peppered him with questions about how to teach the *Short Course*, and heaped flattery on him, such as a Comrade Khomenko, department head of party propaganda, Kiev: "The Short Course is one of the greatest events in the intellectual life of our party, directing our party and primarily the party activists and the nonparty intelligentsia to a still higher intellectual-theoretical level based on the intensive study of the works of Marx, Engels, Lenin, and Stalin."

Politburo sessions were rarely devoted to a single issue, even one of primary importance. The selection of the *Short Course* for discussion, as well as the choice of time, place, and participants, was neither arbitrary nor random. In fact, formal Politburo meetings had become a rarity during the Great Terror. Although the Politburo continued to issue decrees, decisions were made by Stalin himself or by appointed subcommittees, and Politburo members perfunctorily voted by phone or in writing.

Stalin must have regarded the publication of the *Short Course* of sufficient import to call a formal meeting of the Politburo. The presence of invited middle-level party officials was also exceptional. Historically, only top party leaders from the Central Committee or presidium members of control commissions were invited.

This Politburo session on the *Short Course* raises a number of questions, which this essay seeks to answer: What was Stalin's primary message to the party? Why was this revision of "party history" undertaken in the second half of 1930s? Who were the targeted readers of the *Short Course?* What was the plan of action to inculcate workers, peasants, and the intelligentsia with an understanding of this new party history? Can we learn something of value about the state of affairs inside the country and inside the party through the "distorted mirror" of party propaganda?

Why a New Party History?

Although Stalin had expelled his major opponents from the political arena by the end of the 1920s, their physical extermination took place in the period 1936 through the beginning of 1938. In the first show trial, which took place in Moscow August 19–24, 1936, Grigory Zinoviev, Lev Kamenev, and fourteen other purported members of the "Left Opposition" were sentenced to capital punishment. M. N. Riutin,[2] who earlier had had the audacity to challenge Stalin's growing power, and his allies were shot on January 10, 1937. They were followed on January 23–30 by the show trial of the "Parallel Anti-Soviet Trotsky Center," in which Grigory Piatakov, Grigory Sokol'nikov, K. B. Radek, and L. P. Serebriannikov were executed. June 11, 1937 was marked by the executions of M. N. Tukhachevsky, I. P. Uborevich, I. E. Yakir, V. M. Primakov, A. I. Egorov, Y. K. Berzin, and other leading Red Army commanders. Stalin's final blow was directed against the "Rightist-Trotsky Coalition" in the show trial of March 2–13, 1938, which produced the death sentences of Nikolai Bukharin, Aleksei Rykov, N. N. Krestinsky, and eighteen other alleged participants.

Stalin's purges left behind few key players from the October 1917 events and the unfolding history of Bolshevik rule thereafter.[3] The slate was clean for a new history of Soviet communism that could not only justify earlier mistakes committed by the Soviet leadership (Stalin and the Politburo) but also show the wisdom and inevitability of their policies. A "renewed party" should receive a "new history," or as Stalin remarked near the end of the session: "As Jesus said: Do not pour new wine into old wineskins."

The publication of the *Short Course* was feted as a major event in Soviet history. The fanfare was considerable: a publication run of twelve million was ordered along with two million copies in non-Russian languages and more than a half-million copies in foreign languages.[4]

The *Short Course* was to give the Soviet Union a new history and therefore its contents had to be disseminated properly. The Politburo was the highest authority on Soviet ideology and propaganda. It was therefore only fitting that the *Short Course*'s launch should be in a session of the Politburo, the highest authority on ideology and propaganda. The message of the *Short Course* ultimately had to be imparted to the masses by those responsible for propaganda within the party, and wide dissemination required a grassroots effort. The *Short Course* would have to be taught to the intended audience by the same midlevel propaganda operatives invited as special guests to the October 1938 Politburo session.

What Was New in the Short Course?

How did the *Short Course* change Soviet ideology? Stalin's primary goal was to rewrite the history of the revolution, diminishing the true roles of other Old Bolsheviks and exaggerating his own, and to introduce new aspects of party history that would serve his interests.

The elevation of Stalin was achieved by the replacement of the theory of Leninism with the theory of "Marx-Engels-Lenin-Stalin." If prior to the publication of the *Short Course* primarily Lenin's writings were studied, now the role of Marx and Engels was raised significantly, while the main focus of attention was shifted to Stalin, portrayed as a chief creator of party history. The analogy was drawn consistently between Marx and Engels on the one hand, and Lenin and Stalin, on the other. As Engels remained the closest ally of Marx and purveyor of Marx's legacy after his death, so the only possible and legitimate heir to Lenin was Stalin. All others had ostensibly betrayed Lenin's doctrine and deserved to be obliterated from the official history of the party.

Stalin's rewriting of party history aimed at its depersonalization, erasing from it all revolutionaries except Lenin and Stalin. The *Short Course* became an instrument of social engineering and construction of new mentality.[5] The *Short Course* shifts the accent from historical protagonists to abstractions. Responding to the criticism of depersonalization, Stalin in his remarks notes:

"Some say, there is little about individuals in the *Short Course*. Well, we prefer a different approach in our work. . . . A history focused on 'great personalities' teaches our cadres little or nothing at all; history should focus on great ideas."

A depersonalized history that excluded all but the "greats" (Marx, Engels, Lenin, Stalin), with only one conveniently among the living, laid the groundwork for an extreme personality cult, reminiscent of those under oriental despotism. It was this personality cult that Khrushchev sought to dismantle with his secret speech of February 1956.

The Audience

Who was the intended audience of the *Short Course?* Who were the millions of readers to be? In the first decade of Soviet power, the pool of educated citizens was small, but with improving education, an increasing number of citizens were capable of critical appraisal. Although the *Short Course* was also meant for workers and peasants (who might have to be taught by party propagandists), it was directed primarily to the emerging Soviet intelligentsia as the Politburo discussion would show.

Andrei Zhdanov, in his opening remarks, described the *Short Course* as "the basic guide for our cadres in their understanding of Bolshevism, although as Comrade Stalin correctly noted, it can be used in shortened form for unprepared cadres, and it can be used in its entirety for the midlevel of our party." Zhdanov further stressed that "the *Short Course* is targeted primarily at our leading officials, at our Soviet intelligentsia."

In his own remarks, Stalin made the same point: "For whom is this book? It is for the cadres, for our cadres. And what are cadres — they are the command staff, the lower, middle, and higher command staff of the entire state apparatus." If previously, propaganda was targeted primarily at the proletariat, Stalin proclaimed, "from now on our propaganda should address our intellectual cadres."

Increasing bureaucratization combined with a new generation of state and party officials made necessary, as Stalin put it, the task of the "Bolshevization" of administrative workers. Stalin also placed special emphasis on "ideological work" with the rapidly growing student population, the reservoir of future administrative personnel. Publication of the *Short Course,* as the official "civic history" of the Soviet Communist Party, was yet another step in the preparation of qualified intellectual workers.

Stalin's famous motto "cadres decide all" suggests that peasants and the proletariat require strong leadership from an effective bureaucratic apparatus. That state apparatus, however, must be politically loyal. In a mild form of self-criticism, Stalin expressed regret about the loss of some "unreliable" cadres during the purges in a telling remark:

> STALIN: The most serious evil, which we uncovered in the recent past, was that our cadres were not satisfactorily equipped. If "cadres decide all," and this means cadres that work with their minds, these are the cadres that run our country, and if these cadres are poorly equipped in their political understanding, the government is in danger. Take for example the Bukharinites. Their leadership — inbred factionalists — lost their foundation among the people and began to cooperate with foreign intelligence. But besides their leaders — Bukharin and others — there were large numbers of them and not all of them were spies or intelligence agents. We must presume that there were ten to thirty thousand and maybe more who sided with Bukharin. We must conclude that there were as many or more under Trotsky. But they were not all spies. Obviously not. What happened to them? These were cadres that could not digest the sharp turn to collective farms, they could not envision such a change because they were not politically equipped. They did not know the laws of societal development, of economic development, of political development. I am speaking about average Trotskyites and Bukharinites who occupied relatively important positions. One could have been the secretary of a party committee; another may have been a minister; another a deputy minister. How can we explain that some of them became spies and intelligence agents? Some were our own people, who went over to them. Why? It appears that they were not politically equipped, they lacked theoretical foundations; they did not know the laws of political development.

Stalin goes on to assure his listeners that the purges (the "loss" of cadres) was not in vain:

> STALIN: At this time, we lost a part of our cadres, but we gained an enormous number of lower-level workers, we got new cadres, we won over the people to collective farms, we won over the peasantry. Only this explains how easy it was for us to sweep away yesterday's ministers and deputy ministers. We did not waste our time in this period. We won over the working class and the peasantry, but they need direction. They must be directed through the administration but in the administration there were, it appears, the wrong people. . . . In this fashion, in winning the people we let an opportunity slip by for our cadres. We must recognize this fact, and we must correct this mistake.

The implication of Stalin's indirect remarks on the Great Terror is that if there had been a *Short Course* earlier, cadres would have understood his policies better, would have supported them, and mass purges would not have been necessary:

STALIN: [Correcting the mistake] begins with the publication of the *Short Course*. This book demonstrates the basic ideas of Marxism-Leninism on the basis of historical facts. Because it demonstrates its theses with historical facts, it will be convincing for our cadres, who work with their intellects, for thinking people who will not blindly follow. We have not paid sufficient attention to this matter and now we must complete it.

Stalin then offered Nikita Khrushchev as an example of the party creating its own intelligentsia:

STALIN: There is no class that can maintain its domination and rule the state if it is not capable of creating its own intelligentsia, namely, the people who have abandoned physical work and make their living through intellectual labor. Let's take the example of Comrade Khrushchev. He thinks he is still a worker while he is already part of intelligentsia. (Mirth from the audience.)

It is not a coincidence that Stalin's reference to Khrushchev evoked laughter from party functionaries: everyone knew that high intellect was not a quality of which Khrushchev could boast. Despite his short-lived enrollment in a polytechnic institution in Donetsk, he never completed his higher education.

Party Propaganda Workers: Up to the Task?

Stalin's statements make clear why party propaganda workers had been summoned to the Politburo meeting. It was their job to educate "thinking persons" on the principles of the *Short Course*. If they did their job poorly, cadres would not have a grounding in the truth as expressed in the *Short Course*.

STALIN: These are neither workers "at the lathe" nor kolkhoz peasants. . . . an official is an individual who makes conscious decisions. He wants to know what is going on, he raises questions, gets confused because he does not have adequate understanding of politics, preoccupies himself with petty trifles, exhausts himself; finally he loses interest in Marxism and in his "Bolshevization." We ought to compensate for this failure of ours . . . and the best way to begin is to publish the *Short Course*.

Were those party officials responsible for the dissemination of ideology up to the task? The party leadership probably realized the discrepancy between the rising cultural level of the workers and intelligentsia and that of party functionaries. Despite the large number of propaganda workers, there were reasons to doubt their effectiveness, as the Gorky representative, Troshin, went on to explain:

TROSHIN: This is one of our most qualified party organizations. But even here, when we began to discuss their work with learning the *Short Course,* we recognized a fact that speaks to their having watered down the quality of the *Short Course.* On September 20, our House of Party Education called a meeting of seminar leaders and discussed with them how to conduct their first session with propagandists. It turns out that the first chapter, which was already published, was being supplemented by material from the lecturers themselves. This demonstrates that the lecturers moved away from the text and are using their own material.

Although not stated explicitly, the Gorky propaganda workers were not about to change their lectures just because of the release of a new party history. Probably they wanted to continue to use old material with which they were familiar.

Zhdanov himself related two further examples of the "limited preparation of propagandists":

ZHDANOV: A circle is studying the fifth topic of the history of the party. A question about the August Bloc is answered thusly: The bloc did nothing but make noise. On the question of what was the Boxer Rebellion, the propagandist answered: You know what boxing is; this is the origin of the Boxer Rebellion.

What Stalin heard at the meeting from those heading party propaganda departments about the qualifications of propaganda workers was, to say the least, discouraging:

TROSHIN: Often a semiliterate propagandist with secondary education or none at all consults an engineer with higher education, who is well read and has a better understanding of Marxist-Leninist theory; the latter asks questions the educator cannot answer.

Another proof of the poor intellectual level of propagandists was the fact that party organizations had trouble finding specialists on the fourth chapter of the *Short Course,* which contained a rather primitive description of the basics of dialectic and historical materialism and of Lenin's philosophical work *Materialism and Empirio-criticism.* The low intellectual level of propagandists, it seems, existed in almost all regional party organizations. How could the party legitimize itself if its propagandists were not familiar with the theory of Marxism-Leninism, not to mention not understanding its tenets! And these were not rank-and-file instructors but the chiefs of propaganda sections that covered entire regions and republics.

The low cultural level of the propagandists was vividly reflected in the verbatim remarks of the Politburo session participants. The majority could not express themselves well in Russian; theirs was a language filled with poor grammar and bureaucratese. For example, Puzin (chief of the Press Department of the Yaroslavl Regional Party Committee) stated: "Every one of the participants of our group will read a definite sum of literature in a month . . . I think the party committee should have a "fist" (*kulak*) of such qualified individuals/specialists . . . ." "Sum of literature" is not appropriate in the Russian language, nor was the awkward use of "kulak" (a common metaphor in propaganda posters) in "kulak kvalifizirovannikh lydei." Stalin's speech, separately transcribed in the stenogram, was not an exception in respect of the use of poor grammar and bureaucratese.

As the chief of the Propaganda Section of the Voronezh Regional Party Committee Shaposhnikov confirmed, despite the fact that editors and their assistants regularly attended courses for improvement of their qualifications, "the qualifications of the staff in the publishing houses are very poor . . . ; during a test, one of the editors managed to make 40 mistakes in a short dictation."

Voluntarism or Coercion in Learning the Short Course

Stalin called the October 1938 Politburo session to plan the dissemination of a new party history to new and more discriminating cadres. Stalin's Soviet Union was a planned economy that ran on the basis of quantity indicators (such as tons of steel). Judging from Stalin's remarks, he did not wish to spread the word of the new party history superficially to large numbers. Rather he wanted the intelligentsia and those who administered the system to gain a "deep" understanding of its message.

The party propagandists represented at the meeting were, like their industrial counterparts, accustomed to being judged by quantitative indicators. The habit of "quantitative coverage" of propaganda could not be easily eliminated. Even after extensive criticism, the Politburo session participants pointed proudly to the large numbers of "circles" in their territories, most of which, in reality, were either dysfunctional or nonexistent. The chief of the Propaganda Section of the Ivanovo Party Committee, Meltser, for example, boasted: "On July 1 we had 2,800 circles with 48,000 participants. . . . additionally, we had up to 12,000 visitors in the countryside. . . . Among the participants at that time 26,000 individuals were party members, 69,000 were candidates, 4,800 "sympathizers," 3,300 Komsomol members, and 4,700 nonparty visitors. Currently, we have involved in our network 104,000 participants and up to 9,000 nonparty visitors."

The Ivanovo party official did not emphasize that the number of participants had risen from 48,000 to 104,000 in only three months, as a consequence of orders "from above." Nor did he explain that these increases were primarily due to people being forced to attend meetings. Other participants were more candid about the role of force. The Yaroslavl regional party propagandist (Puzin) elaborated: "The majority of listeners have been forced to attend the circles against their will. So the propaganda reports in the course of our party committee meetings discuss not the quality of training, but how many people are involved in it. The subsequent criticism of propaganda work is also based on the numerical data."

The fact that mandatory attendance was required to obtain listeners was not hidden from Stalin:

> STALIN: The consultations. Are they mandatory?
> ANTROPOV (Orel Party Committee): Some of them are voluntary. Sometimes an instructor is compelled to organize them. Not necessarily everyone is dragged there. (Laughter.) But in most cases, it is an obligatory event.
> MOLOTOV: Like any examination.

The chief of propaganda of the Tula region (Kuznetsov) confirmed similar happenings: "The creation of evening schools for the study of party history is a result of pursuit of numbers. Consequently, of those recruited at the beginning of the schools' existence, by the end of the second year only 10 to 15 percent remained enrolled. One can spend an entire lifetime attending school and still learn nothing."

The pattern of forced attendance followed by massive dropouts applied to entire regions. The Tula representative (Kuznetsov) noted there were at one time 1,600 circles in his forty districts. In a four to five month period, 215 of these circles fell apart; in another three to four months 140 more collapsed, despite the fact that the repeated orders of local Party Committees demanded "full involvement" of local Communists. In fact, 30 to 40 percent of Communists did not participate at all.

These anecdotes and figures suggest that even Communist activists did not wish to attend and that coercion worked only for a short period. Nationwide, Zhdanov attested to the collapse of at least every fifth circle soon after its creation. According to Zhdanov, of the 73,000 party history circles that existed in the country (in which mandatory education of more than one million Communists took place) 15,000 had already collapsed.

The reason that so few attended and forced attendance had to be required could be traced, at least in part, to the low educational level of instructors. Many of the participants in the Politburo session, who could hardly be accused of bias against propaganda departments, admitted to the low level and poor training of propaganda workers. Puzin, of the Yaroslavl Party Committee, stated: "Having returned to Yaroslavl upon my graduation after a ten-year absence, I met my colleagues, with whom I had once worked and studied. I was struck by how little progress in personal development these people had made. Despite their long training in conducting party circles, they obviously learned very little."

According to the information provided by the chief of the Propaganda Section of the Kiev Party Committee, Khomenko, in the propaganda circles, most of the participants covered the program up to the third or fourth chapter in an academic year, so the following year it had to be started anew: "Many listeners complain that no matter how often they attend, no matter how much they study, we never get beyond the third or fourth chapter and from this we get very little."

Other regional propaganda officials offered an additional explanation for the boring lectures — fear of misrepresenting the text. The chief of the Propaganda Section of the Kalinin Party Committee, Perepelkin, made clear: "People [who teach party history] fear that they will make mistakes." Therefore instructors have become accustomed to the practice "that at every event there will be exhaustive circulars and instructions, telling them what to do, how to start."

Such extreme reticence spread from the top to the bottom of the propaganda ladder, starting with the Institute of Red Professors, where party cadres were prepared (and where many of them earned promotion through denunciations). In the words of the chief of the Press Section of the Yaroslavl Party Committee, Puzin, "such cowardice and indecisiveness of theoretical thought, especially in the Institute of the Red Professors, is an ordinary phenomenon. . . . If some unanswered question arises [among the students] and they go to the teachers with controversial questions, the teachers often do not give answers. . . . I wrote a report on the uneven development of capitalism and they were dissatisfied that I wrote that tsarist Russia was the most backward capitalist country in Europe. They forced me to renounce this assertion. Even if the student did not understand, there were no efforts to discuss or explain it to him."

The head of the Kiev party propaganda provided yet another example of extreme caution: "In one of our regions, during the work of the circle, a participant asked the propagandist about the possibility of building socialism in one country. At this time, Comrade Stalin's speech on this subject was already known. The propagandist instead of answering immediately said: 'Right now I need to get exact information on this subject and then I'll answer you.' He telephones the regional party secretary and asks: 'Is it possible to build socialism in one country?' The party secretary answers: 'Yes, it is possible.' Then the propagandist returns and answers yes it is possible to build socialism in our country. (General laughter in the hall.)"

To avoid personal responsibility, many instructors resorted to collective readings of the *Short Course*. Consequently, as Zhdanov noted after observing this practice in person, dogmatism became a major factor in indoctrination:

> ZHDANOV: Asking questions, propagandists expect answers in chorus. An instructor from Vyshnyi Volochek addressed his audience with the question: "What did we learn from our discussion?" No one replied, so he went on: "After the discussion the party emerged — what . . . ?" The students replied all together: "More consolidated." (Everyone laughs.)

Organizing Propaganda

A genuine master of political intrigue, Stalin assumed that ideological manipulation in and of itself was not sufficient. For a doctrine to become an official ideology, a specifically trained propaganda apparatus was needed, whose members were willing and capable to propagate its main ideas clearly and diligently among the masses, and consistently arguing its orthodoxy — or, as it was said at the time, "the purity of the doctrine of Marxism-Leninism."

If there were failures in the dissemination of the ideas of the *Short Course*, it would not be due to the limited size of the propaganda apparatus. The enormity of that apparatus was illustrated by the Gorky representative's description of propaganda work at the Gorky Automobile Works: "I'll give you a concrete example — the party organization of the automobile factory. It has a membership of about four thousand engineering and technical persons. There are 207 propagandists and more than 130 study circles on party history."

Stalin and his inner circle ruled so effectively because of their control of the state and party apparatus. Stalin's loyal deputy, Zhdanov, insistently argued for copying the principles of strict subordination and centralized management in teaching the *Short Course* to the people. The Politburo session fully revealed incompetence and multiple deficiencies in the existing propaganda apparatus, as well as the necessity of creating rigid, vertically integrated, and hierarchical system of training and improving the qualifications of its instructors. The so called "circles" (kruzhki), strictly subordinated and controlled by superior party organizations, became the basic unit for *Short Course* studies. The establishment of the Higher School of Marxism-Leninism for training and improving the qualifications of party officials became yet another step in this project. The notion of "party history" replaced "Leninism." Against a back-

drop of intensified censorship, the journal *Bolshevik* became the major theoretical weapon of indoctrination and control of the masses.

The centralized structure of management and control was complemented
by material incentives, in particular, by high salaries. The stenogram shows
that the heads of regional party propaganda departments received the relatively high salary of eight hundred rubles per month.

The unified system of indoctrination of the masses was created through the
special decree of the Central Committee of November 14, 1938 "On Party
Propaganda in Relation to the Publication of the *Short Course of the History of
the All-Union Communist Party (Bolsheviks)*." The decree clarified the chief
function of the *Short Course:* "to endow the party with unified instruction on
party history, providing a legitimized (reviewed by the Central Committee)
interpretation of major questions of party history and of Marxism-Leninism,
that excludes the possibility of arbitrary interpretation."[6] The *Short Course*
was proclaimed an "encyclopedia of the basics of Marxism-Leninism," playing
the role of a dogma that had to be learned not only by the party members but by
everyone else.

Final Thoughts

Dictators have enemies; they are not elected by constituents. They pursue programs that do not please a large part of the citizenry. Dictators have a
number of choices with respect to their enemies. They can eliminate them by
banishment, imprisonment, or execution. They can choose to live with a certain percentage of enemies. Or they can educate or reeducate citizens who are
enemies or who might become enemies. They also might wish to identify those
enemies, actual and potential, who can do them the most harm.

Stalin's message, clearly expressed at the November 1939 Politburo meeting, called in the declining days of the Great Terror, was that he was ready to
turn from physical elimination of enemies to "enemy-prevention." The cadres
that he had to eliminate as enemies during the Great Terror were enemies
because they had not been properly enlightened. That was the mistake of the
party; the party had survived without them and was ready to move on, but
should avoid the mistakes of the past. It needed a doctrine or dogma that
should be understood by all, but most importantly by those "who work with
their minds." If only the citizenry were properly educated in this dogma, there
would be no need to worry about enemies or opposition to the party line.

Stalin's *Short Course* was to be the means to accomplish these goals. It
explained to the intelligentsia and to the masses what they needed to understand. If they understood, they would be active supporters of party decisions.

The Politburo session ended on the usual note. A Politburo commission was to be formed that would deal with the practical implementation of the task of teaching the *Short Course* and would consider all those deficiencies raised by the dialogue with the actual practitioners of official ideology.

Stalin's discussions with propagandists from around the country may or may not have been an eye-opener for him. He may well have known already that most people were not interested in party history or ideology and that they had to be forced to attend sessions. Maybe he knew of the low level of training and intellect of party propagandists. The candor of these low-level party propagandists in pointing out deficiencies is remarkable, because usually such problems were kept from the dictator's view. Either they were new in their positions and could blame deficiencies on their predecessors, or they were simply naïve.

Notes

I want to express my gratitude to Paul Gregory and Yuri Latov for their assistance and advice in preparation of this essay. I would also like to thank an anonymous referee for valuable comments.

1. RGASPI Fond 17, op. 163, del. 1218. Subsequent citations are from this source.

2. M. N. Riutin was known as an ardent opponent of the Trotskyist-Zinovievite coalition, a follower of N. I. Bukharin, the author of the work "Stalin and the Crisis of the Proletarian Dictatorship," and a key figure of the Alliance of Marxists-Leninists. He shared Bukharin's vision of economic policy and Trotsky's criticism of the internal party regime. In September 1932 Stalin issued an order demanding Riutin's execution; however, it did not find immediate support, so Riutin's arrest, exile, and execution were postponed until 1937.

3. By 1938 from Stalin's political rivals only L. D. Trotsky remained alive. He was killed with an ice ax by a Stalinist agent on August, 20, 1940 in his exile in Mexico.

4. Boffa, *Istoriia sovetskogo soiuza*, vol. 1: *Ot revoliutsii do vtoroi mirovoi voiny: Lenin i Stalin, 1917–1941*, p. 534.

5. For more details see Hofstede, *Cultures and Organizations: Software of the Mind*; for his view on Russia, see Hofstede, *Cultures Consequences: International Differences in Work-related Values*. According to Hofstede, the oriental mentality differs from the Western one through the despotism of the rulers and the poorly developed individuality of the ruled. According to this view, depersonalized history of the party can be understood as involving the elimination of "heroes," who previously had constituted an intermediate stratum between "the gods" and "the humans"; and an emphasis on collective actions versus individual deeds.

6. KPSS v rezoliutsiakh, part 2, p. 859.

PART IV

Economic Policy

10

Grain, Class, and Politics During NEP: The Politburo Meeting of December 10, 1925

R. W. DAVIES

The Economic and Political Background

The Politburo session of December 10, 1925, item No. 1, dealt with "The Work of TsSU [the Central Statistical Administration] Concerning the Grain-Fodder Balance." This was a remarkable and rare occasion. Governments in the twentieth century were often anxious to present statistics to their own advantage. In Britain, under the Thatcher government in the 1980s, the definition of "unemployment" was changed on many occasions, resulting in a considerable reduction of the official figure. The falsification of the grain harvest under Stalin after 1932 is notorious. But it is very unusual — perhaps unique — for the supreme policymaking body in a major state to discuss in detail, and with considerable passion, the technicalities of a complex statistical problem, and to resolve the problem by majority vote.

The session took place in the context of the crucial problem of Bolshevik policy during NEP: the relation of the regime to the 23 million peasant households, four-fifths of the population of the Soviet Union. In Marxist studies of the Russian peasantry, three major groups were generally distinguished: kulaks, middle peasants, and poor peasants. The term "kulak" (literally meaning "tight fist") was originally reserved for rural usurers and traders as distinct from rural peasant producers. By the mid-1920s it was generally used more widely to refer to all peasants who hired labor or exploited their neighbors in some other way.

As a result of the October 1917 Revolution and the Civil War economic differentiation in the countryside was considerably reduced. In the early years of the New Economic Policy some differentiation took place, but the degree of petty capitalism in the countryside remained far less than before the revolution.

Measuring the level and dynamic of differentiation was a very difficult problem. The easiest way to divide the peasants into economic groups was by sown area per household, and this also enabled the statisticians to estimate the amount of grain taken to the market by different groups of households. Peasants with more sown area were generally better off. But the sown area did not fully correspond to the wealth of the household. Some more wealthy peasants obtained much of their income from livestock, or trade, or handicrafts, And the classification by sown area did not reveal the number of kulaks exploiting other peasants—these were certainly a fairly small proportion of the peasants in the upper sown-area groups.

In the middle and late 1920s the degree of differentiation was a major issue in the discussion of Soviet policy towards the peasants. The Bolsheviks were preoccupied by the problem of how to ensure agricultural and industrial growth while preventing the emergence of rural capitalism.

The political background in December 1925 was the emerging conflict between the majority of the Politburo and the "New" or "Leningrad" Opposition, in which the controversy about differentiation among the peasantry played a significant role. The majority of the seven-man Politburo included both Stalin and the future Right Opposition, Nikolai Bukharin, Aleksei Rykov, and Mikhail Tomsky. Politburo members Grigory Zinoviev and Lev Kamenev were the leaders of the New Opposition. Until the summer of 1925, these two men, together with Stalin, formed the "Triumvirate" which dominated the Politburo after the death of Lenin in January 1924. Trotsky, the seventh member of the Politburo, and leader of the Left Opposition, was by this time an isolated figure, and had resigned his key post as People's Commissar for Military and Naval Affairs in January 1925. He had been particularly fiercely opposed by Zinoviev and Kamenev, who unsuccessfully called for his expulsion from the Politburo.

Although Stalin cooperated closely with Bukharin, Rykov, and Tomsky, he was his own man, and did not have close allies in the full Politburo. But the candidate members included his staunch ally V. M. Molotov. Valerian Kuibyshev, another reliable associate of Stalin, was head of the powerful joint government-party agency the Workers' and Peasants' Inspectorate and Central Control Commission (known as Rabkrin-CCC). This was responsible for assessing the work of all government and party agencies and increasingly acted as the scourge of dissidence and unorthodoxy. In view of his notionally "independent" role, the head of Rabkrin-CCC was not formally a Politburo member, but he had the status of a member and attended its meetings.

These divisions within the Politburo were strongly influenced by personal antagonisms. The Triumvirate was established because the other leaders were afraid that the charismatic Trotsky would become the Napoleon of the Russian revolution. The New Opposition emerged in the summer and autumn of 1925 partly because Zinoviev and Kamenev feared and were jealous of the growing power of Stalin. The normally mild-mannered Kamenev declared at the Fourteenth Party Congress in December 1925: *"I have reached the conclusion that Comrade Stalin cannot perform the function of uniting the Bolshevik general staff."*[1]

The clash of personalities was intertwined with major policy differences. Trotsky and his supporters believed that the conservatism of the majority of the Politburo was leading to the ossification and bureaucratization of the Soviet Union and the international revolutionary movement. The Politburo majority saw this as a time for the consolidation of the system. While Trotsky stressed the paramountcy of planning, the majority sought to strengthen and deepen the New Economic Policy. In this spirit Zinoviev launched the campaign "Face to the Countryside" in the autumn of 1924. In the spring of 1925 a series of far-reaching measures sought to provide strong economic incentives to the peasants. Bukharin in a famous speech called for the removal of *"many restrictions which put the brake on the growth of the well-to-do and kulak farm."* Specifically, Bukharin stated: "To the peasants, to all the peasantry, we must say: *Enrich yourselves,* develop your farms, and do not fear that constraints will be put on you.[2]

For Zinoviev and Kamenev these policies went too far; the slogan "Enrich yourselves" reflected a dangerous tendency to encourage rural capitalism at the expense of the industrial workers. Zinoviev was supported by the powerful Leningrad party organization, based on the Leningrad proletariat whose support had been indispensable to the victory of the Bolshevik Revolution. But it was Kamenev, who was in charge of the Council of Labor and Defense — the economic committee of the Soviet government — who first drew public attention to the danger of the growing economic differentiation among the peasants. From August onwards, in a series of statements, he expressed alarm about the situation revealed by the grain-fodder balance for 1925–26, prepared by TsSU, which purported to show that 14 percent of peasant households produced 33 percent of the grain harvest and were responsible for 61 percent of the grain surpluses. Kamenev insisted that this reliance on the well-off and kulak peasants for grain supplies had "most serious *social* consequences."[3]

During the autumn, the rift between Zinoviev and Kamenev and the party majority on this and several other issues widened. The TsSU figures became a major center of attention, particularly as a result of the difficulties in collecting grain from the 1925 harvest. The figures were very widely discussed, in daily newspapers as well as in specialized journals. If they were true, did they mean that NEP was leading the country away from socialism, and strengthening capitalism in the countryside? On October 1, contradicting TsSU and Kamenev, a plenum of the party Central Committee authoritatively reasserted the official view that "the mass of grain is produced and thrown on to the market by the mass of middle peasants."[4]

The Central Statistical Administration and the Grain Balance

Prerevolutionary Russia was distinguished for its remarkably strong statistical institutions, both at the level of central government and in the regions. The regional institutions were managed by the semidemocratic local government organizations, the *zemstva*. Within a year of the Bolshevik Revolution of October 1917, the Soviet government, with Lenin's strong support, established the TsSU in Moscow and its network of local agencies based on the prerevolutionary *zemstva* and now attached to the local soviets. Lenin insisted that "statistics must be outside departmental control" and that their main function must be "to express objectively and truthfully the situation as it is, the causes of the present situation and their consequences."[5]

In practice TsSU retained a great deal of independence in the first eight years after its establishment under the directorship of P. I. Popov. Popov, who was supported by Lenin, held this post until December 1925. Before the revolution he had been exiled for revolutionary activities in the 1890s, and between 1909 and 1917 he was head of the Tula *zemstvo* statistical office.[6] He was a man of independent views, rather abrasive in character, and frequently clashed both with other statisticians and the political authorities.

Naturally the crucial issue for the statisticians in this huge and varied peasant country, both before and after the revolution, was grain. Assessing the size of the grain harvest was a major preoccupation.[7] In the early 1920s Popov and TsSU consistently put forward low estimates of the harvest, while Gosplan (the State Planning Commission), supported by rival statisticians, insisted that the peasants for tax and other reasons consistently underestimated the harvest, so that as a result substantial correction coefficients must be applied to the raw data. TsSU reluctantly agreed to correct the harvest data upwards in the course of 1921–25.

All those dealing with the countryside were naturally concerned not only about the total amount of grain produced but also about what happened to it. Well before the revolution, Russian statisticians pioneered the preparation of a "grain-fodder balance" which set out for the agricultural year (July 1–June 30) (1) the stocks of grain held by peasants and others at the beginning of the year; (2) the grain produced during the year; (3) the amounts in which grain was consumed for different purposes during the year; (4) the stock remaining at the end of the year. Item (3) was a particularly complicated matter. Part of the grain was used as seed for the following harvest; part was consumed by its peasant producers; part was consumed by their animals, and part was sold on the market. The part sold on the market was known as "extrarural grain." Extrarural grain was used in a variety of ways. It was the main source of nourishment for the nonrural population, including the army; it provided raw material for a variety of industries, especially for the production of vodka. Grain was also a major item of prerevolutionary export.

There was a further complication. A large amount of grain, which was not part of the category "extrarural grain," was sold by peasants in one region to peasants in another region, or between different peasants within the same region or village. This was known as "intrarural grain." Such rich grain regions as Ukraine and North Caucasus, the "grain-surplus regions," supplied grain to the "grain-deficit regions" such as the more industrialized central and northwestern regions round Moscow and St. Petersburg. Within every region, and often within a village, some peasants, often the poorer peasants, were net purchasers of grain from other peasants.[8]

The estimates made for the different items in the grain-fodder balance came from a variety of sources. "Extrarural grain," with its subdivisions, was known quite accurately. There was, however, a considerable variation between the different estimates of the amount of grain transferred within the countryside, either from peasant to peasant or via intermediaries.

If the Soviet state was to plan the development of agriculture, and of industry and the towns, which depended on agriculture, it needed to know as much as possible about the different items in the balance. All sections of party opinion wanted TsSU to prepare data which showed not only what had happened with previous harvests but also what was going to happen with the present harvest — the grain-fodder *balance* became a grain-fodder *budget*, but without a change of name. The party authorities — and their critics — also wanted to know the role of different social groups in the production and sale of grain, and pressed upon TsSU the need to produce a socially differentiated balance.

Table 10.1. *Percentage Distribution of the Population and of Grain Products [expected in 1925/26] (USSR excluding Turkestan, Transcaucasus, and Kirgizia)*

[(a) For nine sown-area groups]				
Sown area	% of population	% of total production	% of surpluses	% of deficits
1. None	3	—	—	22
2. Up to 1 desyatina	12	3	—	44
3. 1–2 desyatinas	22	12	—	34
4. 2–3 desyatinas	20	16	3	—
5. 3–4 desyatinas	14	15	11	—
6. 4–5 desyatinas	15	21	25	—
7. 6–8 desyatinas	7	12	19	—
8. 8–10 desyatinas	3	7	12	—
9. Over 10 desyatinas	4	14	30	—
Total	100	100	100	100

[(b) For three consolidated sown-area groups]				
Sown area	% of population	% of total production	% of surpluses	% of deficits
1–3. Up to 2 desyatinas	37	15	0	100
4–6. 2–6 desyatinas	49	52	39	—
7–9. 6+ desyatinas	14	33	61	—
Total	100	100	100	100

Note [by Dubenetsky]: This estimate may somewhat exaggerate the surpluses of the larger farms, because we have used an estimate of the grain used for food and to feed livestock (per head of livestock) not on the basis of each province, but of larger regions, but the general picture of the distribution of the harvest and of the surplus is undoubtedly correct.

Note [by present author]: This table appears in an article in *Biulleten' TsSU*, no. 105, pp. 61–73, by N. Dubenetsky, head of the Grain Department of TsSU. dated July 20, 1925. The sown-area figures are per household, the surpluses and deficits are estimated per head of the population of the sown-area group concerned.

I have numbered the rows and rearranged the table to make it easier to follow. The first English translation of the table (slightly simplified) was published in Carr, *Socialism in One Country, 1924–1926*, vol. 1, p. 306 n. 1.[1] Carr's figures are taken from Kamenev, *Stat'i i rechi*, pp. 355–56, which has not been available.

1 desyatina = 1.09 hectares = 2.7 acres.

This was the background to the fateful decision of Popov and TsSU to produce and publish the table showing potential grain sales in 1925–26 in terms of different groups of peasant households (Table 10.1). This table used the standard division of peasant households according to their sown area. The 1925–26 balance, submitted to the Council of People's Commissars in June 1925, before the harvest, divided the peasants into nine groups.

Kamenev's figures were obtained from the last three groups (7–9) in the table. His use of them, to stress the dangers of differentiation, immediately gave rise to angry protests from the party majority, and from Gosplan. The party leaders evidently concluded that this was a good opportunity to get rid of the awkward Popov. Already at the Thirteenth Party Congress in May 1924, Stalin, without naming either Popov or TsSU, had criticized Soviet statisticians who gave different figures for the same phenomenon, contrasting them with statisticians in bourgeois countries, who "respect themselves and retain a certain minimum of professional honor."[9] Between this congress and the publication of the data on differentiation, Popov had further upset the politicians by insisting that a successful policy towards the peasants depended on carrying out a thoroughgoing agriculture census. He also provocatively argued about the grain trade that "private capital must be allowed to penetrate it to a large degree."[10]

Following the attention given to the figures on differentiation by Kamenev and others, in October 1925 Rabkrin established a commission to examine the TsSU grain-fodder balance. It was headed by Yakovlev, Kuibyshev's deputy, and, while it included representatives of TsSU, it was dominated by its critics, notably Vyshnevsky, the principal Gosplan specialist on grain statistics.[11] Unfortunately for Popov, he was abroad during the proceedings of the commission, and returned only shortly before the Politburo meeting of December 10 (Popov's long-standing deputy Pashkovsky acted on his behalf) The findings of the commission were well publicized at the time: they were reported in *Pravda*, in articles by Yakovlev and in a subsequent book. Vyshnevsky published two substantial articles criticizing the methods used by TsSU.[12]

The Politburo Meeting of December 10, 1925: The Debate

The verbatim report of item No. 1 of the Politburo meeting of December 10, 1925, which has now been published from formerly closed archives, does not throw much new light on the validity of the TsSU figures, which were amply discussed in the press. But it greatly illuminates our understanding of the political processes of the mid-1920s and the role and influence of key members of the Politburo.[13]

The meeting was attended by twenty-three people. These included four full members of the Politburo: Kamenev, Rykov, Stalin, and Trotsky (Bukharin, Zinoviev and Tomsky were absent), and three candidate members (Feliks Dzerzhinsky, Molotov, and Jan Rudzutak). Three members of the Central Control Commission were also present, including Kuibyshev; and various members of the party Central Committee, and some experts. It lasted the best part of a day. It heard elaborate reports from Kuibyshev and Yakovlev on behalf of Rabkrin, and a co-report by Popov, who also intervened in the discussion on several occasions. Kuibyshev and Popov both summed up at the end of the meeting. Kamenev, who presided at Politburo meetings at this time, played a prominent part in the discussion. The meeting was addressed by Stalin (three times), Rykov (twice), and Trotsky, and by candidate Politburo members Rudzutak and Molotov. The only expert who spoke, apart from Popov himself, was S. Strumilin from Gosplan, a prominent critic of TsSU harvest statistics.

In their lengthy reports, Kuibyshev and Yakovlev advanced four main arguments against the grain distribution figures. First, according to Kuibyshev the correction coefficients which TsSU added to the sown-area data had not been changed, but they should have been reduced because "there is less incentive now for the peasantry to conceal the sown area." This was the thinnest criticism, because Gosplan and the other agencies had been pressing TsSU ever since the beginning of NEP to increase these coefficients! Secondly, TsSU had used identical consumption norms for all groups of peasants, although "in fact the poor peasant eats less and puts more of his grain on the market than TsSU suggested . . . ; on the other hand the rich peasant eats better and puts less grain on the market." Thirdly, the stocks remaining in the hands of the top groups of peasants had been underestimated, and in consequence the amount of grain they had sold on the market had again been overestimated. Fourthly, the TsSU figures ignored the important point that although the poor peasants purchased more grain than they sold, they did put grain on the market, selling it in the autumn after the harvest and buying it in the spring when they had run short of it. Kuibyshev presented a rival table which purported to show that in terms of the total gross sales of grain the well-off and rich peasants provided not 61 percent but only 29.6 percent of the grain.

In reply, Popov insisted that TsSU reconsidered its correction coefficients each year and only left them constant when there was no evidence for modifying them. In the case of consumption norms they had made it clear that the table issued in June and published later in the *TsSU Bulletin* no. 105 was "only a sketch." On October 9, a new version had been issued in which differentiated norms had been used. As far as stocks were concerned, it was impossible to estimate these accurately in advance because they depended on unknown factors such as the size of the harvest and the price of grain.

Popov rejected the argument about the sale of grain by the poor peasants on the grounds that the grain which was sold within the peasantry "for the most part does not enter the large-scale urban market"; "the circulation of the grain is carried out within agriculture." This was strongly contested by Yakovlev, who insisted that the claim that the poor peasants did not sell to the towns "is not based on any serious foundation." The poor peasants sold from one-third to one-half of their gross harvest in the autumn, and grain was sold within the countryside only in the spring, when the poor peasants purchased more grain than they had sold in the autumn.

Strumilin had long been critical of TsSU. He explained that he did not participate directly in the work of the Rabkrin commission. Instead he was now reporting to the Politburo about the reaction of Gosplan to the TsSU grain figures. The original figures (as in the table above) were "completely unsatisfactory from the point of view of social groupings," because they simply showed the division of the peasants according to sown area. The second version by TsSU tried to deal with criticisms by using different sown-area divisions for different agricultural areas, and as a result had reduced the 61 percent to 52 percent. But this second version was "again completely unsatisfactory," because "the middle peasants of one area could seem to be poorer than the 'poor peasants' of another area, and as a result in the country as a whole poor peasants were lumped together with middle peasants, middle peasants with the better off, and so on." Strumilin concluded on the following note: "No serious Marxist statistician could have produced such a work. This is not only my opinion but also the opinion of everyone with whom the work was discussed in Gosplan." He insisted that the work must be redone before a "more or less true reflection of reality could be obtained."

Trotsky, who a couple of years later treated the alleged increased economic power of the kulaks as a major threat to the Soviet order, might have been expected to applaud the TsSU figures and Kamenev's alarm about them. But on this occasion he was quite circumspect. Following his defeat during 1924, he had taken on secondary government posts in the spring of 1925, and did not yet wish to confront the party majority again. And he was still at loggerheads with Kamenev and Zinoviev. He accused Kamenev of "initially publishing [the TsSU figures] against me," to Kamenev's evident surprise.

> KAMENEV: Against you?
> TROTSKY: Yes, against me, you do that so often, that you may have forgotten it this once.

Trotsky insisted that even if the TsSU figures were correct, which he very much doubted, they did not justify "panic-stricken attitudes." Instead, what mattered was their place in the dynamic of development:

> TROTSKY: If in the following year the same 14 percent of peasants provide 65 percent and then 75 percent, this would obviously be a threatening process. If the figure of 61 percent is true, about which I expressed my emphatic doubt in my report, this does not mean that the same group will have 65 percent in the

following year. On the contrary, from all the data there will be a reduction to say 55 percent or less. The main question is whether we can counterpose a sufficiently rapid growth of industry to the growth of the differentiation of the peasants.

Kamenev, presiding at the meeting, was in an awkward position. He claimed that he had simply drawn attention to figures which had already been reported to the Council of People's Commissars, and had made it clear that they were "preliminary, and needed further elaboration and precision." He maintained that he did not claim that they provided "socio-economic class characteristics":

> KAMENEV: If my article had stated that the 14 percent were well off and had 61 percent of grain surpluses, this accusation could be made. But this statement does not appear in the article.

In the hope of rescuing Popov's position, Kamenev insisted at some length that, whatever he (Kamenev) had said himself, TsSU could not be blamed for it:

> KAMENEV: If, Comrade Yakovlev, you impugn those who drew this kind of conclusion, you should have said that incorrect conclusions were drawn from these figures about the differentiation of the peasantry. That's what you should have said — but you should not have attributed this to TsSU or Comrade Popov. If you want to criticize Kamenev, say so. Why attribute crimes to TsSU which it did not commit, and political acts which it did not undertake? — in these figures there is not the slightest hint that this is a division into kulaks, middle peasants, poor peasants, etc.

Rykov, replying to Kamenev, quoted extensively from Kamenev's pamphlet. The most damning passage he cited was the following:

> RYKOV: There are these five [*sic*] figures [wrote Kamenev]: 37 percent of the peasantry will not only not sell grain, but will buy it; 29 percent will bring to the market a little over one-third of the total marketed commodity, and 14 percent will hand over a little less than two-thirds of the total. These provide the answer to the question: Who received the huge sum of money, and the goods, machinery, etc. which go into the countryside in exchange for the harvest.[14]

Rykov commented sharply: "It is about these figures that you said that the attempt to put a gloss on them is an attempt to put a gloss on the figures about the differentiation of the peasantry."

Following Rykov, Yakovlev again made the claim, crucial to the case against TsSU, that it had treated the figures in its notorious table as recording socio-economic differentiation. He cited an article by the head of the relevant TsSU department (Dubnetsky), which described the sown-area data as referring to "five *social* groups: peasants without sown area, poor, middle, well-off and rich." He also pointed out that in a report to Rabkrin as recently as November 26 Khryashcheva had treated the sown-area data as corresponding to these five main classes. (Everyone at the Politburo meeting knew that Khryashcheva was Popov's wife, though it did not conform with party manners to mention this.) Then Molotov, summing up this line of criticism, credibly suggested that "the data which TsSU provided to the state agencies and to the Rabkrin commission itself slipped from sown-area groupings to class divisions."

In reply, Popov reiterated that he had never intended to take the sown-area groups as a basis for studying classes in the countryside. Instead, TsSU had embarked on an elaborate study which took into account not only sown area but also animal husbandry and artisan activities, and examined the extent to which different groups used hired labor, rented land from other peasants, and owned agricultural equipment. He also insisted, citing a memorandum written by Khryashcheva and himself, that kulaks were a "very small number" (*edinitsy*) of peasants, and could be found in all sown-area groups, though mainly among those with larger sown areas.

Behind these exchanges there lurked substantial differences of view about the situation in the countryside and the policy to be pursued. Earlier in the debate Popov claimed that Rabkrin, by grouping the peasants into only three sown-area groups, thus lumping into a single group all peasants except those with very large sown areas, had made it look as if most grain was sold by this middle group:

> POPOV: I maintain that Rabkrin, consciously or unconsciously, was following the wrong path — the middle-peasantization of households of different economic strengths, and this path is a dangerous one. There is undoubtedly a dangerous deviation here. Here from somewhere or other narodism is breaking in by quiet infiltration [*tikhaia sapa*]. There is a danger here.

The Narodniks (Populists) were the pro-peasant revolutionaries in tsarist times who strongly believed that the equality of the peasant commune could form the basis for socialism. *Tikhaia sapa*, ironically, was the phrase used by Stalin during the agricultural crisis of 1932–33 to describe the conduct of the kulaks who were allegedly sabotaging the collective farms from within.

Molotov in a characteristically blunt speech replied that it was Popov whose view of the middle peasants was erroneous: "It is particularly typical that Comrade. Popov does not notice the role of the middle peasant in the countryside." Molotov addressed Popov as follows:

> MOLOTOV: Comrade Popov, your policy is to defend the poor peasant and besiege the well-off kulak group, and that means you do not see the facts, in particular the results of the October Revolution in the countryside. . . . It is

wrong to take the standpoint that one must follow either a narrow policy in favor of the poor peasants or a policy in favor of the kulaks and well-off peasants. Our policy is to be for the proletariat and the poor peasantry, plus also an alliance with the middle peasantry.

Molotov raised the temperature at the meeting by charging Popov with distorting the statistics to justify his political views. Popov, he declared, sought to show that the reduction of grain prices favored the kulak and the rich peasant: "The impression is that Comrade Popov as it were adjusted his figures to these political conclusions"; "it turns out that the TsSU figures are not just statistical conclusions, but are spoiled by purely political conclusions."

Yakovlev countered Popov's accusation that the orthodox line was tainted with populism by asserting that Popov himself, by refusing to define the kulaks by agricultural criteria, and claiming that they only emerged from trade, loan operations, and so on, was repeating "the old narodnik delusion" that the kulak did not emerge from agriculture as such. Kuibyshev went even further, suggesting that Popov frequently spoke about "the dekulakization of the countryside"; this "political approach" to the problem of placing the peasants in different groups, Kuibyshev maintained, was "a completely wrong method and completely wrong approach." Kuibyshev's insinuation that Popov was in favor of dekulakization had no basis. Ironically, exactly four years later it was Stalin and his supporters who launched the campaign for the elimination of the kulaks as a class.

Stalin, in his contributions to the discussion, was careful not to get involved in the details of the debate about differentiation, but from the outset he made his hostility to Popov abundantly clear. As in 1924, he presented himself as a strong believer in objective statistics:

> STALIN: It is absolutely clear that statistics must be objective, like any other scientific discipline. Here there must be maximum objectivity.

In this context he concentrated his fire on the inconsistencies in the figures, insisting that "we all treated these figures as scientific data, but now it turns out that our TsSU worked with incorrect data." He pointed out that TsSU had produced three different figures for the grain supplied by the top group of households: 61 percent, 54 percent, and 42 percent.[15] But science could not work with "imprecise figures:

> STALIN: You can say what you like about science, but if science works with imprecise figures it is no longer science. I respect science, and TsSU as a citadel of science, but the three different figures which TsSU has brought before us, the gap between which is 19 percent, do not do credit to TsSU, but are an admonishment to it. The conclusion from this is that TsSU uses figures too

arbitrarily, impermissibly arbitrarily, contrary to the requirements of science, contrary to the interests of science.

In his reply, Popov disagreed strongly with Stalin's view of statistics. This important passage is worth reproducing in full, both for its view of statistics and because it was already rare at this time for an official who was not a top politician to criticize Stalin:

> POPOV: All statistical figures are of course provisional [*uslovny*]. Statistical data are provisional, and theory tells us this. Even bookkeepers' records are provisional. The aim we set ourselves in a statistical study is to provide material which approximately describes reality. We have 23 million peasant households — can we really collect precise irrefutable data about these households? Can we really believe that we can give precise figures when we work out the size of the surplus from these 23 million households? Our data are of course approximate, but then we elaborate them, make them more precise and closer to reality. Moreover, the grain-fodder balance is not a purely statistical operation, it is an estimate, although based on statistical data. Comrade Stalin forgets this, supposing that the estimate of the balance is a purely statistical operation, while it is only an estimate. Take the control figures [a form of annual plan] of Gosplan. Can control figures really reflect reality fully? The control figures, like the grain-fodder balance, are not a statistical operation. Comrade Stalin thinks that there is some kind of statistics which gives the most precise figures, which can measure economic phenomena like a pharmacist's scales. There is no such statistics. Statistical data are provisional, but in the course of systematic statistical work we can determine the extent to which it is provisional.

Earlier in the debate, Popov had pointed out that the predictions in the grain-fodder balance of 1925–26, drawn up in June 1925, were also uncertain because of the effect of policy and market conditions:

> POPOV: With one policy grain will be put into reserve stocks to a greater extent than with another policy which leads the peasants to take grain to the market to a greater extent. We argue that there are no grounds for separating out stocks separately from the grain remaining in the hands of the peasants, because stocks entirely depend on market conditions. Can we know market conditions in advance? Who knows this? We said to you: this is the size of the remainder and the surpluses after the normal needs of the agricultural population have been met. . . . Market conditions are a very complicated matter. Everyone thought that this autumn, after a good harvest, grain would come to us at low prices, but an entirely different situation prevailed: grain came very slowly and at a higher price than we supposed. Who could foresee this? Could TsSU have foreseen this? It does not have the data for scientific forecasting.

Can TsSU really dictate the policy which determines the market conditions? You must do this, not TsSU. You can accuse TsSU of many things, but I tell you that TsSU did all it could and provided all it could.

These crucial issues were not further discussed at the Politburo meeting. In his summing up, Popov strongly protested about Molotov's assertion that he had adjusted the figures for political reasons:

POPOV: I have been engaged in scientific statistical work for 27 years and I can assure you that I have never done what you said. . . . I consider you should respect the work of others, and you do not have the right to say that to me, to make such an accusation.

Popov called for the assessment of the work of TsSU by a group of fellow statisticians, the process known as "scientific expertise." He had earlier pointed out that previous assessments of the work of TsSU had been made by specialists capable of judging its work, rather than by Rabkrin and by selected specialists and others who, whatever their other merits, were not qualified to judge the methods used by TsSU. Kuibyshev in his own summing up rejected this proposal, claiming that the principal statisticians in TsSU had accepted Rabkrin's conclusions, and devoted the rest of his speech to repeating the analysis of the TsSU data given in his original report.

The Politburo Meeting of December 10, 1925: The Outcome

The three most powerful figures at the meeting, Rykov, Stalin, and Kuibyshev, had made it abundantly clear that they were in favor of major changes in TsSU, including the removal of Popov. Rykov, as head of the Council of People's Commissars, was, under the direction of the Politburo, in charge of the whole Soviet administrative machine, including TsSU. Quite early in the discussion he demonstrated that as an administrator needing clear guidance from the statisticians he was generally dissatisfied with TsSU:

RYKOV: The table which estimated the harvest was once again miscalculated, and a most unfortunate situation has developed concerning the distribution of commodity grain. The conclusion to be drawn from this is that something must be done, so that everything which occurred this year does not have to be put up with again. Some statistical estimates of the harvest, of the amount of commodity grain, and so on, are of absolutely major significance for our whole policy. It is therefore necessary to carry out changes in TsSU which would prevent us from being placed in such a situation. The work of TsSU cannot be considered satisfactory. Although it should have been heard in the Council of People's Commissars, this report is being heard in the Politburo, because it is connected *with the most important political questions.* The Politburo must give a directive to the Council of People's Commissars that it should take every necessary action to protect the party from the mistakes which are occurring, *and change the leadership of TsSU.*[16]

In his final remarks Kuibyshev, on behalf of the Rabkrin commission, proposed that the Politburo should condemn the "major mistakes" made by TsSU and Popov about the grain balance, and that Popov should be replaced as head of TsSU.

Before the vote, Molotov made a brief personal statement grudgingly apologizing for his attacks on Popov's professional rectitude. Here it is in full: "I am ready to cross out of the stenogram the words which may be interpreted by Comrade Popov as an attack on him personally." (In fact the words remained in the stenogram, as we have seen.)

Popov made a last-minute attempt to save the day for TsSU at the price of sacrificing his own position by proposing "Appoint scientific expertise to investigate the TsSU data, and dismiss Comrade Popov." This was ignored. Kamenev then put Kuibyshev's motion to the vote and it was carried with only Kamenev's vote against. The Politburo decision agreed "in the main" with the conclusions of Rabkrin, and declared that Popov, as director of TsSU, had "permitted major mistakes in the compilation of the grain-fodder balance, making it inadequate for assessing the amount of marketed grain, the surpluses and shortages of grain, and the economic relations of the main strata of the peasantry." Accordingly the Politburo dismissed Popov, and delegated to Rykov and Kuibyshev the search for a new director; their proposal was to be put to the Orgburo and then approved by the Politburo. In the meantime Popov's deputy Pashkovsky was to take charge of TsSU.

Stalin had the last word. After the resolution had been passed, he again demonstrated his devotion to objective statistics:

> STALIN: The main directive to the staff of TsSU: bear in mind that TsSU is a very important scientific establishment of the Republic, the statistical data of which are of prime importance to the ruling agencies of the Republic, and that TsSU is required to produce precise, objectively scientific work, free from political considerations, and that any attempt to adjust the figures to a prejudged opinion will be regarded as a crime.

This clause was promptly adopted and the Politburo moved to the next item on the agenda.

Conclusions

1. The question "On the Work of the TsSU" was placed on the Politburo agenda with the object of removing Popov, the founding director of TsSU, and launching a reform of the statistical administration which would enable the state to adapt it to the interests of Soviet party policy. Two key members of the Politburo — Stalin and Rykov — were unambiguously committed to this verdict in advance, and the party's Control Commission, Rabkrin, provided the data, the arguments, and the recommendations in support of it.

2. This was not a witch-hunting tribunal of the kind represented by the Politburo meeting on the Syrtsov-Lominadze affair five years later.[17] While Popov was subjected to some unjustified political accusations, he himself made similar accusations against the party majority. Basically the case against him had to be made by detailed evidence, and when Molotov accused Popov of political bias, he had to apologize. Popov was given ample time to reply to his accusers, and did not refrain from criticizing Stalin, who presented himself as a firm supporter of scientific objectivity. The Politburo took a vote on the resolution proposed by Kuibyshev on behalf of Rabkrin, and Kamenev voted against it. While the Politburo decision imposed some restrictions on TsSU, the new director continued with some success to struggle for its autonomy.

3. In defending statistics as an objective science which would provide firm clear data to the authorities, Stalin ran roughshod over the complexities of social statistics as they were understood by Popov and his colleagues, and by Western social scientists.

4. The substance of the murky and difficult question of peasant differentiation is still a controversial matter over eighty years later. My own assessment is that TsSU was right in its claim that most of the net extrarural grain was supplied by a relatively small minority of peasant households. A later careful study by A. M. Mikhailovsky, a senior specialist on the grain trade in TsSU, showed that a mere 10–11 percent of households in the European USSR supplied 57 percent of all net extrarural sales of grain in the agricultural year 1927–28.[18] This minority of households, amounting to about two million or so in the whole USSR, was distinct from but overlapped with the smaller "kulak" class. A study based on the 1927 sample census of peasant households was later undertaken by the young Marxist statistician V. S. Nemchinov, who showed that only about half a million households, some 2 percent of the total, could properly be classified as "kulak," and that even in the widest sense the number of kulak households amounted to only 3.8 percent of all peasant households.[19]

5. The Soviet leaders were most unwilling to admit that the supply of grain

depended on a minority of peasants, many of whom were not kulaks but rather relatively well-off grain farmers. Instead, they continued to assert that the middle peasant majority of the peasants provided most of the grain. Stalin, in his famous table of May 1928, purporting to be based on data supplied by Nemchinov, claimed that poor and middle peasant households supplied 74 percent of marketed grain, and that kulaks supplied only 20 percent.[20] But he achieved this result by crudely dividing the peasants into only a couple of groups, the practice to which Popov strongly objected at the Politburo meeting of December 10, 1925.

Notes

I am grateful for comments on an earlier draft of this chapter, and for the supply of material, to Simon Ertz, Yuri Goland, Paul Gregory, Mark Harrison, Oleg Khlevniuk, and Stephen Wheatcroft.

1. *Vsesoiuznaia kommunisticheskaia partiia, XIV s"ezd Vsesoiuznoi kommunisticheskoi partii (b), 18–31 dekabria 1925 g.: Stenograficheskii otchet*, p. 875; emphasis in original.

2. *Pravda*, April 24, 1925; emphasis in original.

3. These statements were published in *Pravda*, August 25, September 17 and 18, and October 24, 1925. On this, see Carr, *Socialism in One Country, 1924–1926*, vol. 1, pp. 292 n. 2, 299, 306 n. 1, and 309.

4. *Pravda*, October 2, 1925.

5. Cited from the archives in *Vestnik statistiki*, 4, 1967, p. 43; see Wheatcroft, "Grain Production and Utilisation in the USSR before Collectivisation," pp. 298–99.

6. Popov (1872–1950) was a Russian from a noble family who studied in Irkutsk and Berlin before the revolution; he began work as a statistician while in exile in Ufa province. He joined the Communist Party in 1924.

7. For a comprehensive study of this question, see Wheatcroft, "Grain Production and Utilisation in the USSR before Collectivisation," pp. 298–99.

8. The above account of the grain balance is simplified. For more details. see Davies, "A Note on Grain Statistics," pp. 314–29, and Karcz, "Back on the Grain Front," pp. 262–94. It was known as the "grain-fodder balance" because it included grain fed to animals, especially horses.

9. Stalin, *Sochineniia*, vol. 3, pp. 214–15, dated May 14.

10. *Ekonomicheskoe obozrenie*, no. 23–24, 1924, p. xxxii; see also Wheatcroft, "Views on Grain Output, Agricultural Reality and Planning in the Soviet Union in the 1920s," pp. 32–35.

11. See Wheatcroft, "Views on Grain Output, Agricultural Reality and Planning in the Soviet Union in the 1920s," pp. 52–53.

12. For details, see ibid., pp. 51–53.

13. This particular stenogram is from the Politburo session of December 10, 1925, "About the Work of TsSU Concerning the Grain-Fodder Balance." It is found in RGASPI Fond 17, op. 3, del. 535. All subsequent quotations are from this source.

14. L. Kamenev, *Nashi dostizheniia, trudnosti i perspektivy,* pp. 24–25 [note by Rykov].

15. The 54 percent was the revised figure provided by TsSU in the autumn following its initial estimate (or rather prediction, as it was made before the harvest) of 61 percent. The 42 percent, as Popov later pointed out, referred to the top two groups, with eight or more desyatinas of sown area per household (see table above, rows 8–9), and thus was consistent with the 61 percent.

16. The italicized phrases were added by Rykov to the final version of his speech.

17. See the chapter by Oleg Khlevniuk in this volume.

18. *Statisticheskoe obozrenie,* no. 5, 1930, pp. 13–49, 142–47.

19. V. S. Nemchinov, *Izbrannye proizvedeniia,* vol. 1, pp. 44–127; see also Davies, *The Socialist Offensive: The Collectivisation of Soviet Agriculture, 1929–1930,* pp. 25–28. In the 1950s Nemchinov was one of the principal founders of the mathematical and econometrics school of economics in the USSR and its application to planning.

20. See Stalin, *Sochineniia,* vol. 11, p. 85. The remaining 6 percent was supplied by collective farms and state farms.

The Politburo on Gold, Industrialization, and the International Economy, 1925–1926

DAVID M. WOODRUFF

The Politburo transcripts for the 1925–26 economic year (October–September) record three sessions on macroeconomic management. The transcripts are broadly consistent with prior historiography, based on both archival and public sources, which has given us a comprehensive picture of policymaking in this crucial year for the fate of the NEP.[1] In the sessions, the Politburo — and invited leaders from the key economic bureaucracies — grappled with the challenges of managing the country's integration into the international economy in light of an unprecedented push for industrial expansion. The challenges were significant, involving an unfavorable trade balance, dwindling gold reserves, and difficulties in securing grain for exports at acceptable prices. Gold shortages were especially hard on industry, which required imports of both raw materials and equipment to meet ambitious goals.

The most forceful and coherent response to the economic challenges was offered by People's Commissar of Finance and Politburo candidate member Grigory Sokol'nikov, who sought a macroeconomic solution through restrictive monetary policy and import cutbacks designed to ensure a favorable balance of trade and an inflow of gold. This approach provoked harsh criticism from Feliks Dzerzhinsky, head of the Supreme Council of the National Economy (Vesenkha), which supervised state-owned industry. Dzerzhinsky received fiery backing from his deputy Georgy Piatakov, who had orchestrated the program of industrial expansion.[2] In this debate — reflecting what Mau has termed the "institutional split" between the industrial bureaucracies and the People's Commissariat of Finance (Narkomfin) — the industrialists failed to prevail.[3] Even after Sokol'nikov's removal from the leadership for his role in the New Opposition at the Fourteenth Party Congress, the Politburo chose macroeconomic restraint over the industrialists' objections.

That this result was possible despite Sokol'nikov's political vulnerability reflected a serious, objective constraint: gold. Excessive industrial ambitions drained gold reserves through two channels. First, they required large imports, especially problematic in the face of weak exports. Second, expansion implied sharp rises in credit to industry, which occurred especially in the early fall of 1925. As the money supply swelled, the finance ministry, Narkomfin, found itself selling more and more gold to maintain the exchange rate. Worried over gold shortages, the Politburo opted for monetary restriction and import cutbacks to ensure a trade surplus, reining in the industrial expansion.

It is striking, however, that in the minds of most leaders macroeconomic policy was not the sole policy needed to address economic difficulties. Macroeconomic forces created problems through their effect on microeconomic decisions — whether of independent peasant producers of grain or of state-controlled economic bodies, both of which reacted to price incentives in ways very visible to the Politburo. Rather than confining itself to changing the macroeconomic environment prompting these decisions, the Politburo also took a number of steps aimed at curtailing the microeconomic autonomy that made them possible. It was this administrative reaction to the economic troubles of 1925–26 that was to have the most lasting significance for what became the Stalinist model of industrialization once monetary restriction was abandoned. Thus, the Politburo record highlights the extreme fragility of the NEP model even as early as the mid-1920's.[4]

An additional lesson of the transcripts is the absolute centrality of the international economy as a concern for Bolshevik policymakers in the period.[5] Deputy industry minister Piatakov set out the stakes most forcefully, calling the lack of hard currency "the fundamental noose that is strangling the development of industry."[6] To get hard currency the Soviets would need to export; to export they needed procurements of grain at prices low enough to make export feasible. But it was not Piatakov alone who saw the dilemma. Again and again, the transcripts reveal, international trade and world prices formed the axis around which policy debate revolved. Indeed, as the discussion below illustrates, efforts to manage the Soviet Union's insertion into the international economy played a crucial role in prompting the policies that were to destroy NEP.[7]

Economic Background

In 1925, Soviet authorities were still committed to a policy of maintaining public faith in the currency by assuring it could be exchanged into gold at a fixed parity. The *chervonets,* or ten-ruble note, bore a specification of its gold content. While citizens could not exchange notes for gold in banks, the People's Commissariat of Finance took pains to ensure that the *chervonets* price of gold on legal or tolerated black markets remained stable — buying gold when its *chervonets* price was cheap and selling it when it was dear.[8] This policy of intervention on the currency markets was a constraint on monetary policy, as an overissue of currency could require sales of gold that drained reserves. Soviet authorities had also made a public, legal commitment to hold gold reserves valued at least a quarter of the currency in circulation — a second way that the availability of gold restricted monetary policy.

However, in the period of the introduction of the *chervonets* (1922–24), and up through the middle of 1925, the gold standard did not in fact force any hard choices about monetary policy. Remonetization of the economy — citizens' willingness to hold more of a currency that they were confident would not depreciate — meant that a great deal of currency could be issued without increasing demand for gold.[9] Indeed, in this period Narkomfin was often a buyer of gold on the markets rather than a seller.[10] Remonetization also broke the link between issue of money and price inflation. From October 1, 1924 to October 1, 1925 the money supply almost doubled with no significant change in observed price levels.[11]

By the summer of 1925, however, the gold standard's constraining effect on monetary policy began to be felt. The period of rebuilding money stocks was over, and further monetary emission did show up as demand for gold. From May of 1925 the state found itself selling more gold coin than it was purchasing.[12] At the same time, the poor harvest of 1924 had led to a decision to spend around 115 million rubles of gold on grain imports, reducing reserves.[13]

The ending of the "free lunch" of noninflationary monetary emission and recent drains of gold reserves did not immediately affect policymaking in the summer of 1925, however. Industrial authorities were poised for an ambitious plan of expansion in the fall, a plan that would require substantial imports of both foreign equipment and foreign raw materials. These plans looked within reach, in part, because of prospects for a very good harvest and, thus, high grain exports. Authorities expected to be able to purchase 780 million poods of grain over the course of the agricultural year, with 380 million poods to go to export.[14] On this basis, the Council of Labor and Defense (STO) approved plans for substantial loans to procurement agencies to facilitate the purchase of grain. Policymakers expected that the good harvest would increase supply and put downward pressure on prices, so possible inflationary effects of this credit expansion were not feared.[15]

In the event, grain prices reached levels much higher than the authorities had anticipated, while procurements were lower.[16] These were the immediate problems that the Politburo would discuss in their late October and early November meetings, covered in the next section.

Some insight into how the summer 1925 decisions were made comes from recriminations over them in the Politburo debates.[17] Demands for gold for industrialization had been intense. Gosplan head Tsiurupa reported that the initial import-export plan, hastily compiled in July, called for 1,059 million rubles of export and 1,009 million rubles of imports — and that even this very large figure involved a cutback of 400 million rubles in import requests by various agencies, especially the Supreme Council of the National Economy.[18] Sokol'nikov complained that the Council of Labor and Defense, where the key decisions were made, was log-rolling its way around credit restrictions: "It's impossible to do anything with you in the Council of Labor and Defense. . . . One can say that the whole policy of procurements before the fall was con- ducted against Narkomfin. I even went to cry into Comrade Stalin's vest . . . about the policy of the Council of Labor and Defense and how it was being conducted. Everybody votes themselves money, the industrialists for the grain procurers, the grain procurers for the industrialists." Dzerzhinsky gave as good as he got, blaming Sokol'nikov's policy of importing goods the preceding economic year for shortages of gold.[19]

Grain Prices and Exports

In a session spread over two dates in late October and early November, the Politburo met to thrash out what to do about flagging procurements and exports and their consequences for industrial expansion plans. The harvest had been good and substantial grain was purchased — well above the amount procured in the preceding year, and 90 percent of the planned amount for the immediate post-harvest months.[20] However, the *price* at which it was pur- chased was well above what had been hoped. Purchasing agents had been given target prices (*direktivnye tseny*) based on world ones, but, armed with ample credit, did not stick to these prices in practice.

By the time the Politburo met, high prices had prompted a dramatic cutback in procurements.[21] People's Commissar of Internal Trade Sheinman reported he now expected 680 rather than 780 million poods for the entire economic year.[22] The cutback was a chaotic process. Sokol'nikov had been away at the start of the procurements campaign, but on his return, shocked by high prices, he took a unilateral decision to curtail credits. He admitted that authorization for this decision came only post hoc, inviting his colleagues to charge him with treason.[23] Supreme Council of the National Economy Deputy Director Kviring complained of the suddenness of the price cutbacks, telling of peasants who had collected sacks from procurement agencies to deliver grain at a price of 1 ruble 60 kopecks a pood, only to be told on their return with grain that they would receive only 1 ruble 15 kopecks: "I have a report that one director of a grain delivery station had to flee from the peasants." The cutback in procurements had important foreign trade implications as well. Freighters that had been contracted for the expected wave of exports were still standing idle in the Black Sea; down payments accepted against the planned shipments had to be returned.[24]

It bears emphasis that it was not so much the volume of grain purchased but rather the price at which it was available *compared to world prices* that was the crucial policy problem the Bolshevik leadership saw itself confronting.[25] Failure to reach the world price levels reflected in the target prices made export unprofitable. Without exports, imports for industry came under threat. The problem of high internal prices reflected what contemporary macroeconomists term an overvalued currency.[26] Simply put, the prices at which Soviet goods entered the world market (their gold prices) were the product of two terms — their ruble prices times the gold value of the ruble. In theory, then, one could reduce gold prices either by reducing ruble prices or by reducing the gold value of the ruble. Strikingly, the second option — devaluation of the *chervonets* — was almost entirely off the table in the Politburo debates: so much so that the need to defend the exchange rate seemed almost taken for granted. It was not only Sokol'nikov who took this position. Stalin warned that "things could end badly for the *chervonets*" without vigorous efforts to accumulate gold reserves by running a trade surplus. Molotov likewise gave a strong statement of the need to defend the *chervonets* in February.[27] (A Politburo commission did debate devaluation in January, but rejected it.[28] See the conclusion for a discussion.)

With devaluation ruled out, debate on high domestic prices for export products centered on two possibilities. Either prices had to come down, or exports would have to take place at a loss. The latter position had some significant support. Internal trade official Sheinman argued that driving procurement prices down to international levels was unrealistic: "in most regions we have reached prices that, although 10–15 percent above the target prices, are acceptable for the internal market. The target prices have a defect, which consists in the fact that we adjust them primarily to world prices. . . . We cannot go to the *muzhik* [the peasant] with [the world] price of 50 kopecks a pood for

rye."[29] (The procurement price for rye in October 1925 was around 75 kopecks per pood.)[30] To earn hard currency, Sheinman argued, some exports
would therefore need to be done at a loss. He complained that a commission
under Kamenev was blocking such efforts. Tsiurupa of Gosplan and Krasin,
the People's Commissar for Foreign Trade, took up the theme more strongly.
Krasin scored the "harm [vred] and defeatism" of discussions on export profitability that were "killing the 'will to export.' "[31] Profitable exports could be
expected only in five to ten years. In the meantime, refusing to export and
expanding internal consumption amounted to a ridiculous policy of "turning
grain into manure [peregona khleba na navoz]." Tsiurupa argued that "export
is necessary and advantageous for us, for without export there is no import; if
we push export, even if it is commercially unprofitable in some cases, we can
cover the losses with the profits from import, which is always profitable."[32]
Organizations resisting unprofitable export should be forced to take into account "the state's overall point of view."

Bureaucratic solutions were also proposed. Gosplan's Tsiurupa reminded
the assembly that even in the summer, in light of the ambitious plans for the
fall, he had called for appointment of a "watchman" (storozh) charged with
"driving export and pressuring exporting organizations." Stalin implied the
split between external and internal prices had institutional roots, and proposed unifying the Commissariats of Internal and Foreign Trade; Kamenev
had a similar position. Dzerzhinsky complained of bureaucratic interference
with the Supreme Council of the National Economy's proposals for ways to
expand exports to fund the imports on which, he stated, industry was critically
dependent. "The requirement for imports . . . is the stimulus that gives us the
possibility of increasing export." Sokol'nikov was scathing in response, keep-
ing monetary issues in the foreground. "And can you pay for anything with a
stimulus?" he asked Dzerzhinsky.[33] As for foreign trade minister, Krasin's
program, it was "senseless," an "effort to evade difficulties in an illusory way."
In order to export at high prices, procurement agencies would have to keep
buying at high prices, and this would mean "throwing an enormous amount of
money into the country," preserving the inflated price level. Instead, Sokol'nikov proposed addressing "the divergence between world and internal prices"
by reducing internal grain prices. This, in turn, would reduce industrial goods'
prices, which, in Sokol'nikov's view were sustained at inflated levels due to the
large incomes peasants derived from high grain prices.

While Sokol'nikov's position against loss-making exports was most forceful, other leaders were also cool to the idea. Rykov accused Krasin of wanting
to turn what should be exceptional into a general rule. How can we push
exports, Stalin asked Krasin, "if prices have leaped and there's nothing to

export?" With some perspicuity, Stalin also noted that relying on imports to compensate for loss-making exports would make it harder to reduce imports in order to husband gold. The eventual decision of a Politburo commission formed to determine policy was to focus on ensuring export profitability while holding loss-making exports to a minimum. This decision seems to have over-ruled a less conservative one issued by some days earlier.[34]

Grain Prices and Procurements

To accept profitability as a criterion for export was to commit oneself to bringing grain prices down. Since this was an achievement that even those willing to countenance loss-making exports would have welcomed, much dis-cussion revolved about how to attain it. In searching for an answer, Bolshevik leaders assessed the roots of high grain prices from both the demand side and the supply side. On the demand side, Sokol'nikov and Rykov articulated a macroeconomic position: high grain prices reflected excessive demand for grain, created by the issue of credit to fund the high plan for procurements and exports. While trade official Sheinman complained in response that he had stuck within strict limits of the finances granted to him, there was general agreement among other leaders that the procurements plan, as Stalin put it, was "inflated [*razdut*]," leading to high prices.[35] At the same time, Sheinman, echoed by Stalin, RSFSR Agriculture Commissar Smirnov, and others, empha-sized the rising price spiral resulting from competition among procurements agents to buy grain. Smirnov even reported that three procurement agents trying to make a purchase from the same peasant had come to blows.[36] Insofar as a bidding war requires resources to bid with, competition among procure-ment agencies was a subordinate problem to that of excess credit. Thus, the whole discussion was another example of the tendency to be scandalized by microeconomic behavior provoked by macroeconomic forces. Even Sokol'ni-kov, who did see the root of high prices in excess credit issued in line with an inflated plan, was happy to mobilize distaste for rivalry among procurement agents to put over his point.[37] To the extent that the problem was too many competing purchasers, additional leverage on prices could be gained by elim-inating private grain purchasers, as Smirnov suggested.[38] Strict policies along these lines were included among the Politburo's final directives.[39] Indeed, a sweeping campaign aimed at driving private grain traders off the market took place through the fall and into the next spring.[40]

On the supply side, the key question was why peasants wouldn't sell grain at lower prices. Here participants began to air the arguments about the procure-ments problem that would be continually rehearsed over the next few years.

Trade official Sheinman gave the basic outlines of the question: "The peasantry sells grain to the extent it needs money: in part for financial needs — taxes, vodka, etc. — and in part to the extent that there are goods available on the market. . . . The stimulus for the peasantry to ship grain lies in industrial goods in two aspects: one aspect is the amount of goods, and the second — the price of goods. . . . If the price is going to be as high as it is now, then the peasantry can get by without some goods, since it's not profitable for it to sell grain at a cheap price and buy goods at an expensive one."[41] In short, peasant sales were held to have two components — an essentially compulsory component based on inflexible monetary obligations, and a voluntary component based on the availability and terms of trade for goods.

On the backdrop of a recent relaxation in tax policy, little attention was devoted to raising the size of peasants' inflexible financial obligations.[42] Sheinman's classing of vodka among these (rather than as a good) proved overoptimistic: Rykov was forced to report in February that receipts were disappointing because "in the village the competition with moonshine is going very poorly."[43] There was also some discussion of revisiting tax or loan policy, but here the leadership was heavily constrained by the publicity with which the conciliatory policies had been announced.[44] Sokol'nikov, who had opposed the tax proposals, presented figures suggesting that the burden of tax policy now fell inappropriately on the poorer peasantry, who had little grain to sell. But this failed to provoke a broader conversation, aside from an ad hominem swipe at Sokol'nikov by Stalin.[45]

If peasants could not be coerced into the market by an incontrovertible need for cash, they would have to be enticed to sell grain by the prospect of making purchases with their receipts. Here the problems were twofold. First, industrial goods' prices were high. Second, goods were often not available, at least at regulated prices in state-controlled cooperative stores — the so-called "goods famine," which began to be noticed from April 1925.[46]

As a baseline for analyzing the Bolsheviks' discussion of these phenomena, it is helpful to consider the unifying, macroeconomic perspective that rising prices and the goods famine were two different forms of inflation. Direct prices rises constituted open inflation, but the goods famine was an example of "repressed" inflation: when prices are unable to rise in line with monetary demand, the result will be that all the goods are bought up and some potential purchasers will be left with money, but nothing to buy.[47] Thus, the goods famine can be seen as a joint result of price controls — initially instituted in response to the "scissors crisis" of 1923 — and excess monetary issue.[48]

In this light, it is extremely significant that no one in the Politburo debates — not even Sokol'nikov — suggested solving the goods famine by liberalizing prices and allowing them to rise. In light of the discussion so far, this consensus is not remarkable. If peasants were going to withhold grain from the market unless they received acceptable terms of trade, allowing industrial products' prices to rise meant allowing grain prices to rise — but this would contradict the desire to maintain low grain prices for export. Many observers have deplored, or even ridiculed, the Bolsheviks' commitment to price controls in this period.[49]

Against the backdrop of the desire to align the domestic price system with the international one, however, the unreflective support price controls received becomes much more comprehensible.[50] Sokol'nikov's diatribe against any suggestion that grain prices should be allowed to rise to match high industrial goods prices is most revealing in this regard:

> SOKOL'NIKOV: We have taken upon ourselves the program of eliminating the scissors, of bringing industrial and agricultural prices to the same level. But what does it mean to carry out this program by way of sanctioning high agricultural prices? It means creating inflation. If your industrial prices are on a level higher than world prices, and if you raise agricultural prices to the same level, your industrial and agricultural prices will turn out to be higher than world prices, i.e. the general price level is higher than the world's, and thus the purchasing power of money is less than the world's. In such a situation, naturally, export is impossible, and with it import. . . . The program of the "scissors," if one regards it as a program that must be carried out via raising agricultural prices to the level of the current industrial prices, is a program for disorganizing our entire economy. We have to correct Comrade Trotsky's program for closing the scissors. . . . We are for elimination of the "scissors," but it isn't needed that the "scissors" be eliminated by raising agricultural prices to the current high level of industrial prices. We must continue and bring to completion the lowering of industrial prices through the lowering of agricultural prices.[51]

In addressing the goods famine, then, Sokol'nikov's primary target was not price caps. While he expressed skepticism about the effectiveness of administrative regulation to overcome market price pressure, he did so in the service of promoting an alternative program of reducing prices via macroeconomic means.[52] With prices falling to match world prices, the price caps would become irrelevant. So it is no surprise that Sokol'nikov glossed over the role of price regulation in giving rise to shortages, stating simply that "a goods famine arises when in the country there is money but no goods,"[53] and concentrated his fire on the sources of excess monetary issue — among them, as in the quote above, issuing credit to fund procurements at high agricultural prices.

In arguing for closing the scissors via downward rather than upward price movements, Sokol'nikov was beating on an open door. Dzerzhinsky, for instance, who was violently opposed to Sokol'nikov on most matters, warned that "We won't get grain from the peasant or anything else for export, if we don't lower retail prices for our products." Even Gosplan's Kviring, who had provoked Sokol'nikov's outburst by noting that high agricultural prices corresponded to high industrial ones, amended his remarks to make clear that both sets of prices should be lower. However, the consensus that prices needed to be lowered still left room for disagreement over how to achieve this aim. There was substantial sentiment that administrative measures curtailing microeconomic autonomy could be an important tool. Kamenev called for resisting inflation "at all costs" and accepted significant restriction in monetary policy to achieve this aim. At the same time he gave much more emphasis to strict limits on cooperative stores' markups over wholesale prices. Sheinman was of similar mind.[54] Sokol'nikov, as noted above, was skeptical on such measures, but did not make them a major target.

Fighting Inflation and the Goods Famine: More Goods or Less Money?

One reason for the fairly marginal role of the debate on administrative measures, no doubt, was that even those most optimistic on their effectiveness conceded that the goods famine and rising prices on industrial goods had an important macroeconomic component. To the extent that both inflation and the goods famine were the result of too much money chasing too few goods, either monetary restriction or an increased supply of goods was a plausible solution. This broad outline of the macroeconomic dilemma was generally shared. As Rykov put it, "the fight with inflation in the presence of a goods famine [implies] that money should be backed by some amount of goods, which can be acquired for this money; since we cannot give goods, we need to reduce the amount of money and lower prices by other means." Kamenev, while also endorsing monetary restriction, advocated policies that would address the problem from the other side by letting "Comrade Piatakov [of the Supreme Council of the National Economy] prepare . . . more calico, leather, and so on and stop up the inflationary hole and the goods famine hole."[55]

Industry officials Dzerzhinsky and Piatakov were, unsurprisingly, likewise advocates of the position that more goods — which they connected with more rapid industrial development — could lead the way out of the country's economic difficulties.[56] However, they too were not entirely indifferent to the effect of monetary forces on inflation and the goods famine. Dzerzhinsky, in particular, accepted that excess credit for procurements had done some harm. "The incorrect grain procurements campaign led to inflation. . . . If inflation had taken place via financing of industry, it would have quickly found a cure, [because] it would have given a commodity equivalent, which would have been on the market. Inflation took place via consumption, and not via production." This argument reflected the viewpoint that insofar as industry was profitable, and paid more into the treasury than it received in return, the net monetary effect of financing industry was deflationary. "Industry practically pumps money out [of the economy]: every pound of sugar, every unit of calico, every pound of kerosene pumps money out, and does not facilitate inflation."[57]

One problem with this economic argument is that it ignores multiplier effects — money that industry spent on inputs and labor could then be spent and respent, so comparing financing to sales or tax payments was neither here nor there. However, it was not until February that anything approaching this logic was articulated — surprisingly enough, by Kuibyshev.[58]

The Gold Budget Constraint

For the course of policy, more significant than these recondite matters of macroeconomic analysis was a real and immediate constraint: the availability of gold. With gold shortages intense, the Bolshevik leadership was greatly concerned about its ability to continue operating in the unforgiving world of international trade finance. Soviet importers often funded their purchases with short-term credit, presumably from sellers, formalized as bills of exchange. If these bills were not paid when due, creditors might formally protest, thereby giving public notice of the Soviets' lack of even short-term creditworthiness. With credit as tight as it was in the aftermath of the Soviet repudiation of tsarist debts, this was an outcome all wished to avoid. As Rykov pointed out, "insofar as our foreign trade is monopolized by the state, a failure to pay due to a lack of hard currency for one or another foreign trade operation is not the bankruptcy of one or another of our organs, which would not be too serious, but the bankruptcy of the state." Stalin and Sokol'nikov sounded similar themes.[59]

Anxiety over the consequences of running out of gold for payments was remarkably deep. In December, Gosplan's Tsiurupa had warned that without reserves, "if some incident happens . . . some payment doesn't get made on time and a bill of exchange gets protested — everything will go head-over-heels immediately." "What's this everything?" asked Rykov. "Do you mean Soviet power, too?" The bare words of the transcript could conceal a sarcastic tone, but Tsiurupa's answer struck a serious note: "No, not Soviet power, but our plans. But I don't know what will happen with us internally when we go bankrupt abroad. This requires additional discussion."[60]

The leadership's anxiety had some real roots: financing for foreign trade operations was clearly balanced on a knife's edge.[61] Trade organs had been issued permission for large imports, based on the receipts envisioned by the ambitious export plans of the summer, and import orders and the accumulation of foreign obligations went forward on this basis. As Krasin noted, "Since you've given us an import program, we are fulfilling it extraordinarily quickly, and every day of delay [in cutting back the import plan] leads to our issuing bills of exchange for millions of rubles, which will need to be paid off."[62]

For October–December 1925, 512 million rubles of import licenses had been issued, even though the Council of Labor and Defense expected export receipts for the quarter to reach only 190 million rubles. Moreover, an estimated 50 million rubles of these receipts would have to go for bills coming due from earlier imports — though Sokol'nikov and others complained that data on these payments was very imprecise. The shortfall was to be made up through short-term trade credit, but as Sokol'nikov noted the huge disparity between hard currency income and expenditure still represented "enormous tension." Gold reserves, meanwhile, were threadbare. One indicator of just how threadbare was the practice of pledging precious metals abroad as collateral on loans, rather than selling them and spending the receipts — an operation whose sole purpose, as Sokol'nikov pointed out, was to avoid showing low levels of reserves.

Sokol'nikov proclaimed that the situation required decisive action to add 200 million rubles in gold reserves, both to ensure stability in foreign payments and to back up the currency. Given expectations of a net increase of over 100 million rubles in foreign credit and various other currency inflows, he suggested this would require a positive trade balance of around 50 million rubles. In this he received full-throated support from Stalin, who with characteristically relentless repetition insisted on the absolute necessity for a positive trade balance, rejecting language from the Council of Labor and Defense that proposed a positive balance "if possible," and offering the much higher figure of 120 million rubles. Perhaps under Stalin's influence, the Politburo commission eventually decided on the still higher figure of 150 million rubles.[63]

The reasons for Stalin's aggressiveness on this point seem to be twofold. The first was his well-known concern about dependence on foreign markets. In the revised transcript, he put this point in words quite similar to those he would use at the Fourteenth Party Congress. "One must bear in mind that the more we export, the more we become dependent on foreign capitalists, and the more vulnerable our economy becomes to blows from the outside. It would be enough, for instance, to boycott our export of say, timber, flax, or grain to a sum of 100 or 200 million — and this is easy for them to do — for our economic plans to become useless and require revision. Therefore we need particular flexibility and caution in foreign trade, and we always must leave ourselves a significant reserve, to protect ourselves from the unexpected."[64] Secondly, Stalin believed that gold reserves were necessary to safeguard the value of the currency. Defending the need for a positive trade balance, he argued, "It is requisite to have a gold reserve to support the exchange rate [*bankovskii kurs*]." In the absence of other sources of gold such as foreign credit, "only with a positive trade balance can we hold off a crisis of the *chervonets* and protect ourselves from inflation and all the perturbations that follow inflation." However, the depth of macroeconomic thinking that underlay this commitment to the gold backing of the currency is open to doubt. In particular there is no evidence of Stalin traversing a chain of logic running from increased monetary issue to the interrelated phenomena of increased demand for gold and inflation in repressed and open forms. Indeed, in February he was to present an entirely nonmonetary analysis of the goods famine (see below). He also confessed confusion over the potential role of reductions in money supply, seeming primarily concerned with whether this could lead to "incineration of money."[65]

In short, while Stalin demonstrated a vigorous commitment to husbanding gold, he showed no signs of a commitment to the gold standard as a nominal anchor and constraint on monetary policy. "The danger [of inflation]," Stalin affirmed, "comes from two sides: on one side from within, because prices for agricultural prices are leaping up — and here it is necessary to take measures to lower prices; on the other side the danger of inflation can come from without, if the trade balance will be negative."[66] Each source of inflationary danger might require its own measures. None of the ones Stalin offered were monetary in character. To lower prices, Stalin called for "elimination of competition among grain procurers" and "measures against the bacchanalia of price rises for manufactured goods by our trade organizations and cooperatives." As noted above, he proposed handling the contradiction between high internal and low external prices by unifying the agencies handling external and internal trade. Even when he approached a demand-driven analysis of the roots of high grain prices, he filtered it through a voluntarist prism: "the peasant completely flipped out [*oshalel*] when he started to get leaned on with requirements for an excessively large amount of grain; he took this all into account and started to be obstinate, and won himself high prices."[67]

Stalin's insistence on a large positive trade balance did not draw a head-on challenge at the November 2 session. His call for import cuts to achieve it was more controversial. Krasin, Piatakov, and Dzerzhinsky emphasized that cutbacks on imports would be painful for industry, and held out hopes for increasing exports by other means. Dzerzhinsky was especially categorical. "And with your formulation, Comrade Stalin, I cannot agree. If we do not take import requirements as our point of departure, we will be slaughtered [*zarezany*], because the fundamental requirements that are being presented must not be cut. . . . For our urgent import requirements we need to seek out [new] categories of export and force exports."[68] Aside from upholding the principle that exports must be profitable, the Politburo commission did not weigh in on this issue. This left the scale of the import cuts implied open to further contention.

Showdown on Industrialization: The Politburo Session of December 12, 1925

By the time the Politburo met again in December of 1925 to discuss procurements and foreign trade, an intense bureaucratic battle over gold had clearly taken place. Tsiurupa—speaking in his new capacity as the head of the newly unified People's Commissariat of Foreign and Internal Trade—reported that there were no less than three distinct proposals for the country's trade and payments balances, and four for the distribution of gold and foreign currency.[69] These came from the People's Commissariat of Foreign and Internal Trade, Gosplan, Narkomfin, and the Supreme Council of the National Economy. The figures were often at great variance. None of the agencies had managed to achieve the trade surplus of 150 million rubles mandated by the Politburo's earlier decision. The proposal of the Commissariat of Foreign and Internal Trade envisioned a surplus of 137 million, that of Gosplan 82 million, and that of the Supreme Council of the National Economy only 21 million. A significant share of this difference could be traced back to disagreements on the import of industrial equipment, with the Supreme Council of the National Economy proposing imports of 116 million rubles versus the 55 million proposed by the Commissariat of Foreign and Internal Trade and Gosplan. Strictures on gold expenditures in the more conservative plans threatened not only capital investment but also current industrial production. Tsiurupa noted that the Commissariat of Foreign and Internal Trade, struggling to maintain a trade surplus, envisioned substantial cutbacks in raw materials imports, "which is, of course, incorrect in essence, for this would mean we would have to go backwards in the development of industry, as a result of which 10, 12, [or] 15 thousand workers would have to be subjected to layoffs."[70]

The bureaucracies also had significant disagreements over how much to build gold reserves. In October, Sokol'nikov had demanded an increase of 200 million in reserves, warning that otherwise the monetary system would "explode."[71] While the Commissariat of Foreign and Internal Trade had drawn up a plan allowing for this, Gosplan's proposal increased reserves only by 119 million, and Supreme Council of the National Economy by only 50 million.

The session shaped up as a battle over whether the rate of expansion of industry was unsustainable, a conclusion for which Kamenev, presiding, plumped in his opening statement, citing the difficulty of drawing up a trade plan that would ensure sufficient growth in gold reserves to back credit emission and a "fairly tense situation with the *chervonets*," probably a reference to increasing intervention on the gold markets.[72]

But it was Sokol'nikov who attacked industrial expansion most fiercely, amplifying and expanding on Kamenev's points. Gold sales in November were 3–4 million rubles, and he expected to spend another 6 million in December. (In October, he had expected to spend 20 million rubles on intervention over the course of the entire coming fiscal year.)[73] He reiterated the case for increased reserves, and called for a cutback in imports of capital equipment. However, in justifying this position he went well beyond the issue of the sufficiency of gold resources, turning to the more general macroeconomic sustainability of the rapid industrial expansion for which this capital equipment was destined. The thrust of Sokol'nikov's critique was that industry had diverted its working capital into investments, draining the state bank of funds that would ordinarily have been held there.[74] As a result, the state bank could not issue long-term loans planned for financing the industrialization campaign. (Dzerzhinsky interrupted with a scornful, and financially ignorant, response: "You want to give us a loan with our own money: take from industry and say, here's your loan."[75] Sokol'nikov's effort, in reply, to give a brief explanation of the role of the banking system as a "reservoir" did not convey the crucial point about fractional reserves.) In short, Sokol'nikov said, plans for an industrial surge relied on triple-counting of working capital resources — one time as immediate capital expenditures, a second time as the reserve base for long-term loans, and a third time when industry assumed increased short-term credit would replace funds diverted to investment. But expanding short-term credit was impossible in view of the broader monetary situation. The only solution was a huge cutback in capital outlays: instead of the nearly 900 million rubles proposed by the Supreme Council of the National Economy one ought to start from 600 million rubles and work up from there.

The industrialists' reaction to Sokol'nikov's onslaught was furious. "The proposal of Comrade Sokol'nikov," said Kviring, "is a proposal to reexamine our party line with respect to the place of industry in the economy." He had a citation from a recent speech by Sokol'nikov and recollections of the decisions of the Twelfth Party Congress to prove it. Rudzutak and Dzerzhinsky ridiculed Sokol'nikov's arguments on multiple counting, and reiterated the point of view that increased production of goods was the key to stabilizing the currency, with Dzerzhinsky even denigrating the role of gold. They also accused Sokol'nikov of a policy that would increase dependence on foreign capital. Dzerzhinsky formulated the alternatives with true Bolshevik starkness. "It's one or the other: either we must orient ourselves to goods from abroad, to finished goods, or we must orient ourselves toward our own goods." Kviring went further, suggesting that Sokol'nikov's planned accumulation of gold reserves, at the expense of industry, would end up with a new decision to spend these reserves for imports of finished goods.[76]

Sokol'nikov expressed some bewilderment at the character of attacks on him, protesting that conducting a general argument about the relative development of industry and agriculture was entirely beside the point.[77] The real questions were more urgent and practical. "We can find ourselves in a situation where an avalanche of layoffs of factory workers lands upon us, if the exhaustion of the working capital of industry and the credit resources of the banks will reach the scale of an industrial crisis. That's the potential danger that needs to be eliminated firmly and in good time. What's the point of mixing in the question about industry [and] agriculture in general? When we have to find a concrete solution for the present day, are we really going to engage in pseudoscientific chatter [*boltologiia*]?"[78]

In the context of the Politburo, this focus on practical concerns carried the day. Dzerzhinsky had struck an uncompromising tone: "Our industrial requirements must be satisfied, at all costs [*vo chto by to ni stalo*]. This is the instruction the Politburo must issue." When Sokol'nikov added, "in line with the available possibilities," Dzerzhinsky was dismissive: "No, at all costs." The Politburo sided with Sokol'nikov. Rykov and Stalin emphasized that the Supreme Council of the National Economy was operating on the basis of plans that had not received official approval, and that approval for too aggressive a plan would not be forthcoming. As Stalin told Dzerzhinsky, "Our current pace [*razbeg*] does correspond to the state of our economy, and we can collapse [*sorvat'sia.*]" The Politburo explicitly voted language that mandated fitting industrial development plans to available resources. Though there was no clear endorsement of Sokol'nikov's point of view on monetary issues, the Politburo rejected the Supreme Council of the National Economy's figures on the trade balance, choosing a far higher figure, closer to Narkomfin's, that would allow for accumulation of reserves.[79]

As a party veteran, Sokol'nikov must of known he could not opt out of ideological casuistry for long. The Fourteenth Party Congress was only a week away. In practical policies, Stalin's position at the Congress differed in no way from those he had defended in the narrower confines of the Politburo. He spoke of the need for a positive trade balance, restraint in the pace of industrialization, and the importance of avoiding inflation.[80] But as a political weapon against Sokol'nikov, who had joined with Kamenev and Zinoviev in the "New Opposition," Stalin adopted at the Congress precisely the *boltologiia* of the industrial lobby. Stalin singled out a publication of Sokol'nikov's subordinate Shanin, whom he accused of wanting to maintain the USSR as an "agrarian country that must export agricultural products and import equipment."[81] This was the charge that Kviring had leveled against Sokol'nikov in the Politburo. Rudzutak, the only member of the industrial lobby to speak at the Congress, was only too happy to pile on, rehearsing the critiques the industrialists had already aired in the Politburo. In an implicit retort to Sokol'nikov's accusation of triple-counting working capital, Rudzutak suggested it was Sokol'nikov who wanted "to hatch the same egg two times" by rechristening short-term credit as long-term credit.[82] Of the policy matters on which the industrialists had sharp disagreements with Stalin, not a word was spoken.

After Sokol'nikov: The Meeting of February 25, 1926

Sokol'nikov's support for the opposition led to his removal as a candidate member of the Politburo and from his post at Narkomfin.[83] In the immediate aftermath of the downfall of its nemesis, the industrial faction had launched a new push to get its monetary theories accepted, but monetary policy was in practice conservative (see Figure 11.1 on growth of Gosbank credit). In January, the Politburo considered, and rejected, a devaluation of the currency pushed by Dzerzhinsky and Piatakov.[84] The transcript of the February 1926 Politburo meeting provides a helpful opportunity to assess how the leadership approached economic policy in the absence of Sokol'nikov's forceful focus on monetary issues.

Stalin, for his part, continued to insist on the need for a trade surplus as a guarantee against inflation, and spoke for a conservative budget policy.[85] At the same time, he explicitly embraced the "disproportion" theory of the goods famine, which saw its source in the more rapid growth of agricultural production compared to that of industry. Echoing both Preobrazhensky and Gosplan economists, Stalin suggested "the goods famine will grow, if we do not move industry forward to the utmost."[86] This theory relied on the assumption that increased agricultural *production* meant increased agricultural *income*, which would show up as excess demand for industrial products. Sokol'nikov had railed against precisely this assumption in November, in view of the fact that

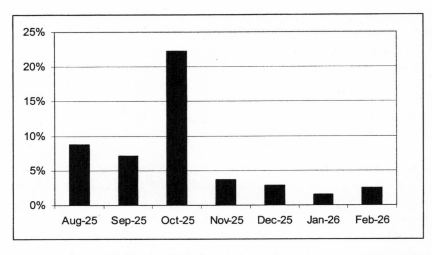

Figure 11.1. Growth of Gosbank Credit (percentage increase over previous month)
Source: Kon"iukturnyi Institut data from Johnson and Temin, "Macroeconomics of NEP," 757.

lower prices could cancel out the potential effects of higher production on demand.[87] In February, even without him, skepticism was widely aired. Kalinin pointed out that the disproportion theory ought to imply a collapse in grain prices as supplies grew — repeating a point Sokol'nikov had made in public the previous year.[88] Rykov pointed out that using the disproportion thesis to explain a changing economic situation amounted to explaining a variable with a constant.[89]

Most surprisingly, both Kuibyshev and Molotov challenged Stalin's point of view. Kuibyshev, while proclaiming Stalin's view "entirely correct," implicitly devalued its importance by stressing that financing capital investment in industry would worsen disproportions by increasing demand and inflationary pressure. Molotov was less tactful: "Some comrades are exaggerating the presence of a tendency to disproportion between agriculture and industry. And this can lead to incorrect and dangerous conclusions, violating the general policy of the party as a whole."[90] He proceeded to identify an overambitious rate of industrialization as a key problem, defense of the exchange rate as a key priority, and restriction of money issue as a key policy.

In short, despite the elimination of Sokol'nikov, the industrialists found the situation in the Politburo no more congenial. Piatakov's effort to demonstrate that industry could supply most of the finance for its own capital expansion was slapped down by Kuibyshev, who noted that Piatakov's calculations involved a massive expansion of short-term credit to replace working capital diverted to investment. Dzerzhinsky conceded that while investments were below what would be wished, "it is clear that you cannot pour anything from an empty vessel." The Politburo approved only 95 million rubles of capital equipment imports, against the 222 million the Supreme Council of the National Economy had requested as recently as December.[91]

Conclusion

Humor was rare in the Politburo sessions. One recorded instance of laughter was when Sokol'nikov satirized what he called the "bureaucratic [*vedomstvennoe*] enthusiasm" of the industrialists: "Comrade Krasin wants to ship goods in, Comrade Dzerzhinsky to ship goods out, and Comrade Rudzutak thinks the main thing is his transport and wants to ship goods around."[92] The significance of such bureaucratic lobbying has been a major emphasis of recent historiography on economic policy in the 1920s.[93] Sokol'nikov's joke highlights the important institutional role of the Politburo in economic regulation. As has been clear at several points in the above narrative, the Politburo took a more cautious line than the Council of Labor and Defense, which, as Mau notes, "had not been able to become a true planning and economic center of the country standing above the individual economic bureaucracies — it remained, as in the times of war communism, an interbureaucracy commission."[94] Sokol'nikov and others disappointed with decisions emerging from the Council of Labor and Defense, including Stalin, clearly sought to push the Politburo to bring the bureaucracies to heel, and in this they had some success. In November, the Politburo revised Council of Labor and Defense decisions to strengthen the importance of export profitability and the push for a positive trade balance. The December session, in which the Politburo made its choice from among three distinct agency proposals on the trade balance, shows it playing the role of a court of final appeal in interbureaucratic quarrels.[95] (This role perhaps helps to explain the almost total silence of Bukharin, who had no economic bureaucracy to represent, and made no attempt whatever to affect practical policy at any of the three sessions.[96] Bukharin's extremely prominent public role as a theorist of development notwithstanding, no one with access to these transcripts would have been tempted to describe the operation of anything like a Stalin-Bukharin "duumvirate.")[97]

As the record shows, the ability to understand macroeconomic matters from a monetary perspective was clearly not limited to Sokol'nikov. Rykov, Kamenev, Molotov, and Kuibyshev all produced relatively coherent macroeconomic analyses drawing a connection between monetary emission, inflation, and the goods famine. Nevertheless, Sokol'nikov's departure was significant.

He was the only participant in any of the meetings to express any skepticism about the effectiveness of microeconomic regulation as a tool for reining in prices. But focused as he was on macroeconomic issues, he made no effort to derail policies restricting retail price markups and repressing private grain purchasers. It was these policies that were the wave of the future. Within a year after his departure, the Politburo held an entire session on "lowering retail prices" without mentioning the money supply as an issue even once.[98]

Thus, in 1925–26, clear portents of the shift of the center of gravity from macroeconomic to microeconomic regulation, which was eventually to destroy NEP, were already visible. Even though Sokol'nikov's policy position carried the day in late 1925, his broader intellectual framework did not. Running out of gold was a danger all could understand, and one on which Stalin was fixated, but reacting to this danger required no decisions on the relative weight of macro-and microeconomic factors in determining prices. Husbanding gold likewise required no general determination on whether or not to accept profitability as the criterion of foreign trade. For Stalin, the decision to reject unprofitable exports stemmed from concerns that the desire to cover losses would prompt excessive imports, and not, as for Sokol'nikov, the need to avoid further stoking excess demand. But with imports centrally managed, and monetary issue as an alternate way of covering losses, husbanding gold could be made consistent with unprofitable exports, and so, over the next several years, it was.[99]

The role of the gold standard itself in the slide to an administered price system must also be recognized.[100] It was the exchange rate of the *chervonets* that determined the target prices for grain and, because of the desire to offer acceptable terms of trade to the peasant, for industrial goods. Even in Western Europe in the 1920's, Karl Polanyi argued, efforts to enforce deflation as the gold standard required led to "authoritarian interventionism" and "governmentally adjusted prices and wages."[101] Under the direction of a party taught by experience that "the 'invisible hand' was not on the tiller," this dynamic could only be more intense.[102]

By successfully defending a disequilibrium, overvalued exchange rate in January 1926, advocates of market equilibrium won a pyrrhic victory. As the Politburo struggled with the consequences of overvaluation in 1925–26, grim omens of what was to come could be heard. Complaining about the difficulties of making grain purchases at low prices despite the presence of peasant stocks, Tsiurupa asked whether Dzerzhinsky might be helpful in his role as head of the OGPU.[103] Molotov reported that grain prices had been driven down in Ukraine only by "only thanks to a number of measures of a semi–War Communist character."[104] And Kamenev reacted to the crowding out of exports by domestic consumption — funded by the valuable *chervonets* — in words that can only have a chilling resonance now: "How can we conduct the sort of policy Witte discussed: we don't eat enough ourselves, but we export? There are no methods to do this; we haven't felt our way to these methods."[105] It would not take long.

Notes

1. Nonarchival sources that remain extremely valuable are Carr, *Socialism in One Country, 1924–1926,* vol. 1, and Dohan, "Soviet Foreign Trade in the NEP Economy and Soviet Industrialization Strategy." Outstanding archival work on the period includes: Graziosi, " 'Building the First System of State Industry in History': Piatakov's VSNKh and the Crisis of the NEP 1923–1926," pp. 539–80; Mau, *Reformy i dogmy, 1914–1929: Ocherki istorii stanovleniia khoziaistvennoi sistemy sovetskogo totalitarizma;* Goland, "Currency Regulation In the Nep Period," pp. 1251–1296; and Goland, *Krizisy, razrushivshie NEP; Valiutnoe regulirovanie v period NEPa.*

2. On Piatakov and the industrial program, see Graziosi, " 'Building the First System of State Industry in History': Piatakov's VSNKh and the Crisis of the NEP 1923–1926," pp. 539–580.

3. Mau, *Reformy i dogmy, 1914–1929: Ocherki istorii stanovleniia khoziaistvennoi sistemy sovetskogo totalitarizma,* pp. 137–151.

4. Graziosi, " 'Building the First System of State Industry in History': Piatakov's VSNKh and the Crisis of the NEP 1923–1926," p. 556.

5. Certainly, no scholar of the economic dilemmas and debates of the period has entirely ignored international trade and finance, but they have often not received the centrality they deserve. See, for instance: Nove, *An Economic History of the U.S.S.R.;* Erlich, *The Soviet Industrialization Debate, 1924–1928;* Lewin, "The Immediate Background of Soviet Collectivization"; and Carr, *Socialism in One Country, 1924–1926,* vol. 1. By contrast, studies that give international factors pride of place in understanding the economic dilemmas of NEP gain additional luster from the new evidence. See Dohan, "Soviet Foreign Trade in the NEP Economy and Soviet Industrialization Strategy"; Day, *Leon Trotsky and the Politics of Economic Isolation:* Goland, "Currency Regulation in the Nep Period," pp. 1251–1296; and Goland, *Krizisy, razrushivshie NEP; Valiutnoe regulirovanie v period NEPa.*

6. RGASPI Fond 17, op. 3, del. 533.

7. For a related argument based solely on remarkably diligent pursuit of published sources, see Dohan, "Soviet Foreign Trade in the NEP Economy and Soviet Industrialization Strategy."

8. Goland, "Currency Regulation in the Nep Period," pp. 1251–1296; Barnett, "As Good as Gold? A Note on the Chervonets," pp. 663–669.

9. Johnson and Temin, "The Macroeconomics of NEP," p. 755.

10. Goland, "Currency Regulation in the Nep Period," pp. 1258–1259.

11. For the money supply (defined here as deposits held with and notes issued by Gosbank), see Arnold, *Banks, Credit, and Money in Soviet Russia,* pp. 246–247, quoted in Johnson and Temin, "The Macroeconomics of NEP," p. 754. For price levels, see Malafeev, *Istoriia tsenoobrazovaniia v SSSR, 1917–1963 gg.,* pp. 378–379.

12. Goland, "Currency Regulation in the Nep Period," p. 1261.

13. RGASPI Fond 17, op. 3, del. 533. Figure given by Sokol'nikov.

14. RGASPI Fond 17, op. 3, del. 533. Figures given by Sheinman.

15. Carr, *Socialism in One Country, 1924–1926*, vol. 1, p. 292. RGASPI Fond 17, op. 3, del. 533. Remarks by Dzerzhinsky.

16. Carr, *Socialism in One Country, 1924–1926*, vol. 1, p. 293.

17. See also Goland, "Currency Regulation in the Nep Period," p. 1262.

18. RGASPI Fond 17, op. 3, del. 533.

19. RGASPI Fond 17, op. 3, del. 533.

20. RGASPI Fond 17, op. 3, del. 533. Figure from Kamenev.

21. Carr, *Socialism in One Country, 1924–1926*, vol. 1, p. 293.

22. RGASPI Fond 17, op. 3, del. 533. Sheinman's office from Ivkin, *Gosudarstvennaia vlast' SSSR: Vysshie organy vlasti i upravleniia i ikh rukovoditeli, 1923–1991 gg., istoriko-biograficheskoi spravochnik*, p. 598.

23. RGASPI Fond 17, op. 3, del. 533.

24. RGASPI Fond 17, op. 3, del. 533. Remarks by Rudzutak, Kamenev, and Sokol'nikov. Kviring's office from www.hrono.ru/biograf/kviring.html.

25. RGASPI Fond 17, op. 3, del. 533. Kamenev, for instance, lapsed into repetition to convey the severity of the situation: "In these circumstances it is extremely difficult to make the necessary exports. Prices on the external market are falling, whereas ours remain extremely high. This is an extremely worrisome signal." Stalin, Rykov, Sheinman, and Sokol'nikov also explicitly discussed the issue. For the extra-Politburo discussion see Dohan, "Soviet Foreign Trade in the NEP Economy and Soviet Industrialization Strategy," p. 246.

26. On the significance of the overvalued ruble see especially Dohan, "Soviet Foreign Trade in the NEP Economy and Soviet Industrialization Strategy," p. 3 and throughout. The intellectual framework for understanding currency overvaluation was available to the Politburo, especially via the work of Iurovskii. See Goland, "Currency Regulation in the Nep Period," and Iurovskii, *Denezhnaia politika sovetskoi vlasti 1917–1927: Izbrannye stat'i.*

27. RGASPI Fond 17, op. 3, del. 680.

28. Goland, "Currency Regulation in the Nep Period," p. 1267.

29. RGASPI Fond 17, op. 3, del. 533.

30. Calculated from Johnson and Temin, "The Macroeconomics of NEP," p. 755, Table 2.

31. RGASPI Fond 17, op. 3, del. 533.

32. RGASPI Fond 17, op. 3, del. 533. Exporting at a loss and compensating with import profits had already been practiced as early as the 1924–25 economic year. See Dohan, "Soviet Foreign Trade in the NEP Economy and Soviet Industrialization Strategy," pp. 226–27.

33. These exchanges are from RGASPI Fond 17, op. 3, del. 533.

34. RGASPI Fond 17, op. 3, del. 533. Remarks by Stalin and concluding "Directives for Soviet Organs," section V, point 3.

35. RGASPI Fond 17, op. 3, del. 533.

36. RGASPI Fond 17, op. 3, del. 533. Compare Carr, *Socialism in One Country, 1924–1926*, vol. 1, pp. 295–97, 321.

37. RGASPI Fond 17, op. 3, del. 533. *Sokol'nikov:* "But you have seen perfectly clearly

what happens when we put forward an enormous plan, how a race among the grain procurers begins, how on this basis a wild [*beshenaia*] competition between procurers forms and how prices begin to jump."

38. RGASPI Fond 17, op. 3, del. 533. *Smirnov:* "If we do not take the internal market into our hands, then it will be a command, when the peasant brings grain and sells it for a ruble, while right nearby a private purchaser is paying a ruble ten. This will be a command, and the peasant will understand it that way. Thus we need to add: in developing our plan we need to decisively adopt the task of organizing our grain market, so that [the People's Commissariat of Internal Trade] can dictate in some measure grain prices."

39. RGASPI Fond 17, op. 3, del. 533. Concluding "Directives to Soviet Organs," Part A, Section 3.

40. Goland, *Krizisy, razrushivshie NEP; Valiutnoe regulirovanie v period NEPa*, p. 20; Dohan, "Soviet Foreign Trade in the NEP Economy and Soviet Industrialization Strategy," pp. 268–69. RGASPI Fond 17, op. 3, del. 680. Remarks by Kamenev.

41. RGASPI Fond 17, op. 3, del. 533. Compare Preobrazhensky's view as expressed in Erlich, *The Soviet Industrialization Debate*, p. 35.

42. Carr, *Socialism in One Country, 1924–1926*, vol. 1, pp. 249–56.

43. RGASPI Fond 17, op. 3, del. 680.

44. Carr, *Socialism in One Country, 1924–1926*, vol. 1, pp. 267–75. Kamenev argued against accelerating deadlines for tax payments as a form of financial pressure, citing public promises. RGASPI Fond 17, op. 3, del. 533. Stalin, however, spoke for tax acceleration, though he struck his suggestion from the final transcript.

45. RGASPI Fond 17, op. 3, del. 533.

46. Johnson and Temin, "The Macroeconomics of NEP," p. 755.

47. For a general introduction to the phenomenon of repressed inflation see Peebles, *A Short History of Socialist Money.*

48. Johnson and Temin, "The Macroeconomics of NEP," p. 755. For background on the evolution of price policy see ibid., Carr, *Socialism in One Country, 1924–1926*, vol. 1, pp. 435–38, and Mark Harrison's essay in this volume.

49. For example, Johnson and Temin, "The Macroeconomics of NEP"; Nove, *An Economic History of the U.S.S.R.*

50. For less categorical suggestions in this vein, see Dohan, "Soviet Foreign Trade in the NEP Economy and Soviet Industrialization Strategy"; and Goland, *Krizisy, razrushivshie NEP: Valiutnoe regulirovanie v period NEPa.*

51. RGASPI Fond 17, op. 3, del. 533.

52. RGASPI Fond 17, op. 3, del. 533. *Sokol'nikov:* "I am not entirely agreed with what Comrade Sheinman said about administrative action regarding prices. At a certain level the contradiction between the situation on the market and administrative measures begins to paralyze measures of administrative regulation . . ."

53. RGASPI Fond 17, op. 3, del. 537.

54. These exchanges are from RGASPI Fond 17, op. 3, del. 533.

55. RGASPI Fond 17, op. 3, del. 533.

56. RGASPI Fond 17, op. 3, del. 533. For Sokol'nikov's analysis of these arguments after the fact, see Sokol'nikov, *Novaia finansovaia politika: Na puti k tverdoi valiute*, pp. 324–26.

57. RGASPI Fond 17, op. 3, del. 533.

58. RGASPI Fond 17, op. 3, del. 680.

59. RGASPI Fond 17, op. 3, del. 533.

60. RGASPI Fond 17, op. 3, del. 537. Compare Rykov's earlier comments, RGASPI Fond 17, op. 3, del. 533: "After all, we are in the sort of situation that a crisis even with the payments of the Cotton Committee is not just a crisis of the Cotton Committee but a crisis of Soviet power," though here he seems to be discussing a crisis of commercial reputation rather than a political crisis.

61. Goland, "Currency Regulation in the Nep Period," p. 1264.

62. RGASPI Fond 17, op. 3, del. 533.

63. These exchanges are from RGASPI Fond 17, op. 3, del. 533, concluding "Directives," section V, point 1.

64. RGASPI Fond 17, op. 3, del. 533. The unrevised text, just prior in the transcript, makes a similar point, though it draws the connection to reserves less directly. For Stalin's extremely similar remarks at the Fourteenth Party Congress, see Vsesoiuznaia kommunisticheskaia partiia, *XIV s"ezd Vsesoiuznoi kommunisticheskoi partii (b), 18–31 dekabria 1925 g.: Stenograficheskii otchet,* p. 29.

65. RGASPI Fond 17, op. 3, del. 533.

66. RGASPI Fond 17, op. 3, del. 533.

67. RGASPI Fond 17, op. 3, del. 533.

68. RGASPI Fond 17, op. 3, del. 533.

69. For Tsiurupa's office and the unification, see Ivkin, *Gosudarstvennaia vlast' SSSR: Vysshie organy vlasti i upravleniia i ikh rukovoditeli,* pp. 130–31.

70. RGASPI Fond 17, op. 3, del. 537.

71. RGASPI Fond 17, op. 3, del. 533.

72. RGASPI Fond 17, op. 3, del. 537.

73. RGASPI Fond 17, op. 3, del. 533.

74. On this phenomenon, see Goland, "Currency Regulation In the Nep Period," p. 1266, and more generally Graziosi, " 'Building the First System of State Industry in History': Piatakov's VSNKh and the Crisis of the NEP 1923–1926," p. 579 n. 143.

75. RGASPI Fond 17, op. 3, del. 537.

76. RGASPI Fond 17, op. 3, del. 537.

77. RGASPI Fond 17, op. 3, del. 537.

78. These exchanges are from RGASPI Fond 17, op. 3, del. 537.

79. RGASPI Fond 17, op. 3, del. 537.

80. *Vsesoiuznaia kommunisticheskaia partiia, XIV s"ezd Vsesoiuznoi kommunisticheskoi partii (b), 18–31 dekabria 1925 g.: Stenograficheskii otchet,* pp. 28, 30, 35–36, 49–50.

81. Ibid., pp. 27–28.

82. Ibid., p. 339.

83. Genis, "Upriamyi Narkom s Il'inkoi," p. 23; Goland, "Currency Regulation in the Nep Period," p. 1267.

84. Goland, "Currency Regulation in the Nep Period," pp. 1267–79.

85. RGASPI Fond 17, op. 3, del. 680.

86. RGASPI Fond 17, op. 3, del. 680. For background on the disproportion theory, see Erlich, *The Soviet Industrialization Debate,* p. 35; and Goland, *Krizisy, razrushivshie NEP: Valiutnoe regulirovanie v period NEPa,* pp. 25–32.

87. RGASPI Fond 17, op. 3, del. 533.

88. RGASPI Fond 17, op. 3, del. 680. Compare Sokol'nikov, *Novaia finansovaia politika: Na puti k tverdoi valiute,* p. 276.

89. RGASPI Fond 17, op. 3, del. 680. Compare Sokol'nikov, *Novaia finansovaia politika: Na puti k tverdoi valiute,* p. 326.

90. RGASPI Fond 17, op. 3, del. 680.

91. RGASPI Fond 17, op. 3, del. 680. Concluding "Resolution of the Politburo," Section I.B., items b and v. Compare RGASPI Fond 17, op. 3, del. 537, where Tsiurupa reported Vesenkha's request.

92. RGASPI Fond 17, op. 3, del. 533. English does not permit a particularly felicitous rendering of the joke, which plays on a common root: "т. Красин хочет ввозить, т. Дзержинский вывозить, а т. Рудзутак считает, что самое основное—это его транспорт и хочет перевозить."

93. Mau, *Reformy i dogmy: Ocherki istorii stanovleniia khoziaistvennoi sistemy sovetskogo totalitarizma;* Shearer, *Industry, State, and Society in Stalin's Russia, 1926–1934.*

94. Mau, *Reformy i dogmy: Ocherki istorii stanovleniia khoziaistvennoi sistemy sovetskogo totalitarizma,* p. 155.

95. Thus Dzerzhinsky at the December session: "I all the same request that we hear from the main agencies: Gosplan, Vesenkha, Narkomfin. Limit the time maybe, but put the whole picture before the Politburo." RGASPI Fond 17, op. 3, del. 537.

96. The Politburo transcripts thus confirm the picture of Bukharin's passivity in the face of the Vesenkha industrialization drive drawn in Graziosi, " 'Building the First System of State Industry in History': Piatakov's VSNKh and the Crisis of the NEP 1923–1926."

97. Cohen, *Bukharin and the Bolshevik Revolution: A Political Biography, 1888–1938,* pp. 213–42.

98. RGASPI Fond 17, op. 3, del. 703. See Mark Harrison's essay in this volume.

99. Dohan, "Soviet Foreign Trade in the NEP Economy and Soviet Industrialization Strategy," p. 297, 482.

100. Cf. ibid.

101. Polanyi, *The Great Transformation,* pp. 233–34.

102. Rosenberg, "The Problem of Market Relations and the State in Revolutionary Russia," pp. 356–96, 377. I have used Rosenberg's description of October 1917 to summarize his broader thesis applying to the 1920s.

103. RGASPI Fond 17, op. 3, del. 537.

104. RGASPI Fond 17, op. 3, del. 680.

105. RGASPI Fond 17, op. 3, del. 533.

12

Prices in the Politburo, 1927:
Market Equilibrium versus the Use of Force

MARK HARRISON

The Politburo met on January 3, 1927, to discuss progress towards cutting the retail prices of industrial commodities.[1] The meeting itself had no great influence on events. The policy of cutting retail prices had been previously adopted — at the party Central Committee plenum in April 1926 — and was already in effect. The policy was supported by a broad consensus of those present, although the Left Opposition was no longer represented in the Politburo.[2] The main purpose of the meeting was evidently to review progress, which had been difficult. The main outcome was to refer the discussion to a subcommittee that already existed, and to reinforce its membership. The discussion is of interest today because it shows the Bolshevik leaders debating the role of market equilibrium versus the use of force in the allocation of resources.

The transcript teases us with fleeting glimpses of individual leaders at work. The discussion is led by Anastas Mikoyan (Politburo member and trade commissar), and chaired actively by Aleksei Rykov (Politburo member and head of the government). These come across as worthy prefects, able to manage detail, and to make a point sharply, but with no great sense of occasion or mission. Stalin is already the teacher, disciplining the classroom from time to time by bringing the pupils back to fundamentals when they stray from the point: "It should be emphasized," he demanded, that the matters under discussion "present a most serious danger, that the struggle against this danger is one of the most important tasks of our party. All this should have been emphasized, but this, unfortunately, Comrade Mikoyan's report does not do." Nikolai Bukharin (Politburo member and *Pravda* editor) is the class wit; his classmates laugh at his jokes, but he also makes a clever, substantive intervention that wins Stalin's approval. Mikhail Kalinin (Politburo member and titular head of state) is the boy who would like everyone to be nice. Stanislav Kosior (then a secretary of the Central Committee) is the voice of the real world outside the classroom: there's trouble in the playground; something must be done. Others help to carry the drama along but do not stand out for their roles in the plot.

The wider context is this. After nearly three years of suspension during the Russian Civil War the Bolsheviks returned the urban-rural market to legality in March 1921 — too late to avert a bitter famine in the winter of that year that may have cost six million lives.[3] Agriculture was in ruins; so was industry. After that, the economy recovered.

A core process driving the recovery was the restoration of urban-rural exchange. Peasants grew foodstuffs, tobacco, fibers, and by-products of animal husbandry such as wool and leather, which they sold on the market to urban consumers and producers for cash. They used this cash to buy industrial commodities: salt, refined sugar, matches, fabrics, metal goods, and farm implements. Firms located in the towns and cities, often state-owned, supplied these goods for cash; in turn, they and their workers were able to purchase the unprocessed foods and materials they required of agriculture. This classical process of Smithian specialization and exchange returned the Soviet economy to something close to prewar levels of output and employment by the later 1920s.[4]

The recovery process was marked by two crises in the urban-rural market, the "scissors" crisis of 1922–23 and the grain procurement crisis that began at the end of 1927. How the scissors crisis got its name is shown in Figure 12.1: in the second half of 1922 there was a rapid divergence of relative prices of immense proportions that, when illustrated on a graph, looked like a pair of scissors with the blades opening. Ever after, commentators referred to the real price of industrial goods as the "scissors." When the price rose, the scissors opened; when it fell, they closed. Participants in the Politburo meeting also extended the metaphor to other contexts: the "wholesale-retail scissors," for example, meant the gap between wholesale and retail prices of the same goods; another "urban-rural" scissors involved higher prices for the same goods in villages compared with urban retail outlets.

The course of the scissors crisis was as follows.[5] The Civil War was over. Agricultural production was recovering from the famine of 1921, while industry struggled to reorganize and recover. Industrial prices rose and agricultural prices fell away. By October 1923, the real price of industrial goods, measured

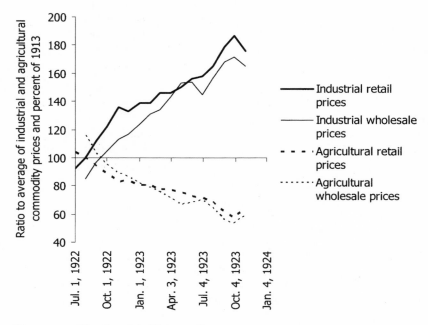

Figure 12.1. The Opening "Scissors," 1922–1923
Source: Based on the data underlying a similar figure reproduced by Strumilin, *Na plano-vom fronte*, p. 64, from *Biulleten' Gosplana*, no. 10 (1923).

in food units, reached more than three times the prewar relativity. (This was true of both retail and wholesale prices, but the chart reminds us that the retail and wholesale scissors could and did move independently in some degree.) Faced with such disadvantageous terms, the peasants failed to return to the market with their food supplies for the hungry towns. The Soviet state took action to close the scissors and this brought the peasants back to the market. But the scissors were not shut completely. For this reason and others, food marketing never recovered to the levels witnessed before the World War and revolution.[6] During 1925 and 1926, moreover, the scissors tended to spring open again. As Figure 12.2 suggests, wholesale prices were not such a source of concern, at least by the standards of 1922–23, but the divergence of retail prices became quite marked again in the mid-1920s and this was both a worry and a puzzle.

When the Politburo met in January 1927 a second crisis, the food marketing crisis of 1928 and 1929, lay just around the corner. Unlike the first, it would prove terminal; it provoked suspension of the market followed by the eventual destruction of the entire system of peasant farming.

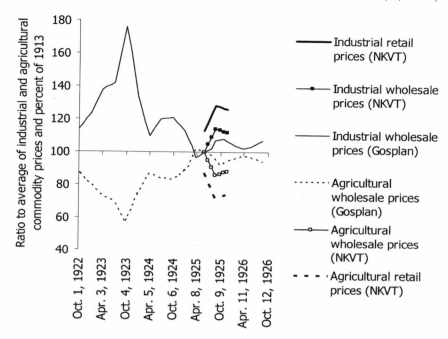

Figure 12.2. The Scissors Open, Close, and Reopen, 1922–23 to 1925–26
Source: Based on the data underlying a similar figure produced for the Central Committee plenum, October 9, 1925, found in RGASPI Fond 17, op. 2, del. 197, l. 66. Thanks to Simon Ertz for this reference. The long series are by Gosplan; the short series, July 1925 to January 1926, are by the Ministry of Internal Trade (NKVT).

The food marketing crisis of 1928 and 1929 and the scissors crisis of 1922–23 bear superficial similarities. In each crisis peasants became unexpectedly reluctant to bring their products to the market; this threatened the supply of food and raw materials to industry, urban households, and the armed forces, as well as exports that were urgently needed to earn scarce foreign currency. In each crisis the relative price of manufactures on the urban-rural market appeared to be excessively high. The first crisis was apparently resolved when the authorities intervened to force down the price of industrial commodities; following this intervention, food marketing recovered and economic expansion was resumed. The authorities concluded that they had succeeded in mastering the laws of the market.

Yet when the same policies were applied in an apparently similar context a few years later the results were exactly opposite: industrial prices were pressed down, but this time food supplies deteriorated. In short, an intervention that stabilized the economic recovery in 1923 proved destabilizing when attempted a second time in 1927, with far-reaching consequences: eventually the lives of 100 million people were turned upside down, and a significant proportion of them were tragically curtailed. When the Politburo met in January 1927, however, the consequences lay in the future.

I will focus on three aspects of the discussion that took place in this context: the motivations behind the policy of price reductions, its feasibility given the resistance encountered in attempting to implement it, and the range of methods that were contemplated to enforce the policy.

Motivations

In calling for retail price cuts in 1926–27 the Bolshevik leaders were intervening against the market. At a general level, the motivation for cutting industrial prices does not emerge strongly from the Politburo debate. Mikoyan's written report mentioned it only briefly before launching into the technicalities of price measurement. "The huge significance of the level and trend of retail prices for the national economy, for determining the purchasing power of the *chervonets* [ruble], for determining the real level of the workers' wages, and for determining economic relations between town and country," he wrote, "is obvious to all."

This neglect of fundamentals was a source of impatience to at least one participant, Stalin: the wide-open scissors, he insisted in debate, "are opening up a rich field for private capital and are establishing favorable conditions for disruption of the alliance [between the peasants and workers]." He quoted lengthily from the Central Committee resolution of the previous April: "the success of the further progress of grain procurements — including fulfilment of the export plan and the real growth of wages, and accomplishments in the struggle with private capitalist accumulation — depends completely on the continued reduction of retail prices for industrial goods and agricultural products. The attention of the trade unions, state industry, state agencies, and especially cooperatives, should be focused on this struggle in the immediate future."

Although the overarching aims of the policy of price cuts were not strongly articulated in the Politburo, where they did emerge there was a rough consensus. Cutting industrial prices was intended to draw both the workers and the peasants into the process of socialist industrialization and economic development. The "alliance" of the peasants and workers envisaged urban-rural trade as a cooperative, positive-sum game: through trade, the peasants could obtain the industrial commodities that they needed, and supply the state in return with food and raw materials for the urban workers and soldiers, industrial production, and exports. Cutting retail prices of industrial commodities could raise real wages, reduce worker discontent, and offer the peasants more advantageous terms on which to engage in trade.

Or could it? Outside the Politburo, this policy was criticized from the left and from the right. Expert advice from the Finance Ministry was to allow prices to find their equilibrium level.[7] Some basic economic reasoning (set out in more detail in the appendix to this chapter) suggests why. If the price of a good falls, the quantity demanded will increase. The market will remain in balance only if there is a matching increase in supply. In 1923 the Bolsheviks had forced down the prices of industrial goods against the resistance of the newly formed syndicates, or wholesale supply monopolies, in state industry. The price cuts had promoted the recovery of industry *because its spare capacity could support a large increase in supply.*

But the same did not happen a second time. What the Bolsheviks had not fully realized was that in 1923 they had managed to cut prices *and* preserve equilibrium because the price cuts were accompanied by a rise in industrial production that was immediate, not planned hopefully for the distant future. By 1927, the progress of the industrialization program was already imposing strains on industrial capacity. State industry generally had much less spare capacity than four years before. The rapid growth of capital goods production to meet the needs of the investment program left little capacity to meet the needs of the retail market. As a result, the output of consumer goods and farm implements was restrained.

What was to be expected in 1927 if the policy succeeded and prices were cut, *but the supply of manufactures did not respond?* Growing shortages were inevitable; indeed, by 1926–27 there were already widespread shortages of manufactures, known at the time as the "goods famine" — a famine of industrial goods as opposed to a conventional food famine. Particular shortages could be met to a limited extent by forced substitution: the head of Tsentrosoiuz, the central union of consumer cooperatives, Isidor Liubimov, told the Politburo how industrial suppliers were compelling retail networks to substitute unwanted fish products, soap, and glassware for those ordered. But the fact is that the policy of price cuts was deliberately focused on those mass consumption goods that were already *least* available. The previous decisions of the Council of Labor and Defense, Mikoyan reported, had singled out for 10 percent price reductions "the following *deficit* commodities: fabrics, leather, nails, iron, and so forth," which he also described as *the most widely sold* (emphasis added). They were selected for price cuts, apparently, on the grounds that trade markups were already higher for deficit goods and gave the most scope for reduction. This ignored the probability that higher markups reflected greater scarcity; price cuts for deficit commodities also offered the greatest scope for further unbalancing the market.

Given the goods famine, there was more than one possible outcome. One alternative was simply to accept a policy defeat, abandon the price cuts, and allow the market to return to equilibrium. There would have been a political cost, however: the Bolsheviks would be seen to have broken a promise.

Alternative outcomes were arguably as bad or worse. One claimed purpose of the policy of price cuts was to create advantageous terms for the peasants to sell food to the state. But there was no advantage to the peasants if, beyond a point, they could not buy manufactures at *any* price. Beyond that point, the only effect of industrial price cuts would be to reduce the sums the farmers would need to raise to buy the manufactures actually available, and so cut the quantities of food that the farmers would bring to the market. In a market that was already out of equilibrium, cutting the prices of industrial goods would be actually counterproductive in terms of stimulating food supplies.

There could be further unintended consequences. The state could lose control of the market for industrial goods, and even of industrial production. The widening shortages of industrial goods would create strong incentives for private traders and private producers to enter the market. Even if supply remained unchanged, it would be advantageous for traders to buy up state goods at low official prices and sell them on to consumers at high equilibrium prices. Consumers would end up paying the same prices as before. The private traders would collect some or all of the profits that could have been made by the state. The Politburo debaters called this "speculation": thus, Mikoyan declared, "I am not against accumulation [i.e. profit seeking], I am for accumulation." Voice: "Obviously." Mikoyan: "If it's on the basis of properly organized work, not through price inflation and speculation."

The gap between low official prices and high market prices could also motivate private producers to enter the market and supply the missing manufactures, aided by the fact that "the peasant sells his wares at half the factory price at most" (Rykov). Private industry supplying the retail market would grow while the socialist sector would remain static. This shift in relative proportions was what Stalin feared when he mentioned the "struggle with private capitalist accumulation" and the threat to the "alliance" between the peasants and workers": when the peasants were selling to private traders and artisans, not to the state, they were at risk of becoming detached from the alliance.

It is generally understood that prices play a number of roles in a market economy: ideally they signal scarcities; attract resources to high-profit uses; balance supply and demand so that markets are cleared without undesired excess capacity or frustrated consumers; and they distribute income between wages, profits, and rents. The Politburo discussion was almost exclusively focused on the distributive aspect of prices; participants saw high industrial commodity prices primarily as redistributing income away from urban and rural households to profits, and they were not thinking at all about the need to balance supply and demand. Although nobody in the Politburo quoted Marx, this emphasis was, perhaps, characteristically Marxian.

The other voice excluded from the Politburo was the defeated Left Opposition's. In earlier years both Iury Piatakov (deputy commissar of state industry) and leftist theoretician Evgeny Preobrazhensky had urged that industrial prices should be maintained or increased. This was because they favored the redistribution of income towards industrial profits in order to finance industrialization; they were not concerned about market equilibrium. The attitude of Leon Trotsky, leader of the Left Opposition, was equivocal: he was against an increase in industrial retail prices on tactical political grounds, but he did favor an increase in wholesale industrial prices so as to channel profits out of trade into industry. During 1926 Piatakov also advocated this intermediate position. One result of the hedging and fudging was that the opposition came to appear divided and without a clear alternative to that of the leadership.[8]

In terms of market equilibrium, however, the policy of actually reducing retail prices made sense only if the state sector could respond by rapidly increasing the supply of products to the market. This was expected to be the result of the industrialization program — eventually. In fact, however, the discussion reflects profound disappointment with the immediate results. Rykov complained:

> Does industrialization offer anything for price cuts this year? It doesn't. Not even in the branches of industry, such as glass, that we have mechanized more than others. The Council of Labor and Defense was told recently that mechanization has been carried out in such a way that glass prices will rise this year.
> VOICE: Why?
> RYKOV: I asked the same question myself, but I got no clear answer. Sergo [Ordzhonikidze, Politburo member, at the time head of the party control commission] is currently in correspondence with the glass factories on this issue. We've built factories that are better than "in Europe" but glass prices have become even more expensive.

Kosior reported that

> the workers asked me: "Why are prices for baked bread not coming down, when we can buy grain more cheaply?" I myself don't know why bread prices are unchanged.
> RYKOV: It's the "mechanization" of baking.
> KOSIOR: We see this sort of thing everywhere.

Stalin was the only one to suggest an explanation: mechanization of industry, coupled with outdated work norms and piece rates, often "progressive," was driving wage earnings upward faster than worker productivity. In other words, the workers were capturing the gains from industrialization at the expense of the state.[9]

To summarize, the Bolsheviks had adopted a policy of industrial price cuts in the belief that it would reconcile the competing interests of workers, peasants, and the state. This belief was ill-founded. It rested, however, on recent experience: in 1923 the Soviet leaders had implemented a similar policy with apparent success. In 1927, the same leaders felt they now understood the market economy and had proved their ability to manipulate it. They did not see that circumstances had changed: their previous success had depended on expanding industrial production of consumer goods to keep pace with the market expansion that price cuts enabled. In 1927 a significant range of consumer goods was already in short supply and these shortages would soon worsen.

If, in 1927, Mikoyan, Rykov, and Stalin had listened more carefully to those with a better understanding of market economics, would they have chosen differently? We cannot know for sure.

Possibly, they did not yet have the full courage of their convictions. In April 1928, for example, Bolshevik policy wavered briefly away from confrontation with the market and back to accommodation. "It would be premature," historians Carr and Davies concluded, "to assume that at this time a majority of the leaders, or Stalin in particular, was committed to coercion, or had decided to abandon the methods of the market for a policy of direct action."[10]

But we do know this: by 1929 they could see the consequences of their actions in full measure, and they did not draw back. This is because they attached no importance to market equilibrium. They were looking not for equilibrium, but for direct control over prices and allocations. In early 1927 it frustrated them that they were nowhere near achieving this, and in early 1928 they vacillated. In 1929, faced with a naked choice between market equilibrium and going over to a command system ruled by force, they chose force.

The fact that this crisis was not precipitated even more rapidly can be ascribed to a simple fact that occupied much time in the Politburo: in January 1927 the policy of industrial retail price cuts was proving extremely difficult to implement, and was encountering resistance from many sources. Whether or not price cuts were desirable, it was not clear that they were feasible. The difficulties evoked two lines of discussion: What were the main obstacles to implementation of the policy? And by what means should it be enforced?

Feasibility

If retail prices were so stubbornly high, what was the reason? Simplifying a little, Figure 12.3 shows how the retail prices of state manufactured goods were formed in the 1920s. There are four preliminaries to note.

First, the government directly determined some costs, for example freight charges and sales taxes; the government could cut prices by reducing its levies, but then it lost budgetary revenue as a result. Second, profits were accounted for, properly, within the markups that producers and sellers claimed at each stage. The Bolsheviks were not against profits as such, but they generally wanted profits to be made out of trading at approved prices using approved markups. Third, the producers and sellers themselves reported production and distribution costs, so there was scope for inflating costs at each stage. The inflation of costs could be real, in the sense that resources were used up inefficiently, the gain to the producer being a quiet life; equally it might take the form of concealed profit-taking, so that costs were exaggerated and cash flows diverted into unauthorized institutional accounts or private pockets.

Fourth, it is clear that most participants had little or no confidence in the quality of the price data they were discussing. They wanted to make a policy instrument out of a variable that most believed they could observe only poorly, with a wide error margin. Mikoyan discussed measurement explicitly and came armed with tables of trends in factory, wholesale, and retail prices, the accuracy of which Liubimov defended — but no one else did, and even Mikoyan conceded: "I don't know how reliable these figures are but their sources are all documented and more precise data are not to be found anywhere." There was also understandable concern that the averages neglected significant variation between town and country and among regions. Whether or not Mikoyan's figures were accurate, they were not politically credible. The discussion was relatively uninformed about trends in productivity, costs, or other relevant price-forming variables. In addition the concept of markups on costs proved intractable for nonspecialist discussion; some participants struggled to understand what was included in this markup or that, while others lacked any clear way of expressing a change over time in a share of a variable that was itself changing.

Starting from the top, we have already mentioned one factor in the retail price level: the persistently high production costs of industry. Russian Republic trade official N. B. Eismont (later a member of the Smirnov-Eismont-Tolmachev conspiracy),[11] for example, pointed out that existing retail margins were simply not large enough to explain more than a small part of the widening of the scissors compared with the prewar period. Industrial production

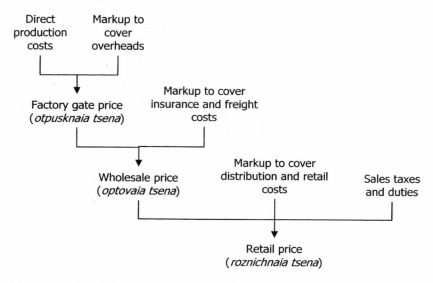

Figure 12.3. Retail Price Formation

costs were the elephant in the room. They were not completely ignored; as we have seen, both Rykov and Stalin made the point that industrialization was not cutting production costs as fast as expected. Other speakers focused on lesser issues, perhaps because they were looking for quicker results. More common was the standpoint of industry official V. N. Mantsev, who asserted plainly that "if industry wholesale prices went up over this period, then they went up by 1 to 2 percent overall. [Mikoyan's reply inaudible.] . . . What influence could this have on the retail price level? Absolutely none. The increase in retail prices has not been caused by the ill will of industry. We have made some mistakes, of course, but in this respect it is not our fault."

Much discussion was devoted to the size of wholesale and retail trade costs and markups, the "wholesale-retail" scissors, and the scope for pressing them shut. On this, Mikoyan's written report is uninteresting; it deals only with technicalities such as credit costs and freight charges. His speech set a sharper tone, and his first significant point was that trade markups were higher than they should be, especially for deficit commodities:

> MIKOYAN: Just in relation to manufactures, especially in retail trade, we have extremely high markups compared with both prewar and normal contemporary ones. Private traders in particular have big markups, but that's fully understandable. It's extremely expensive for the private trader to acquire goods, he has no direct channel for getting goods. If you look in any large private store you won't find goods in big batches, just remnants that the

unemployed, janitors, and others have bought up on commission for the private trader. In cooperation there are also big markups and in state trade too, but nonetheless all the evidence I have shows that these are not bad compared with the prewar years for commodities *not* in short supply. On the other hand, insofar as our trade system is structured more rationally than the private trader's, and we have centralized trade, large-scale associations, and so on (the socialist system ought to be rational, and we ought to be establishing a transitional distribution apparatus), we can't define prewar markups as our ideal; we ought to squeeze them.

Mikoyan went on to suggest that profit seeking in trade organizations was the main obstacle to price cuts: "our [Ministry of] Internal Trade," he complained, "isn't able to make people cut prices because they often think price cutting is good, but accumulation is better. (Laughter.)" Stalin labored the same point:

> STALIN: Among cooperative workers and our trade workers there have recently formed a dangerous psychology and a dangerous aspiration toward achieving "glittering" bottom lines (*balansy*) with "glittering" profits. The cooperative workers are more and more aiming not to strengthen the alliance of worker and peasant consumers, but to accumulate more profit and then glitter with the bottom line. This, comrades, is a dangerous psychology and a dangerous aspiration that can lead to no good. We need neither glittering bottom lines nor high profits. This is not our policy. We need an alliance of the broad mass of consumers of the towns and countryside. Let there be less profits and let there be no glittering bottom lines, but let us strengthen the alliance of our industry, through the trading agencies, with the mass consumer. This is our policy. Unfortunately, our cooperatives do not understand or do not want to understand this. And this is now the main danger.

Others also singled out profit seeking for criticism. The outstanding contribution on this score was Bukharin's. "Industry is developing more rapidly than agriculture," he began,

> but the state of affairs . . . in the field of relations between the working class and the peasantry is standing still. Explain what's the matter? I know of no other explanation [but that] we have hidden accumulation that is not being passed on to us.
> VOICE: True.
> BUKHARIN: There is accumulation in the field of industry, and in the field of trade, and cooperation, and they are hiding this accumulation from us. The business stinks not of tens but of hundreds of millions.

By "hidden accumulation," Bukharin evidently meant profits that were not being reported to the government but held in secret.

Then, a verbal auction took place over the hidden profits of Tsentrosoiuz, the central cooperative trading agency, that Stalin won:

> BUKHARIN: In my view it must be generally acknowledged that there is hidden accumulation, but it's not being reported to us.
> STALIN: There is, without doubt, there is.
> BUKHARIN: It's a question of profits.
> STALIN: 120 million.
> MIKOYAN: 175.
> BUKHARIN: About 200.

But a few minutes later Stalin placed the winning bid:

> STALIN: I think if you count the hidden profit too, the profit can go to 250, maybe to 300 million. Who needs this deception and what are these super-profits for? Who can be unaware that these superprofits can lead only to the decay of our commodity supply network and the detachment of the party and state from the mass of consumers numbered in millions?

Not all of those present were opposed to profit seeking. Valerian Kuibyshev, the minister for state industry, first complemented Mikoyan's argument by suggesting that deficit commodities typically commanded huge markups, especially in the free market; he went on to point out that cooperatives could then profit by slightly undercutting free market prices. When challenged, however, Kuibyshev would not speak out against profit as such. He argued that *trade* profits were a problem because they were lost to industry; *industrial* profits were needed to finance industrialization. This argument came close to that of Piatakov and the Left Opposition at the time, but the closeness arose partly because the Left had deliberately blurred its own line. Ordzhonikidze, head of the party Control Commission, also spoke up for industrial profits: "About hidden accumulation . . . Certainly they hide it. Of course not for themselves, but in order to expand local industry. You can cut wholesale prices but I believe that if our goods distribution network will absorb the same amount as now, no matter how much you cut, nothing will come out. I worry that we will tell Kuibyshev to cut [prices] but the reduction will not reach the consumer." Going further, the light industry commissar, Liubimov, was willing to stand up for trade profits too: "If you make us sell 10 or 50 commodities at a loss, and forbid us to make a profit on the other 10, it's obvious that our organization will fly away, carrying a loss overall."

Other participants were concerned not about high profits in trade but about high costs. Politburo member Andrei Andreev noted a rapid growth of total employment in cooperative trade in 1925 and 1926, despite frequent complaints that the shortage of commodities left the cooperatives underemployed. Ordzhonikidze gave anecdotal support to this. He described a typical rural cooperative store staffed by four workers, in place of one before the war; when asked the reason, he was told that "one can steal, whereas these will watch each other." But "if all three conspire to steal," he retorted, "there'll be nothing left in the shop. . . . let Comrade Liubimov or someone prove to me that this is not the case." *Liubimov*: "I haven't proved it." But Liubimov *had* argued that commodity shortages themselves were raising the search costs that trading agencies had to bear, since their procurement agents now had to travel far and wide to locate supplies.[12]

Towards the end, Stalin weighed in decisively. It did not really matter whether the problem was high profits or high costs in the retail sector. "At the expense of what must the policy of retail price cuts be implemented? At the expense of the apparatus of the trading agencies, at the expense of cutting their staff, at the expense of cutting their overhead costs, at the expense of cutting their profits. There are no other sources. This we must understand and from this we must proceed. This is why cutting markups is the immediate task." Stalin concluded with a brutality of expression that was already his characteristic: "We must, before anything else, implement a serious reduction of retail prices for industrial commodities of a mass character both in the countryside and in the towns, *beating down the markup*, reducing the markup, *breaking the resistance of the cooperatives* and other trading agencies *at all costs*" (emphasis added).

If Stalin felt that he had closed the debate, Kalinin, the final speaker, did not seem to notice. He was clearly skeptical of the Politburo policy; "A while ago," he confessed, "we thought that retail price cuts were literally the panacea that would save us, but now we see that this is not so." He was for cooperatives' profit seeking: "profit is not a dangerous thing in cooperation," he argued on the grounds that cooperatives pay a dividend to their members, returning the profit to the consumers. As for high trade costs, Kalinin talked about how the revolution had improved the position of service sector workers, disproportionately raising trade costs; "Why do we pay 5 kopecks for bread? Because that's what it costs." This dissent did not meet with any rejoinder or rebuke, although it is reported at one point that Kosior interrupted by coughing "ironically."

Enforcement

Mikoyan appeared to believe that the policy adopted the previous spring of cutting key commodity prices by 10 percent could not be driven further. He put this down to the fact that the Bolsheviks were not yet really in control of the market for manufactures. He suggested this by contrasting the bad state of the market for manufactures with the good state of the grain market; this also usefully illustrates what kind of control the Bolsheviks aspired to:

MIKOYAN: "We have reached a point such that peasant muddle and the peasant grain market are wholly and completely in our hands, we can raise or lower grain prices at any time, and we have all the levers of influence in our hands. But in relation to state trade and the cooperatives, we don't have these levers for industrial commodities, or, more accurately, we utilize them badly. At present it is easier to raise or lower grain prices in a short period of time across the entire Union territory; and more difficult, and it demands unbelievably more effort, to cut prices for industrial commodities in the state-trading or cooperative sphere, because no one stands up for the peasant [*muzhik*] and gets in our way, whereas various organizations stand up for cooperation and state trade and defend them. Some comrade or other turns up from cooperation and state trade and says we can't cut prices just like that, there has to be a profit, all are good guys — and the result is none of the necessary pressure and none of the necessary results.

Here we have the situation that state and cooperative organizations, that are socialist-type organizations, are less subject to the influence of the state and its leadership than the private market for grain.

. . . It may be that the upper layer of the cooperatives has recently been supporting us and wants a reduction, but this is not true of the whole cooperative system and all local agencies.

Mikoyan had reached a surprising conclusion: it was easier for the state to control millions of farmers through the market than to exercise effective authority over a dozen or so ministries and a few hundred industrial trusts. His words have the sound of reality knocking at the Bolsheviks' door. They wanted to socialize the market economy. Now they had a new problem: Who controls the agencies of socialization?

Given his sense of the limits of state power, Mikoyan was apparently opposed to calls for radical price cuts and wanted to pursue a realistic target of a 2 to 3 percent overall reduction. His interventions are pervaded by a sense of bureaucratic impotence; even if "state and cooperative organizations . . . are less subject to the influence of the state and its leadership than the private market for grain," he lamented, it was also true that "we have few means of influence over private capital." He described his own trade ministry as not only "weak in the center" but also understaffed locally; each provincial office employed no more than "15 to 20 persons including messengers, cleaners, and others." He believed little could be achieved without the involvement of local party organizations and the mobilization of mass pressure on trade costs and prices. Later in discussion Liubimov pointedly criticized party and trade union organizations for "frosty" (*prokhladnoe*) neglect of the policy of price reductions.

They could only get so far with what an industry representative, Mantsev, ridiculed as an "evangelical" style of work: "we recommend, we request, we suggest." Stalin suggested adding public pressure through use of the press to expose pricing abuses. But in closing the debate, Mikoyan made a striking admission of weakness that Central Committee secretary Kosior immediately rejected:

> MIKOYAN: I want to say one thing — whatever measures we adopt, whatever proposals all the Politburo members agree on for cutting prices by squeezing trade costs, we cannot achieve the kind of retail price reductions now, or within two or three months, that can pacify the workers and peasants in the smallest degree.
>
> KOSIOR: That's not proven.

But if not party mobilization and public pressure, then what? The alternative was police measures and repression. The new RSFSR criminal code that came into effect on January 1, 1927 made the "malicious raising of prices of merchandise by way of buying up, concealing, or withholding from the market" an offence punishable by imprisonment.[13] Several of the papers received by the Politburo dealt with local party organizations' involvement in discussion and implementation of price cuts. The last of these is entitled "Holding to Account of Organizations and Persons Not Implementing the Directives of Party Agencies on the Reduction of Retail Prices." It lists a dozen regional committees that had issued resolutions calling for reprimands, dismissals, and prosecutions for lack of whole-hearted compliance with the policy.

While it is not clear that these threats specifically had been carried out, something was going on. Early in the discussion, Mikoyan noted that while some were "complaining that repressive measures have not been applied . . . there are already 600 cases of repressive measures against trading agencies in the [Russian Republic]. There is no solution," he warned, "in repressions alone, since repression is an auxiliary weapon that cannot replace all the forms of economic positions in the market." Eismont confirmed subsequently that the six hundred cases of "repression" were indeed prosecutions.

Stalin's various contributions show three recurrent themes. First, he resolutely defended the role of the party, rejecting all criticisms. Second, it was not enough for state or party to make decisions; they must also monitor progress towards implementation. Stalin saw a pattern, wider than the narrow issue of retail prices, in decisions that disappeared into an administrative vacuum. The Council of Labor and Defense had adopted a resolution calling for shorter retail supply chains. "Is this decree of the Council of Labor and Defense being implemented?" he asked, giving the answer: "No, it is not being implemented"; and another question: "Why?" Again, the Council of Labor and Defense had adopted a resolution to close state trading outlets where they duplicated cooperative networks. "Is this decree of the Council of Labor and Defense being implemented? No, it is not being implemented. Why?" He criticized Mikoyan for not providing evidence of whether a decision of the Council of Labor and Defense to reconstitute trading agencies that resisted the price cuts had been carried through.

Stalin's third preoccupation was with the power of state to force radical change. This is where his dispute with Mikoyan emerged most clearly. Mikoyan wanted to set a realistic target of a 2 to 3 percent overall reduction. Stalin wanted more and did not see why it should not be imposed by force, by an act of political will. This led to a satirical exchange:

> MIKOYAN: . . . generally, on average, prices can be cut by 2 to 3 percent.
> STALIN: By two kopecks off the ruble?
> MIKOYAN: Roughly. That's in the immediate future.
> STALIN: It's not enough.
> MIKOYAN: I would like it to be more, but I can't issue instructions that no one can fulfil. I am a supporter of those instructions for our administration that have 80 to 90 percent feasibility. If you issue an instruction in which 60 percent is feasible and 40 percent is infeasible, then this will disorganize the administration. We are currently shouting that they are not implementing the directive, but they are not arresting us and jailing us for it; Comrade Liubimov is not in prison and I haven't been arrested. They aren't carrying out all instructions, but no one has been handed over to the courts to answer for it. But when it comes to grain, and Lobachev [head of grain marketing] doesn't comply with an order, they dismiss him and jail him.
> VOICE: What do you want, for them to jail you, and then everything will be all right?
> MIKOYAN: Arrest me, I'll happily go to prison so as to sleep well.
> VOICE: How long do you want to go to prison for?
> MIKOYAN: About six months.

Finally, how did the Bolshevik leaders see the expected consequences of failure? The Bolshevik leaders clearly expected to pay a political price if they did not press on with the policy they had previously announced. They also no doubt feared what the opposition would say if the policy failed. Mikoyan worried that, with no results in six months, "the masses will say that we deceived them and that prices haven't been cut enough." Kosior warned explicitly of the likely damage to the party's credibility: "Our discussions today remind me of what's happening at meetings where we talk about our achievements and about how prices have come down and so on, and the workers grumble: 'The devil take you, you have all those achievements and we don't feel a thing.' A few days ago in Kazan' I was demonstrating that we have cut prices but the workers don't believe it."

Implicitly, Kosior sided with Stalin against Mikoyan on the size of cuts that were required; the public would simply not notice a deflation of the order of 2 or 3 percent. "In the Trade Ministry," he mocked, "you weigh price cuts on a pharmacist's scales, and you calibrate them in units of the order of 0.05, but in life it looks otherwise." He concluded: "We have talked about price cuts for a whole year. They are looking to us now for actions, not resolutions."

The Politburo meeting was indeed followed by action. Between January and October 1927 there was a concerted campaign of decrees, propaganda, and mobilizations in which Mikoyan and his Ministry of Trade played a leading role. It had the effect of lowering official retail prices of industrial goods by more than 7 percent — much more than the "2 to 3 percent" that Mikoyan had modestly urged in January. As a result, shortages multiplied; the peasants became increasingly unable to buy from the state and increasingly reluctant to sell to it.[14] Mass operations of the OGPU security police and mass arrests in the countryside formed the core of the "extraordinary measures" adopted at the end of 1927 to bring in the grain from that year's harvest.[15]

In 1926–27 the Bolsheviks were pursuing a policy of downward pressure on retail prices of industrial commodities. In the Politburo there was broad agreement in support of this policy in principle, but clear differences over how far it should be pursued and where to accommodate to economic and social resistance. Some special interests were voiced; there was a clear tendency for those with an interest in industry, such as Ordzhonikidze and Kuibyshev, to seek to push the burden of adjustment onto trade, and for those with interests in trade or cooperatives, such as Liubimov and Kalinin, to defend them. A significant middle ground wished to pursue price cuts only in moderation and within limits. On one side, Stalin rejected all compromise; on the other side, only Kalinin expressed reservations that could be construed as reasonable.

The party's policy of industrial retail price cuts was a significant factor undermining the market economy and contributing to its eventual replacement by a command system in which resources were allocated by force. It worked at four different levels. Each can be seen clearly in the minutes of the Politburo.

First, the policy promoted market disequilibrium. This in itself was not of concern to the leadership core, which did not set any special value on a balanced economy. However, the particular form of disequilibrium that the policy promoted was that state-supplied manufactures became increasingly unavailable at the low prices resulting from downward pressure. Shortages spread, with predictably adverse effects on the peasants' willingness to bring their food to the market. Eventually, the threat to agricultural supplies for urban households, state industry, the Red Army, and exports led the Bolshevik regime into a direct confrontation with the peasantry that ended in collectivization and famine.

Second, the policy was a step in the process that made price setting a political, not economic decision. Once the state took responsibility for setting prices, it had to accept that industrial managers could no longer be held accountable for profits or losses, and would become indifferent to costs. Thus the government's price controls promoted the softening of budget constraints faced by state-owned enterprises and encouraged them to use up resources in production and distribution that might otherwise have been available for raising living standards and developing the economy. It led directly, therefore, to the inefficiencies of the command system.

Third, the party's policy evoked resistance; the resistance evoked a search for the people impeding the policy in the private market, in the cooperative trading agencies, and in the state retail sector. This search was accompanied by calls not only for mass pressure to counteract the resistance, but also for direct repression of the resisters. The politicization of price setting in general led, by this direct route, to the criminalization of the specific pricing decisions that the party perceived as undermining its policies.

Fourth and finally, Stalin was able to exploit the issue to promote his claim to personal leadership. As we watch the Politburo members debate the issues, Stalin emerges as the chief defender of the party, its policies, and its organizations. We see Stalin's rhetoric at work in this role. It is like a bulldozer. Link by link, its metal tracks crush all obstacles. The party must hold its line at all costs. The resisters are a source of danger; those who cover for them have misplaced their loyalties and priorities. The resistance must be broken, by persuasion if possible, by force if necessary. That is all.

Appendix: Price Cuts and Market Equilibrium

This appendix sets out explicitly the reasoning used in the first section of this essay to explain the effects of industrial price cuts in the Soviet retail market. In Figure 12.4 peasant farmers supply food which, measured vertically, is traded against state-manufactured goods, measured horizontally. The equilibrium is found where two lines or "offer curves" intersect at point A, and the state exchanges M_0 manufactured goods for F_0 food. The slope of the line from the origin to A, measured by the angle σ, measures the real price of industrial goods: when the scissors open, σ increases and the line becomes steeper, and conversely when the scissors close.

The analysis takes the nominal price of food as given, as the Politburo had to, since grain prices were to be considered in a separate report. They assumed

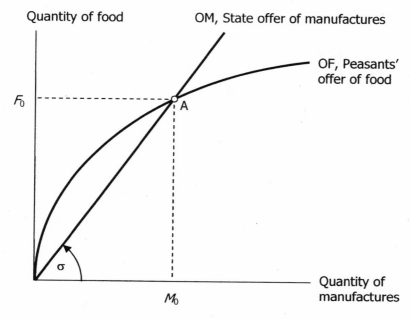

Figure 12.4. State Industry and Peasant Farmers in Equilibrium
Note: The angle σ measures the scissors, or the price of manufactures relative to food.

that a cut in the nominal price of a manufactured item measured in rubles and kopecks is also a cut in its relative price measured in food units; and in our model σ is therefore the relative price.

The convex OF curve shows the peasants' offer of food in return for manufactured goods; it is convex because of diminishing marginal utility, which made the peasants increasingly reluctant to give up food in return for manufactured goods as their consumption basket shifted away from food to manufactures. An increase in agricultural productivity would shift the OF curve upwards, since cheaper food would make farmers willing to give up more food for an item of manufactured goods. In equilibrium, the size of the urban-rural market would grow.

The straight, upward-sloping OM line shows the manufactured goods that state industry was willing to offer the countryside in return for food. Its slope measures the price at which manufactures were offered. It is straight because the price was fixed independently of quantities: state industry had market power and used this power to preset the price of manufactures before going to the market. The basis of price-setting was a markup on costs. Real costs were determined by industrial productivity. The size of the markup on costs then

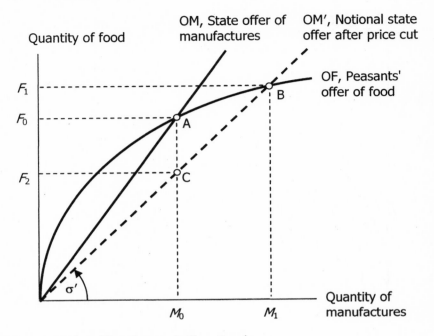

Figure 12.5. State Manufactures in Short Supply

depended on the state's use of its market power. A reduction in the markup and a reduction in industrial costs would each close the scissors and swing the urban offer curve to the right; either of these would expand the urban-rural market. This theoretical proposition, once much debated, has been verified empirically for the Soviet economy in the 1920s.[16]

The background to policy discussion in January 1927 is illustrated in Figure 12.5. Starting from point A, the leadership had decided to expand the market by cutting the price of industrial goods, reducing the slope of the OM curve to σ' and shifting the curve to OM'. At the new price σ' the peasants would offer to exchange F_1 food for M_1 manufactures. Provided the state could increase the supply of manufactures to match, the market equilibrium would shift from A to point B. With more food available, real wages could rise and industrial employment could grow. This is what had happened in 1923, when the Bolsheviks had managed to cut prices *and* preserve equilibrium because the price cuts were accompanied by a simultaneous rise in industrial production.

In 1927, however, prices were being cut without a simultaneous increase in the supply of manufactures, which was fixed by the state at M_0. In Figure 12.5 the OM' curve is only the state's *notional* offer. Its slope is the price at which industry offers manufactures to the countryside, but beyond the quantity M_0 the state offers no more goods at any price. There is a shortage of manufactures: the "goods famine." In this context there are four possible outcomes, shown in the figure:

1. Abandon the policy of price cuts and accept the political damage of a policy defeat. The market returns to equilibrium at A.

2. Hold the price of manufactures to σ'. With manufactures available only up to the quantity M_0, farmers will be forced off their offer curve to point C. They will sell only the food required to purchase M_0, since M_0 is the maximum they can buy at any price. In fact, they will sell only F_2 which is not only less than F_1 but even less than F_0. The party has saved its political capital but the price cuts have been counterproductive in terms of the supply of food.

3. The gap between the state price and the equilibrium price may now encourage the reselling of manufactures, allowing private individuals to collect the gap in the form of rents or bribes. The market returns to equilibrium at A, but the state, buying and selling at C, has lost revenue to the private resellers, who collect part of the food that might otherwise have gone to the state.

4. The gap between the state price and the equilibrium price may also encourage private producers to enter the market and supply the unsatisfied consumers. The state is no worse off absolutely, since it continues to buy and sell at A. But the private sector will grow, so the state sector's share will shrink proportionally.

Notes

I thank the Hoover Institution and Archive for their hospitality in July 2006 when this paper was written, the University of Warwick North America Travel Fund for financial support, and R. W. Davies, Michael Ellman, Simon Ertz, Paul Gregory, and Peter Law for advice and comments.

1. RGASPI Fond 17, op. 163, del. 703. Files 701 and 702 contain the transcript in the original and showing the editorial and authors' corrections.

2. The background to the policy of price reductions in 1926 and 1927 is covered in more detail by Carr and Davies, *A History of Soviet Russia: Foundations of a Planned Economy, 1926–1929*, vol. 1, pp. 715–37.

3. Davies and Wheatcroft, "Population," p. 64.

4. Gregory, "National Income," p. 247; Harrison, "National Income," pp. 41–42.

5. The classic account is by Carr, *A History of Soviet Russia: The Interregnum, 1923–1924*.

6. Harrison, "The Peasantry and Industrialisation."

7. Carr and Davies, *A History of Soviet Russia: Foundations of a Planned Economy, 1926–1929*, vol. 1, p. 716.

8. Ibid., pp. 717–23.

9. Work norm revision would remain a critical issue for Soviet industrial policy and labor relations through the following decades; see e.g. Arnot, *Controlling Soviet Labour: Experimental Change from Brezhnev to Gorbachev,* pp. 84–87; Davies and Khlevnyuk, "Stakhanovism and the Soviet Economy."

10. Carr and Davies, *A History of Soviet Russia: Foundations of a Planned Economy, 1926–1929,* vol. 1, pp. 65–66; for a fuller account of this episode based on the archives see Manning, "The Rise and Fall of 'the Extraordinary Measures,' January–June, 1928: Towards a Reexamination of the Onset of the Stalin Revolution."

11. See the essay by Charters Wynn in this volume.

12. This seems to be an early reference to the role of the *tolkach* in the Soviet economy later described by Joseph Berliner, *Factory and Manager in the USSR,* and others.

13. Carr and Davies, *A History of Soviet Russia: Foundations of a Planned Economy, 1926–1929,* vol. 1, p. 724.

14. Ibid., pp. 724–30.

15. Manning, "The Rise and Fall of 'the Extraordinary Measures,' January–June, 1928: Towards a Reexamination of the Onset of the Stalin Revolution."

16. Gregory and Mokhtari, "State Grain Purchases, Relative Prices, and the Soviet Grain Procurement Crisis."

Bibliography

Adibekov, G. M., et al., eds. *Politbiuro TsK PRP(b)-VKP(b) i Evropa: Resheniia "osoboi papki," 1923–1939.* Moscow: Rosspen, 2001.

Adibekov, G. M., K. M. Anderson, and L. I. Rogovaia, eds. *Politbiuro TsK RKP(b)-VKP(b): Povestki dnia zasedanii.* Vol. 1: *1919–1929.* Moscow: Rosspen, 2000.

———, eds. *Politbiuro TsK RKP(b)-VKP(b): Povestki dnia zasedanii.* Vol. 2: *1930–1939.* Moscow. Rosspen, 2001.

———, eds. *Politbiuro TsK RKP(b)-VKP(b): Povestki dnia zasedanii.* Vol. 3: *1949–1952.* Moscow. Rosspen, 2001.

Arnold, Arthur, *Banks, Credit, and Money in Soviet Russia.* New York: Columbia University Press, 1937.

Arnot, Bob. *Controlling Soviet Labour: Experimental Change from Brezhnev to Gorbachev.* Basingstoke: Macmillan, 1987.

Artizov, A. N., ed. *Reabilitatsiia: Kak eto bylo.* Vol. 3. Moscow: Materik, 2004.

"Assessing the New Archival Sources." Special issue of *Cahiers du Monde Russe,* nos. 1–2, 1999.

Avtorkhanov, Abdurakhman. *Stalin and the Soviet Communist Party: A Study in the Technology of Power.* New York. Praeger, 1959.

Banac, Ivo, ed., *The Diary of Georgi Dimitrov.* New Haven: Yale University Press, 2003.

Barnett, V. "As Good as Gold? A Note on the Chervonets." *Europe-Asia Studies,* vol. 46, no. 4, 1994, pp. 663–69.

Bazhanov, Boris. *Bazhanov and the Damnation of Stalin.* Translated by David Doyle. Columbus: Ohio State Press, 1990.

——. *Vospominaniia byvshego sekretaria Stalina*. Moscow: Terra, 1997.

Berliner, Joseph S. *Factory and Manager in the USSR*. Cambridge, Mass.: Harvard University Press, 1957.

Bogdanov, Iu. N. *Strogo-sekretno: 30 let v OGPU-NKVD-MVD*. Moscow: Veche, 2002.

Boffa, Dzh. *Istoriia sovetskogo soiuza*. Vol. 1: *Ot revoliutsii do vtoroi mirovoi voiny: Lenin i Stalin, 1917-1941*. Moscow: Mezhdunarodnye otnosheniia. 1990.

Broue, Pierre. "Party Opposition to Stalin (1930–1932) and the First Moscow Trial." In John W. Strong, ed., *Essays on Revolutionary Culture and Stalinism*. Columbus: Ohio State University Press, 1990.

Carr, Edward Hallett. *Socialism in One Country, 1924–1926*. Vol. 1. London: Macmillan, 1958.

——. *A History of Soviet Russia: The Interregnum, 1923–1924*. Harmondsworth: Pelican, 1969.

Carr, E. H., and R. W. Davies, *A History of Soviet Russia: Foundations of a Planned Economy, 1926–1929*. Vol. 1. Harmondsworth: Pelican, 1974.

Chuev, F., ed. *Molotov: Poluderzhavnyi vlastelin*. Moscow: Olma Press, 1999.

Citrine, Walter McLennan. *A Trade Unionist Looks at Russia*. London: The Trades Union Congress General Council, 1936.

Cohen, Stephen. *Bukharin and the Bolshevik Revolution: A Political Biography, 1888–1938*. Oxford: Oxford University Press, 1980.

Conquest, Robert. *The Harvest of Sorrow: Soviet Collectivization and the Terror-Famine*. New York: Oxford University Press, 1986.

——. *Stalin and the Kirov Murder*. New York: Oxford University Press, 1989.

——. *The Great Terror: A Reassessment*. New York: Oxford University Press, 1990.

——. *Stalin: Breaker of Nations*. New York: Viking, 1991.

Corney, Frederick C. *Telling October: Memory and the Making of the Bolshevik Revolution*. Ithaca: Cornell University Press, 2004.

Courtoise, Stephane, et al., eds. *Black Book of Communism: Crimes, Terror, Repression*. Translated by J. Murphy and M. Kramer. Cambridge, Mass.: Harvard University Press, 1999.

Dallin, Alexander, and F. I. Firsov, eds. *The Dimitrov-Stalin Correspondence*. New Haven: Yale University Press, 2000.

Daniels, Robert Vincent. *The Conscience of the Revolution: Communist Opposition in Soviet Russia*. Cambridge: Cambridge University Press, 1960; reprint ed., New York: Simon and Schuster, 1969.

Danilov, V. P., et al., eds. *Tragediia Sovetskoi derevni: Kollektivizatsiia i raskulachivanie*. Vol. 1. Moscow. Rosspen, 1999.

Davies, R. W. "A Note on Grain Statistics." *Soviet Studies*, vol. 21, no. 4, 1967, pp. 14–29.

——. *The Socialist Offensive: The Collectivisation of Soviet Agriculture, 1929–1930*. London: Macmillan, 1980.

——. "The Syrtsov-Lominadze Affair." *Soviet Studies*, vol. 33, no. 1, January 1981, pp. 29–50.

——. *The Soviet Economy in Turmoil, 1929–1930*. Basingstoke: Macmillan, 1989.

——. *Crisis and Progress in the Soviet Economy, 1931–1933*. Basingstoke: Macmillan, 1996.

———. "Making Economic Policy." In Paul Gregory, ed., *Behind the Façade of Stalin's Command Economy.* Palo Alto: Hoover Institution Press, 2001.

Davies, R. W., Melanie Ilic, and Oleg Khlevnyuk, "The Politburo and Economic Policy Making." In E. A. Rees, ed., *The Nature of Stalin's Dictatorship: The Politburo, 1924–1953.* New York. Palgrave Macmillan, 2003.

Davies, R. W., and Oleg Khlevnyuk. "Stakhanovism and the Soviet Economy." *Europe-Asia Studies,* vol. 54, no. 6, 2002, pp. 867–903.

Davies, R. W., Oleg V. Khlevniuk, and E. A. Rees, eds. *The Stalin-Kaganovich Correspondence 1931–1936.* New Haven: Yale University Press, 2003.

Davies, R. W., and S. G. Wheatcroft. "Population." In R. W. Davies, Mark Harrison, and S. G. Wheatcroft, eds., *The Economic Transformation of the Soviet Union, 1913–1945.* Cambridge: Cambridge University Press, 1994.

———. *The Years of Hunger: Soviet Agriculture, 1931–1933.* Basingstoke: Palgrave Macmillan, 2004.

Day, Richard. *Leon Trotsky and the Politics of Economic Isolation.* Cambridge: Cambridge University Press, 1973.

"'Delo M. N. Riutina' v sud'be G. E. Zinovieva i L. B. Kameneva, Oktiabr 1932," *Istoricheskii arkhiv,* no. 1, 2006.

Derendiger, E. *Erzählungen aus dem Leben: Als Graphiker in Moskau 1910 bis 1938.* Zürich: Chronos Verlag, 2005.

Desiatyi s"ezd RKP(b), Mart 1921 goda: Stenograficheskii otchet. Moscow: Gospolitizdat, 1963.

Deutscher, Isaac. *Stalin: A Political Biography.* 1949; reprint eds., London: Oxford University Press, 1961; New York. Oxford University Press, 1966.

———. *The Prophet Unarmed: Trotsky, 1921–1929.* London: Oxford University Press, 1959.

Dohan, Michael. "Soviet Foreign Trade in the NEP Economy and Soviet Industrialization Strategy.". Ph. D. diss., Massachusetts Institute of Technology, 1969.

"Dve 'besedy's professorom V. N. Slepkovym: Iz 'reabilitatsionnogo dela' M. N. Riutina, 1932." *Istoricheskii arkhiv,* no. 5, 2003.

Egorova, A. G., and K. M. Bogoliubova, eds. *Kommunisticheskaia partiia Sovietskogo Soiuza v rezoliutsiiakh i resheniiakh s"ezdov, konferentsii i plenumov TsK.* Vols. 2 and 6. Moscow: Politizdat, 1953, 1985.

Ekonomicheskoe obozrenie, no. 23–24, 1924.

Erlich, Alexander. *The Soviet Industrialization Debate, 1924–1928.* Cambridge, Mass.: Harvard University Press, 1960.

Fel'shtinskii, Iu., ed. *Kommunisticheskaia oppozitsia v SSSR: Iz arkhiva L'va Trotskogo;* Vols. 1–4. Benson, Vt.: Chalidze Publications, 1988.

Filtzer, Donald. *Soviet Workers and Stalinist Industrialization: The Formation of Modern Soviet Production Relations, 1928–1941.* Armonk: M. E. Sharpe, 1986.

Firsov, F. I. "K voprosu o taktike edinogo fronta v 1921–1924 gg.," *Voprosy Istorii KPSS,* no. 12, 1987, pp. 121–22.

Fitzpatrick, Sheila. *Education and Social Mobility in the Soviet Union, 1921–1934.* Cambridge: Cambridge University Press, 1979.

———. "The Great Departure: Rural-Urban Migration in the Soviet Union, 1929–33," In William G. Rosenberg and Lewis H. Siegelbaum, eds., *Social Dimensions of Soviet Industrialization,* pp. 28–33. Bloomington: Indiana University Press, 1993.

———. *Stalin's Peasants. Resistance and Survival in the Russian Village after Collectiviza-tion.* London: Oxford University Press, 1994.

———. *Tear Off the Masks! Identity and Imposture in Twentieth-Century Russia.* Prince-ton: Princeton University Press, 2005.

"Fragmenty stenogrammy dekabr'skogo plenuma TsK VKP(b), 1936 goda." *Voprosy istorii,* 1995, no. 1.

Furet, Francois. *The Passing of an Illusion: The Idea of Communism in the Twentieth Century.* Translated by Deborah Furet. Chicago: Chicago University Press, 1999.

Fursenko, A. A. *Prezidium TSK KPSS 1954–1964: Chernovye protokolnye zapisi zase-danii, stenogrammy, postanovleniia v 3 Tomakh.* Moscow: RAN, 2003.

Genis, V. L. "Upriamyi Narkom s Il'inkoi." In G. I. Sokol'nikov, ed., *Novaia finansovaia politika: Na puti k tverdoi valiute.* Moscow: Nauka, 1995.

Getty, J. Arch. "The Politics of Repression Revisited." In J. Arch Getty and Roberta T. Manning, eds. *Stalinist Terror: New Perspectives.* New York: Cambridge University Press, 1993.

———. "Russian Archives: Is the Door Half Open or Half Closed?" *Perspectives of the American Historical Association,* vol. 34, no. 5, May–June 1996.

Getty, J. Arch, and Oleg V. Naumov. *The Road to Terror: Stalin and the Self-Destruction of the Bolsheviks, 1932–1939.* New Haven: Yale University Press, 1999.

Getty, J. Arch, and Roberta T. Manning, eds. *Stalinist Terror: New Perspectives.* New York: Cambridge University Press, 1993.

Gill, Graeme. *The Rules of the Communist Party of the Soviet Union.* Basingstoke: Macmillan, 1988.

Gleason, Abbott. *Totalitarianism: The Inner History of the Cold War.* New York: Oxford University Press, 1995.

Goland, Iurii. "Currency Regulation in the Nep Period." *Europe-Asia Studies,* vol. 46, no. 8, 1994, pp. 1251–96.

———. M. *Krizisy, razrushivshie NEP: Valiutnoe regulirovanie v period NEPa.* 2d. enl. ed. Moscow: Fond ekon. knigi "Nachala," 1998.

Gorelov, O. I. *Tsugtsvant Mikhaila Tomskogo.* Moscow: Rosspen, 2000.

Gorlizki, Yoram, and Oleg Khlevniuk, "Stalin and His Circle." In Ronald Grigor Suny, ed., *The Cambridge History of Russia: The Twentieth Century,* pp. 243–58. Cam-bridge: Cambridge University Press, 2006.

Graziosi, Andrea. " 'Building the First System of State Industry in History': Piatakov's VSNKh and the Crisis of the NEP 1923–1926." *Cahiers du Monde russe et soviétique,* vol. 32, no. 4, 1991, pp. 539–80.

Graziosi, Andrea, et al., eds. *Bolshevistskoe rukovodstvo: Perepiska, 1912–1927: Shor-nik dokumentov.* Moscow. Rosspen, 1996.

Gregory, Paul R. "National Income." In R. W. Davies, ed., *From Tsarism to the New Economic Policy: Continuity and Change in the Economy of the USSR.* Basingstoke: Macmillan, 1990.

———. *The Political Economy of Stalinism: Evidence From the Soviet Secret Archives.* Cambridge: Cambridge University Press, 2004.

Gregory, Paul R., and Manouchehr Mokhtari. "State Grain Purchases, Relative Prices, and the Soviet Grain Procurement Crisis." *Explorations in Economic History,* vol. 30, no. 2, 1993, pp. 182–94.

Gurovich, P. V. *Vseobschaia stachka v Anglii 1926 g.* Moscow: Izdatel'stvo Akademii nauk, 1959.

Halfin, Igal. *Terror in My Soul: Communist Autobiographies on Trial.* Cambridge, Mass.: Harvard University Press, 2003.

Harris, James R. *The Great Urals: Regionalism and the Evolution of the Soviet System.* Ithaca: Cornell University Press, 1999.

Harrison, Mark. "The Peasantry and Industrialisation." In R. W. Davies, ed., *From Tsarism to the New Economic Policy: Continuity and Change in the Economy of the USSR.* Basingstoke: Macmillan, 1990.

——. "National Income." In R. W. Davies, Mark Harrison, and S. G. Wheatcroft, eds., *The Economic Transformation of the Soviet Union, 1913–1945.* Cambridge: Cambridge University Press, 1994.

Haslam, Jonathan. "Russian Archival Revelations and Our Understanding of the Cold War." *Diplomatic History,* vol. 21, no. 2, Spring 1997, pp. 217–28.

——. *The Vices of Integrity: E. H. Carr, 1892–1982.* New York: Verso, 2000.

Heinzen, James W. *Inventing a Soviet Countryside: State Power and the Transformation of Rural Russia, 1917–1929.* Pittsburgh: University of Pittsburgh Press, 2004.

Hellbeck, Jochen. *Revolution on My Mind; Writing a Diary under Stalin.* Cambridge, Mass.: Harvard University Press, 2006.

Hoffmann, David. *Peasant Metropolis: Social Identities in Moscow, 1929–1941.* Ithaca: Cornell University Press, 1994.

Hofstede, G. *Cultures and Organizations: Software of the Mind.* New York: Harper-Collins, 1994.

——. *Cultures Consequences: International Differences in Work-related Values.* Beverly Hills: Sage, 2001.

Hughes, J. "Patrimonialism and the Stalinist System: The Case of S. I. Syrtsov." *Europe-Asia Studies,* vol. 48, no. 4, 1996, pp. 551–68.

Humbert-Droz, Jules. *De Lénine à Staline: Dix ans au service de l' Internationale communiste, 1921–1931.* Neuchâtel: La Baconnière, 1971.

Iakovlev, A. N., ed. *Reabilitatsiia: Politicheskie protsessy 30–50-kh godov.* Moscow: Politizdat, 1991.

——, ed. *Kak lomali NEP: Stenogrammy plenumov TsK VKP(b) 1928–1929gg.* Vol. 4. Moscow: Fond Demokratii, 2000.

Ilizarov, Boris. *Tainaia zhizn' Stalina: Po materialam ego biblioteki i arkhiva.* Moscow: Veche, 2002.

Iurovskii, L. N. *Denezhnaia politika sovetskoi vlasti 1917–1927: Izbrannye stat'i, Ekonomicheskaia istoriia Rossii.* Moscow: Izdatel'stvo Nachala, 1996.

Ivkin, V. I. *Gosudarstvennaia vlast' SSSR: Vysshie organy vlasti i upravleniia i ikh rukovoditeli, 1923–1991 gg., istoriko-biograficheskoi spravochnik.* Moscow: Rosspen, 1999.

Ivnitskii, N. A. *Sudba raskulachennikh v SSSR.* Moscow: Sobranie, 2004.

Johnson, Simon, and Peter Temin. "The Macroeconomics of NEP." *Economic History Review,* vol. 46, no. 4, 1993, pp. 750–67.

Jones, S. F. *Socialism in Georgian Colors: The European Road to Social Democracy, 1883–1917.* Cambridge, Mass.: Harvard University Press, 2005.

Kaganovich, L. M. *Pamiatnye zapiski*. Moscow: Vagrius, 1996.

Kamenev, L. *Nashi dostizheniia, trudnosti i perspektivy*. Moscow, 1925.

Karcz, J. F. "Back on the Grain Front." *Soviet Studies*, vol. 22, no. 2, 1970, pp. 262–94.

Khaustov, V. N., V. P. Naumov, and N. S. Plotnikova, eds. *Lubianka: Stalin i VChK-GPU-OGPU-NKVD, ianvar' 1922–dekabr' 1936*. Moscow: Fond Demokratiia, 2003.

Khlevniuk, O. V. *1937: Stalin, NKVD, i sovetskoe obshchestvo*. Moscow: Respublika, 1992.

———. *Politbiuro: Mekhanizmy politicheskoi vlasti v 1930-e gody*. Moscow: Rosspen, 1996.

———. "Sovetskaia ekonomicheskaia politika na rubezhe 40–50 godov i delo Gosplana." Working Paper, Florence, March 2000.

———. *The History of the Gulag: From Collectivization to the·Great Terror*. Translated by Vadim Staklo. New Haven: Yale University Press, 2004.

Khlevniuk, O. V., A. V. Kvashonkin, L. P. Kosheleva, and L. A. Rogovaia, *Stalinskoe Politbiuro v 30-e gody*. Moscow: AIRO-XX, 1995.

Khlevniuk, O. V., P. Gregory, and A. Vatlin., eds. *Stenogrammy zasedanii Politbiuro TsK VKP(b), 1923–38*. Moscow: Rosspen, 2007.

Khlevniuk, O. V., R. W. Davies, E. A. Rees, and L. A. Rogovaia, eds. *Stalin i Kaganovich: Perepiska, 1931–1936 gg*. Moscow: Rosspen, 2001.

Khlevnyuk, Oleg. "The First Generation of Stalinist 'Party Generals.' " In E. A. Rees, ed., *Center-Local Relations in the Stalinist State, 1928–1941*. New York: Palgrave Macmillan, 2002.

Khrushchev, Sergei, ed. *Memoirs of Nikita Khrushchev*. Vol. 1: *Commissar (1918–1945)*. Translated by George Shriver. University Park: Pennsylvania State University Press, 1999.

Kitaeff, Mikhail. *Communist Party Officials*. New York: Research Program on the U.S.S.R, 1954.

Kislitsyn, S. A. *Variant Syrtsova (iz istorii formirovaniia antistalinskogo soprotivleniia v sovestkom obschestve v 20–30e gg.)*. Rotsov on Don: Nauchno-metodicheski tsentr "Logos," 1992.

Koenker, Diane P., and Ronald D. Bachman, eds. *Revelations from the Russian Archives: Documents in English Translation*. Washington, D.C.: Library of Congress, 1997.

Kommunisticheskii Internatsional v dokumentakh, 1919–1932. (Moscow: Partiinoe izdatel'stvo, 1933)

Kosheleva, L., V. Lel'chuk, V. Naumov, O. Naumov, L. Rogovaia, and O. Khlevniuk, eds. *Pis'ma I. V. Stalina V. M. Molotovu, 1925–1936 gg: Sbornik dokumentov*. Moscow: Rossiia molodaia, 1995.

Kotkin, Steven. *Magnetic Mountain: Stalinism as a Civilization*. Berkeley: University of California Press, 1995.

———. *Armageddon Averted: The Soviet Collapse 1970–2000*. New York: Oxford University Press, 2001.

KPSS v rezoliutsiakh. Moscow: Politizdat, 1953.

Kuromiya, Hiroaki. *Stalin's Industrial Revolution: Politics and Workers, 1928–1932*. Cambridge: Cambridge University Press, 1988.

———. *Freedom and Terror in the Donbas: A Ukrainian-Russian Borderland, 1870s–1990s*. New York: Cambridge University Press, 1998.

——. *Stalin: Profiles in Power.* London: Longman, 2005.

Kvashonkin, A. V., et al., eds. *Sovetskoe rukovodstvo: Perepiska, 1928–1941.* Moscow: Rosspen, 1999.

Laqueur, Walter. *Stalin: The Glasnost Revelations.* New York: Macmillan, 1990.

Larina, Anna. *This I Cannot Forget: The Memoirs of Nikolai Bukharin's Widow.* Translated by Gary Kern. New York: Norton, 1993.

Lenin, V. I. *Collected Works.* Moscow: Progress, 1966.

——. "Letter to the Congress" (1922–1923). In *Complete Works*, vol. 45, pp. 343–48. Moscow: Politicheskaia literatura, 1970.

Lewin, Moshe. *Lenin's Last Struggle.* New York: Pantheon, 1968.

——. *Russian Peasants and Soviet Power: A Study of Collectivization.* Translated by Irene Nove. Evanston: Northwestern University Press, 1968; reprint ed., 1975.

——. "The Immediate Background of Soviet Collectivization." In M. Lewin, ed., *The Making of the Soviet System.* New York: Pantheon, 1985.

——, ed. *The Making of the Soviet System: Essays in the Social History of Interwar Russia.* New York: Pantheon, 1985.

Lih, Lars T., Oleg V. Naumov, and Oleg V. Khlevniuk, eds. *Stalin's Letters to Molotov, 1925–1936.* New Haven: Yale University Press, 1995.

Linz, Susan J., ed. *The Impact of World War II on the Soviet Union.* Totowa: Rowman & Allanheld, 1985.

Malafeev, Aleksei Nikolaevich. *Istoriia tsenoobrazovaniia v SSSR, 1917–1963 gg.* Moscow: Mysl, 1964.

Malia, Martin. *Soviet Tragedy: A History of Socialism in Russia, 1917–1991.* New York: Free Press, 1994.

Manning, Roberta T. "The Rise and Fall of 'the Extraordinary Measures,' January–June, 1928: Towards a Reexamination of the Onset of the Stalin Revolution." *The Carl Beck Papers in Russian & East European Studies,* no. 1504. Pittsburgh: University of Pittsburgh, Center for Russian & East European Studies, 2001.

Martin, Terry, *The Affirmative Action Empire: Nations and Nationalism in the Soviet Union, 1923–1939.* Ithaca: Cornell University Press, 2001.

Mau, V. A. *Reformy i dogmy, 1914–1929: Ocherki istorii stanovleniia khoziaistvennoi sistemy sovetskogo totalitarizma.* Moscow: Izdatel'stvo "Delo," 1993.

McDermott, Kevin. *Stalin: Revolutionary in an Era of War.* New York: Palgrave Macmillan, 2006.

Medvedev, Roy. *Nikolai Bukharin: The Last Years.* Translated by A. D. P. Briggs. New York: Norton, 1980.

——. *All Stalin's Men.* Translated by Harold Shukman. Garden City: Anchor Press, 1985.

——. *Let History Judge: The Origins and Consequences of Stalinism.* Edited and Translated by George Shriver. New York: Columbia University Press, 1989.

Merridale, C. *Moscow Politics and the Rise of Stalin.* London: Macmillan, 1990.

Mikoian, A. I. *Tak bylo: Razmyshleniia o minuvshem.* Moscow: Vagrius, 1990.

Molotov, Vyacheslav Mikhailovich. *Molotov Remembers: Inside Kremlin Politics: Conversations with Felix Chuev.* Edited by F. Chuev and Albert Resis. Chicago: Ivan Dee, 1993.

Montefiore, Simon Sebag. *Stalin: The Court of the Red Tsar*. London: Weidenfeld & Nicholson, 2003.

Nabokov, Vladimir. *Pnin*. Harmondsworth: Penguin, 1957.

Naidich, Larisa. *Sled na peske: Ocherki o russkom iazykovom uzuse*. St. Petersburg: St. Petersburg State University, 1995.

Naimark, Norman M. "Cold War Studies and New Archival Materials on Stalin." *Russian Review*, vol. 61, no. 1, January, 2002, pp. 1–15.

———. "Stalin and Europe in the Postwar Period, 1945–53: Issues and Problems." *Journal of Modern European History*, vol. 2, no. 1, 2004.

Neizvestnaia Rossiia, no. 1, 1992.

Nemchinov, V. S. *Izbrannye proizvedeniia*. Vol. 1. Moscow: Nauka, 1967.

Nevezhin, V. A. *Zastol'nye rechi Stalina*. Moscow: AIRO-XX, 2003.

Nove, Alec. *An Economic History of the U.S.S.R.* Harmondsworth: Penguin, 1972.

Novoe vremia, no. 11, 29, 2003 (Iurii Bogomolov).

"O dele tak nazyvaemogo 'soiuza marksistov-lenintsev,'" *Izvestiia TsK KPSS*, no. 6, June 1989.

Orlov, Alexander. *The Secret History of Stalin's Crimes*. New York: Random House, 1953.

"O tak nazyvaemoi 'antipartiinoi kontrrevoliutsionnoi gruppirovke Eismonta, Tolmacheva i drugikh,'" *Izvestiia TsK KPSS*, no. 11, November 1990.

Peebles, Gavin. *A Short History of Socialist Money*. Sydney: Allen & Unwin, 1991.

Pipes, Richard. *The Unknown Lenin: From the Secret Archive*. New Haven: Yale University Press, 1996.

Polanyi, Karl. *The Great Transformation*. Boston: Beacon Press, 1957.

Pollock, Ethan. *Conversations with Stalin on Questions of Political Economy*. Cold War International History Project Working Paper no. 33. Washington, D.C., 2001.

Pravda. April 24, August 25, September 17 and 18, and October 2 and 24, 1925.

"'Pust' kazhdyi otvechaet za sebia' (Materialy partiinoi chistki M. P. Tomskogo)." *Kentavr*, July-August, 1992.

Rayfield, Donald. *Stalin: The Tyrant and Those Who Killed for Him*. New York: Random House, 2004.

Ree, Erik van. *The Political Thought of Joseph Stalin: A Study in Twentieth-Century Revolutionary Patriotism*. London: Routledge, 2002.

Rees, E. A. "Stalinism: The Primacy of Politics." In John Channon, ed., *Politics, Society and Stalinism in the USSR*. New York: St. Martin's Press, 1998.

———. "The Changing Nature of Centre-Local Relations in the USSR, 1928–36." In E. A. Rees, ed., *Centre-Local Relations in the Stalinist State, 1928–1941*. New York: Palgrave Macmillan, 2002.

———. "Stalin as Leader 1924–1937: From Oligarch to Dictator," In E. A. Rees, ed., *The nature of Stalin's Dictatorship: The Politburo 1928–1953*. Basingstoke: Palgrave Macmillan, 2003.

———, ed. *Decision-Making in the Stalinist Command Economy, 1932–1937*. London: Macmillan, 1997.

Reswick, William. *I Dreamt Revolution*. Chicago: Henry Regnery, 1952.

Rigby, T. H. *Communist Party Membership in the U.S.S.R. 1917–1967*. Princeton: Princeton University Press, 1968.

Roberts, Geoffrey. *Stalin's War: From World War to Cold War, 1939–1953.* New Haven: Yale University Press, 2006.

Rogovin, Vadim. *A byla li alternative? "Trotskizm": Vzgliad cherez gody.* Moscow: Terra, 1992.

———. *Vlast' i oppozitsii.* Moscow: Teatr, 1993.

Rosenberg, Alexander. "The Problem of Market Relations and the State in Revolutionary Russia." *Comparative Studies in Society and History,* vol. 36, no. 2. 1994, pp. 356–96.

Rossman, Jeffrey J. "A Workers' Strike in Stalin's Russia: The Vichuga Uprising of April 1932." In Lynne Viola, ed., *Contending with Stalinism: Soviet Power and Popular Resistance in the 1930s,* pp. 44–83. Ithaca: Cornell University Press, 2002.

Rumiantsev, Viacheslav. *Khronos: Biograficheskii ukazatel' 2006.* Available from *www. hrono. ru* (accessed 23 October 2006).

Sakharov, V. A. *"Politicheskoe zaveshchanie" Lenina: Real'nost' istorii i mify politiki.* Moscow: Izdatel'stvo Moskovskogo Universiteta, 2003.

Schapiro, Leonard. *The Communist Party of the Soviet Union.* New York: Random House, 1960.

Selishchev, A. *Iazyk revoliutsionnoi epokhi: Iz nabliudenii nad russkim iazykom poslednikh let 1917–1926.* Moscow: Rabotnik prosveshchenia, 1928.

Serge, Victor. *Russia Twenty Years After.* New York: Pioneer Publishers, 1937.

Sergeev, Artem, and Ekaterina Glushik. *Besedy o Staline.* Moscow: Forum, 2006.

Service, Robert. *The Bolshevik Party in Revolution: A Study in Organisational Change.* London: Macmillan, 1979.

———. *Stalin: A Biography.* London: Macmillan, 2004.

Shearer, David R. *Industry, State, and Society in Stalin's Russia, 1926–1934.* Ithaca: Cornell University Press, 1996.

Shestnadtsaty s"ezd VKP(b): Stenograficheskii otchet. Moscow, 1930.

Shishkin, I. V. "Delo Riutina." *Voprosy istorii,* no. 7, 1989.

Simonov, Konstantin. *Glazami cheloveka moego pokoleniia.* Moscow: Kniga, 1989.

Slezkine, Yuri. *Arctic Mirrors: Russia and the Small Peoples of the North.* Ithaca: Cornell University Press, 1994.

Sofsky, Wolfgang. *The Order of Terror: The Concentration Camp.* Translated by William Templer. Princeton:Princeton University Press, 1996.

Sokol'nikov, Grigorii Iakovlevich. *Novaia finansovaia politika: Na puti k tverdoi valiute.* Moscow: Nauka, 1995.

Sorenson, Jay B. *The Life and Death of Soviet Trade Unionism, 1917–1928.* New York: Atherton Press, 1969.

Sotsialisticheskii vestnik. July 23, 1928, August 30, 1936.

Stalin, I. V. *Sochineniia.* Vol. 3. Moscow, 1947.

———. *Sochineniia.* Edited by R. H. McNeal. 3 vols. Stanford: Hoover Institution Press, 1967.

———. *Sochineniia.* Vol. 11. Moscow, 1949.

Stalin, J. V. *Works.* Vols. 6, 9, 13. Moscow: Foreign Languages Publishing House, 1953, 1954, 1955.

Statisticheskoe obozrenie, no. 5, 1930.

"Stenogrammy ochnykh stavok v TsK VKP(b), Dekabr' 1936 goda." *Voprosy istorii,* no. 3, 2002.

Strumilin, S. *Na planovom fronte, 1920–1930 gg.* Moscow: Gospolitizdat, 1958.

Suny, Ronald G. *Revenge of the Past: Nationalism, Revolution, and the Collapse of the Soviet Union.* Stanford: Stanford University Press, 1993.

——, ed. *The Cambridge History of Russia: The Twentieth Century.* Cambridge: Cambridge University Press, 2006.

"Tainyi agent Iosifa Stalina: Dokymental'naia o donosakh i donoschike." *Neizvestnaia Rossiia.* no. 1, 1992.

Talbott, Strobe, ed. *Khrushchev Remembers.* Boston: Little Brown, 1970.

Terayama, Kyosuke. "Sutarin to Manshu: Sen hyaku sanju nen dai zenhan no Sutarin no tai Manshu seisaku" (Stalin and Manchuria: Stalin's policy towards Manchuria in the first half of the 1930s), *Tohoku Ajia Kenkyu,* no. 9, 2005, pp. 89–110.

Trinadtsatyi s"ezd RKP(b): Stenograficheskii otchet (1924). Moscow: Gosudarstvennoe izdatel'tsvo politicheskoi literatury, 1963.

Todorov, Tzvetan. *Hope and Memory: Lessons from the Twentieth Century.* Princeton: Princeton University Press, 2000.

Trotskii, L. B. *Moia zhizn': Opyt biografii.* Berlin: Granit, 1930.

——. *Portrety revoliutsionerov.* Compiled by Iu. Felshtin'skii. Benson, Vt.: Chalidze Publications, 1988.

——. *Voprosy britanskogo rabochego dvizheniia.* In Y. Felshtinskii, ed., *Kommunisticheskaia oppozitsia v SSSR, 1923–1927.* Vol. 1. Benson, Vt.: Chalidze Publications, 1988.

Trotsky, Leon. *The Revolution Betrayed: What Is the Soviet Union and Where Is It Going?* Translated by Max Eastman. New York: Doubleday, 1937.

——. *Stalin: An Appraisal of the Man and His Influence.* Edited and translated by Charles Malamath. London: Harper, 1941.

Trotsky to Bukharin, March 4, 1926. Hoover Institution Archives, Trotsky Collection, box 9, folder 48.

Tucker, Robert C. *Stalin as Revolutionary 1879–1929: A Study in History and Personality.* New York: Norton, 1973.

——, ed. *The Lenin Anthology.* New York: Norton, 1975.

Tucker, Robert C., and Stephen F. Cohen, eds. *The Great Purge Trial.* New York: Norton, 1965.

Ulam, Adam B. *Expansion and Coexistence: Soviet Foreign Policy, 1917–1967.* New York: Harcourt Brace, 1967.

——. *Stalin: The Man and His Era.* Boston: Beacon, 1989.

Vaiskopf, Mikhail. *Pisatel' Stalin.* Moscow: Novoe literaturnoe obozrenie, 2002.

Vatlin, A. Iu. "Rozdenie politiki edinogo fronta: 'Russkoe izmereniie.'" In *Rabochii klass i sovremennyi mir,* no. 1, 1990.

——. *Komintern: Pervye desiat let.* Moscow: Rossiia molodaia, 1993.

——. "Iosif Stalin auf dem Weg zur absoluten Macht: Neue Dokumente aus Moskauer Archiven." *Forum für osteuropäische Ideen- und Zeitgeschichte,* vol. 4, no. 2, 2000.

Vert N., and S. V. Mironenko, eds. *Massovye repressii v SSSR.* Vol. 1 of V. P. Kozlov, ed., *Istoriia Stalinskogo Gulaga.* Moscow: Rosspen, 2004.

Viola, Lynne. *The Best Sons of the Fatherland: Workers in the Vanguard of Soviet Collectivization.* New York: Oxford University Press, 1987.

———. *Peasant Rebels under Stalin: Collectivization and the Culture of Peasant Resistance*. New York: Oxford University Press, 1996.

Viola, Lynne, V. P. Danilov, N. A. Ivnitsky, and Denis Kozlov, eds. *The War against the Peasantry, 1927–1930*. New Haven: Yale University Press, 2005.

Volkogonov, Dmitri. *Stalin: Triumph and Tragedy*. Translated by Harold Shukman. Rocklin, Calif.: Prima, 1991.

Vilkova, V. P., ed. *RKP (b) i vnutripartiinaia bor'ba v dvatsatye gody, 1924: Dokumenty i materialy*. Moscow: IOM, 2004.

Vsesoiuznaia kommunisticheskaia partiia, XIV s"ezd Vsesoiuznoi kommunisticheskoi partii (b), 18–31 dekabria 1925 g.: Stenograficheskii otchet. Moscow: Gosudarstvennoe izdatel'stvo, 1926.

Warth, Robert D. *Leon Trotsky*. Boston: Twayne, 1977.

Watson. Derek. *Molotov: A Biography*. New York: Macmillan, 2005.

Weiskopf (Vaiskopf), Michael. "Leon Trotsky's Family Romance." *Partial Answers*, vol 4, no. 1, 2006, pp. 21–40.

Wheatcroft, S. G. "Views on Grain Output, Agricultural Reality and Planning in the Soviet Union in the 1920s." M.Soc.Sci. thesis, Centre for Russian and East European Studies, University of Birmingham, 1974.

———. "Grain Production and Utilisation in the USSR before Collectivisation." Ph.D. thesis, Centre for Russian and East European Studies, University of Birmingham, 1980.

Zelenin, I. E., ed. *Tragediia Sovetskoi derevni: Kollektivizatsiia i raskulachivanie, 1930–1933*. Vol. 3. Moscow: Rosspen, 2001.

Zhuravlev, V. V., and A. N. Solopov. *Bukharin: Chelovek, politik, ucheny*. Moscow: Politizdat, 1990.

Zhuravlev, V. V., et al., eds. *Vlast' i oppozitsiia: Rossiiskii politicheskoi protsess XX stoletiia*. Moscow: Rosspen, 1995.

Contributors

R. W. DAVIES is Emeritus Professor of Soviet Economic History and Senior Fellow, Centre for Russian and East European Studies, University of Birmingham, UK.

PAUL R. GREGORY is Cullen Distinguished Professor of Economics, University of Houston, and a Research Fellow at the Hoover Institution on War, Revolution, and Peace, Stanford University.

MARK HARRISON is Professor of Economics at the University of Warwick, UK, Senior Research Fellow of the Centre for Russian and East European Studies, University of Birmingham, and Distinguished Visiting Fellow of the Hoover Institution on War, Revolution, and Peace, Stanford University.

OLEG KHLEVNIUK is a Senior Researcher of the Russian Archival Service.

HIROAKI KUROMIYA is a Professor of History at Indiana University.

NORMAN NAIMARK is Robert and Florence McDonnell Professor of East European Studies and a Senior Research Fellow at the Hoover Institution on War, Revolution, and Peace and the Freeman-Spogli Institute for International Studies, Stanford University.

RUSTEM NUREEV is Professor of Economics at the Higher School of Economics, Moscow.

ROBERT SERVICE is Professor of Russian History at Oxford University, Director of the Russian and Eurasian Studies Centre at St Antony's College, Oxford, a Fellow of the British Academy and a Distinguished Visiting Fellow at the Hoover Institution on War, Revolution, and Peace, Stanford University.

LEONA TOKER is Professor of English in The Hebrew University of Jerusalem.

ALEXANDER VATLIN is Professor of History at the Lomonosov Moscow State University.

DAVID M. WOODRUFF is Lecturer in Comparative Politics at the London School of Economics and Political Science.

CHARTERS WYNN is Associate Professor of History at the University of Texas at Austin.

Index

Muralov, Nikolai, 124, 129, 152–53, 157

Narkomfin (People's Commissariat of Finance), 200, 201, 212
Narodniks, 191
Naumov, Oleg, 98, 113
Nechaev, I. P., 103
Nemchinov, V. S., 196
New Economic Policy (NEP), 10–11; crucial problem of Bolshevik policy during, 181; deepening of, 183; destruction of, 200; fragility of model, 200; *smychka* as central feature of, 12; turning against objectives of the October Revolution, 122
"New Opposition," emergence of, 62, 91, 183
Nikolsky, Nikolai, 100
"normal," use of, in Politburo members' statements, 147–48
Nureev, Rustem, 13
Nusinov, I. S., 82, 83–84

OGPU, 92, 100–101, 103
OGPU-NKVD, 137
Operation Barbarossa, 115n24
Ordzhonikidze, Sergo, 31; discussing cutting retail prices of industrial commodities, 236; during Smirnov-Eismont-Tolmachev affair, 104; involvement in the Syrtsov-Lominadze affair, 79, 81, 85

Parallel Anti-Soviet Trotsky Center, 167
"party," use of, in Politburo members' statements, 149–50
Party Congress, 124
party discipline, 25
Pashkovsky, 195
peasantry, three major groups of, 181–82
People's Commissariat of Finance. *See* Narkomfin
People's Commissariat of Foreign and Internal Trade, 212, 213

Perepelkin, 175
Piatakov, Grigory (Iury), 64, 145, 167, 211–12; fighting inflation and the goods famine, 208; on industrial capital expansion, 216; response to economic challenges, 199–200; on Soviets' need for hard currency, 200
Polanyi, Karl, 218
Politburo, 26; anger in members' discourse, 125–26; approach to economic policy in Sokol'nikov's absence, 215–17; atmosphere of, under Kamenev-Zinoviev-Stalin troika, 26–27, 61–64; clash of personalities intertwined with policy differences, 183; coercing opposition within into recanting, 137–38; curtailing microeconomic autonomy, 200; debate in, tone of, 27–28; decrees of, resulting from compromise, 24–25; disagreements in, over gold and trade/payments balances, 212–13; discourse in, similar to public speeches, 133; dissent in, 27; economic discussions of, 23–25; emerging conflict with "New" or "Leningrad" Opposition, 182; establishment of, 121; financial support for British strikers, 64, 65–66; function of, 121; as highest political authority, 16–17; increasingly violent metaphors used in, 158; language used in intraparty struggles, 137; leadership of, treating factions in personal terms, 128; linguistic battles within, 12–13; linking meetings with Central Committee actions, 19; lists of meetings, 19; meeting agendas of, 18–19, 20; meetings of, rarity during the Great Terror, 167; members of, catching others in verbal traps, 152–53; members of, speaking within Marxist-Leninist framework, 125; members' fear of Trotsky, 121–22; mock-ceremonial language in, 137, 146; political discussions of, 25; power structure altered after Lenin's death, 121–22; proceed-